Cape Breton University Press recognizes the support of the Province of Nova Scotia through the Department of Tourism, Culture and Heritage. We are pleased to work in partnership with the Culture Division to develop and promote our cultural resources for all Nova Scotians.

NOVA SCOTIA
Tourism, Culture and Heritage

Cover Design: Cathy MacLean, Pleasant Bay, NS
Layout: Gail Jones, Sydney, NS
Printing by Kromar Printing Ltd., Winnipeg, MB

First Publication in 1984 as ISBN: 0-920336-26-4

Library and Archives Canada Cataloguing in Publication

Newton, Pamela, 1938-
The Cape Breton book of days / Pamela Newton. — Updated and expanded.

ISBN-13: 978-1-897009-03-1

ISBN-10: 1-897009-03-8

1. Cape Breton Island (N.S.)—History—Miscellanea. 2. Cape Breton Island (N.S.)—History—Anecdotes. I. Title.
FC2343.4.N49 2005 971.6'9'002 C2005-904636-8

Cape Breton University Press
PO Box 5300
Sydney, NS B1P 6L2
Canada
www.cbupress.ca

The Cape Breton Book of Days

Revised Edition

by

Pamela G. Newton

Cape Breton University Press
Sydney, Nova Scotia
Canada

To my husband David

and to my children and grandchildren

Foreword

When the first edition of Pam Newton's *Cape Breton Book of Days* appeared in 1984, it was the first annals of events relating specifically to Cape Breton's rich and colourful past. At the time, we were on the verge of our bicentennial, celebrating the founding of Sydney in 1785, and as we reflected on our history we realized that information about many events had previously been under-recognized, only vaguely remembered, difficult to access or even overlooked completely. Pam painstakingly and, I must say, lovingly went about correcting the situation, pouring over thousands of newspaper articles, manuscripts and books to produce an exciting chronicle of events – major and minor – that are our past.

But who would use it? Cape Bretoners being who they are, argumentative about dates, times and locations of past events (not to mention family connections), the book proved to be a great asset. Not only did newspapers, radio, authors and teachers depend upon the book for information, the general public read it simply to be familiar with – and perhaps to marvel at – the events of our past.

Since 1984, Pam has collected more information and events to add to this amazing journal. As well, inquisitive Cape Bretoners queried her earlier material and offered addenda. As a result, and as a stickler for detail, Pam has blessed us with this revised and updated edition. In my introduction to the first edition, I trusted that the *Book of Days* would spur further investigation of our Island's remarkable history, a prediction that proved correct. I know this edition will draw further attention to past events with the same happy result.

Robert J. Morgan

Acknowledgements

Many people helped me with the original *Book of Days*. I would especially like to thank once again the Cape Bretoners I met through my work with the CBC radio show *Fresh Air*. I also want to thank the following for their very generous assistance: the staffs of the Beaton Institute, the Cape Breton University Library and the McConnell Library, the Fortress of Louisbourg National and Alexander Graham Bell historic sites of Canada. My thanks to the Cape Breton University Press, formerly UCCB Press, and its former editor Tim Belliveau, and its present editor, Mike Hunter for their help in monitoring the book and getting the original and this updated and expanded version into print. Thanks also to Gail Jones at CBU Press. I should also acknowledge with great respect the many newspapers which serve our communities so well and which, literally, write our history as we live it. Much of the information in this book is paraphrased from newspaper accounts.

I want to particularly thank my husband David for all his help. Also, thanks to Kenneth Donovan and John Johnston, my French connection with the Fortress of Louisbourg and to the Alexander Graham Bell museum and Jack Stephens. Thanks to Ken Lynds, Diana Schwartz, Don Burns, Ron Caplan, Ray Fahey, Simon Gillis and Jeff Martin and Anne MacLean of the treasure trove that is the Beaton Institute. Most of the photographs are from their general collection, but specifically I want to mention the Cabot Archives and Owen Fitzgerald. Thanks to the *Cape Breton Post*, the Old Sydney Society, James St. Clair and the late Elva Jackson, those goldmines of Cape Breton history. Doug MacPhee, Allister MacGillivary and Sheldon MacInnes are thanked for their assistance with the musical history of the island. Thanks to Dr. Robert Morgan, for his constant support for his kind words, and to all the other Cape Bretoners too numerous to detail who were always ready to respond to my requests for information.

Much has happened in the past twenty years. There are events we wish had never happened, like the McDonald's murders and the closure of the coalmines, but there are many triumphs – a new convention centre, a new hospital, new homes for the mentally disabled and adolescents at risk. And there are personal triumphs – the heart transplant recipient who climbed a mountain in Africa, the lifesaving volunteer fireman from Ingonish, the nine year old girl from North Sydney who became the Canadian Monopoly champion, the New Waterford brothers who are horseshoe champs.

Many events in the long and colourful history of Cape Breton are included in this book, but many have been omitted, either deliberately or through ignorance. And so it is quite possible that incidents which should properly have a place here have been left out. The entries offer glimpses into our past. Big and small events, happy and sad ones, all play a part. We may have been personally involved or perhaps just involved by reading about events in our newspapers. But all are points of reference for our lives.

In the tradition of the original *Cape Breton Book of Days*, this updated and expanded version continues as a daily journal of life here. As before, the present tense is used and word spellings and expressions remain as they were on the date reported.

P.G.N.

The Calendar

On September 3, 1752, England and its colonies switch to the Gregorian calendar. Today is now September 14. In different countries, and in some cases different parts of the same country, years begin at different times. In 1582, in an attempt to sort out the confusion, Pope Gregory XIII reformed the calendar, but it isn't until today that Protestant England officially accepts his calendar.

France and its colonies, including Louisbourg, have been using the New Style Gregorian calendar for years. According to the French, Louisbourg fell in the first siege on June 28, 1745, but according to the English and the New Englanders, it was June 17.

The dates used in this book, except if otherwise marked, have all been changed to the New Style Gregorian Calendar, the one we all use now.

"The main of life is composed of small incidents and petty occurrences; of wishes for objects not remote, and grief for disappointments of no fatal consequence; of insect vexations which sting us and fly away, impertinences which buzz a while about us, and are heard no more; of meteorous pleasures which dance before us and are disapated; of compliments which glide off the soul like other music, and are forgotten by him that gave and him that received them.

"There is nothing too little for so little a creature as man. It is by Studying little things that we attain the great art of having as little misery and as much happiness as possible."

Samuel Johnson (1649-1703)

The Island

January

We come from the countries all over the world
To hack at the forests to plow the land down
Fishermen, farmers and sailors all come
To clear for the future this pioneer ground.

Chorus:
We are an island, a rock in a stream
We are a people as proud as there's been
In soft summer breeze or in wild winter wind
The home of our hearts, Cape Breton.

Kenzie MacNeil

Fig. 1.1 Collage of subjects interviewed for CBC Fresh Air *in the 1970s and '80s. Pamela Newton.*

January 1

1790 The great moose massacre
This is the winter of the great Cape Breton Moose Massacre. Supplying the settlers with fresh moose or caribou meat isn't depleting the large herds in northern Cape Breton. But the demand for hides is. Moose hides are fetching ten shillings a piece—and hunters have flocked from all over, including Newfoundland, to make a killing in more than one way.

Before the winter is over, more than 9,000 moose carcasses are left rotting and the stench makes the air rancid for miles around. Passing ships' captains and crews complain of the foul smell coming from Cape Breton.

Fig. 1.2

1862 Source of tension
Nine young men from Main-a-Dieu and Louisbourg join the crew of the American fishing vessel, *Hir Crue*. Local fishermen don't like the American fishing fleet coming into local ports and recruiting the young men to join their crews. In fact, local fishermen don't care for Americans and Europeans fishing in their waters at all.

1899 Community takes the pledge
One hundred fifty-nine men of St. Peter's Parish in Ingonish take pledges promising "to abstain from all intoxicating liquors for the time set opposite our names or until we will have our names removed from the book." In front of the parish priest, the men pledge not to drink for anywhere from six months to life. (Eight men take the pledge for life.)

1950 Coal to the rescue
Drastic coal shortages force CNR to cut train schedules throughout Canada. The largest shipment of coal from Cape Breton ever recorded in a 30-day period leaves for coal-hungry eastern Canada.

1985 Celebrations begin
Anniversary celebrations get underway as Cape Breton and Sydney celebrate their Bicentennials and North Sydney its Centennial. Two hundred years ago, Cape Breton was a separate colony with its own capital at Sydney.

Fig. 1.3 Sydney bicentennial celebrations, 1985.

1997 Tragic dip

This year's Polar Bear Club's traditional New Year's Day dip in South Bar (Sydney) Harbour turns to tragedy. Minutes after leaving the minus 7° C water, 65-year-old Bill Jamieson, a veteran of the Club and one of 29 people who "swim" today, suffers a fatal heart attack.

2001 Gone fishin'

Winter sports-fishing is expanded. Selected lakes and streams are now open to anglers fishing for chain pickerel, white and yellow perch and stocked rainbow trout.

January 2

1940 Sword fishery sharp

A year-end report on the expanding sword-fishing industry reports that about 75 per cent of the swordfish from Canadian waters were landed at Glace Bay, where they were prepared for the Boston market. The catch of 1,778,700 pounds is the largest in the history of the industry. Captain Ernie Billard, a Glace Bay fisherman on his way to Morien, caught the first fish of the season.

Average price throughout the summer was 10 cents per pound, resulting in an income locally of $146,000. Fish livers brought an added $4,867.

1941 Convoys to England

The departure of a 23-ship convoy from Sydney Harbour marks the end of the first convoy season in which, during roughly five months of operation, some 967 ships sailed in 48 convoys to Britain.

1964 Family court

Nova Scotia's first family court starts in Cape Breton.

1970 Blast furnace coal

The Cape Breton Development Corporation's Coal Division officials announce that last year's production of 616,548 tons of blast furnace coke was the highest in the history of the coke ovens, and more Cape Breton coal is being used in the process.

1987 Jeux Canada Winter Games

The new games facility at the University College of Cape Breton is officially opened by athletics director, Dr. Carl "Bucky" Buchanan. This top-flight facility has seating for 2,000 fans and an Olympic-sized ice surface. It also houses a sports medicine wing and a Hall of Fame. The Games will be opened by the prime minister in February, kicking off two weeks of sporting and cultural events.

January 3

1882 Moses Coady

Moses Coady is born in North East Margaree. Educated at St. Francis Xavier University and in Rome, where he was ordained a priest, he began the most dynamic phase of his career in

1928 when he was appointed director of the St. FX Extension Department. A year later he organized the fishermen of Eastern Canada and formed the United Maritime Fishermen.

The "Man from Margaree" became a recognized authority on rural problems. He was active in Adult Education, receiving the American Carnegie Award for his work, and was appointed Vice-President of the American Association for Adult Education. His book, *Masters of Their Own Destiny,* was published in 1939. After the war, Pope Pius XIII raised him to the rank of Domestic Prelate. Named President of the Canadian Association of Adult Education in 1949, he later accepted an invitation from Trygve Lie to address the Plenary Session of the United Nations.

1950 Propane here

The first propane plant in Nova Scotia starts at Leitches Creek. Although a newcomer to the Maritimes, propane is an old story in the U.S.

1989 Happy 100th birthday

Sydney Mines marks the start of its 100th birthday since incorporation with a Gala Ball at Memorial High.

January 4

1928 Coal on Charlotte Street

The Board of Works in Sydney passes a resolution that no coal can be unloaded into chutes on Charlotte Street between Wentworth and Nepean Streets after noon. Local residents are complaining that coal is being unloaded at all hours of the day.

1937 Permission to bootleg coal

The Victory Mine Local of Glace Bay decides to ask the government to allow bootleg mining in Wadden's Cove and District Six.

1999 Enterprising youth

The YMCA Enterprise Centre in Glace Bay has trained and placed 111 youth as part of the federal Public Youth Internship Program.

January 5

1759 Highlanders ready

Fraser's Highlanders are recruited for service in Cape Breton and North America.

1843 Threatened with "annihilation"

The newspaper *Spirit of the Times,* published in Sydney, is threatened with "annihilation" because the editor, J. D. Khun, recommends the Militia Law be repealed.

1903 Biggest yet

The world's largest shipment of steel, 5,252 tons, leaves Sydney on the steamer *Bergenhus,* bound for Philadelphia.

1927 Closed

The U.S. Consulate closes in Sydney.

1942 Major population shift

Towns throughout Cape Breton suffer considerable reductions in population:

	1881	1941
Framboise	680	397
Grand Narrows	1,464	852
Judique	2,027	904
Loch Lomond	437	170
Margaree	1,246	731
North River	697	327
Whycocomagh	1,787	696

1959 News

Radio Station CBI starts daily news bulletins.

1963 500th game

Sydney native, Danny Gallivan broadcasts his 500th National Hockey League game. Danny Gallivan started as a baseball pitcher, invited to the NY Giants' training camp in 1939, but by the next year his arm gave out, and a new career had to be found. This started events that led him to the broadcasting booth "high over the ice" at the Montreal Forum. He won an ACTRA Sportscasting Award in 1974 and was inducted into the NS Sports Hall of Fame in September 1980.

1984 Lingan No. 3 opens

The Nova Scotia Power Corporation's newest source of electrical power, Lingan No. 3 unit, is fully operational. This is the third 150-megawatt coal-fired unit to become commercial since October 1979. Lingan, along with units 1 and 2, is now the largest generating station in the province at 450 megawatts. Lingan is the latest part of the corporation's plans to reduce its dependency on imported oil to produce electricity.

2004 You're the tops!

The Cabot Trail is named as one of North America's top six scenic drives in Canada by the Michelin North America 2004 Road Atlas.

Fig. 1.4 Cabot Trail, n.d.

January 6

1832 In and out

Trade statistics for the last three months of 1831 include, among other imports to Cape Breton, 35,392 cwt. of tobacco and 47,980 gallons of rum. Exports ranged from coal and fish to barley, sheep, gypsum, cattle, oats and potatoes and were sold as far away as Britain, Spain, Brazil and the West Indies.

1915 War preparations

Exhibition directors okay the proposed use of the Cape Breton Exhibition buildings in Sydney as barracks for a mobilization center.

1923 To popularize radio

Local radio pioneers, G. A. Edwards, George D. Crowell of Sydney, M. J. Cleary of North Sydney and M. Bateson of Sydney Mines, officers of the Cape Breton Amateur Radio Association which wants to popularize radio, write to Ottawa for improvements in the local Marconi Station.

1951 Bell of *Baddeck*

From now on, the bell of the corvette *Baddeck* will open the sessions of the Victoria County Council meetings.

January 7

1840 Yields bring prizes

The first premiums are given to the prize winners of last summer's Agricultural Society's Fair in Sydney. First prize of a cradle scythe for the finest and heaviest bushel of wheat, weighing 60 1/2 pounds, goes to Alexander Grant of North West Arm. Second prize, a Buck Harrow, for the finest and heaviest bushel of oats, weighing 44 pounds, is awarded to William McLeod of the same community. Third prize, a cultivator, is won by Michael Mullins of Low Point for the largest crop of potatoes from two measured square rods. His yield averaged 520 bushels to the acre. 1984 averages are 375 bushels to the acre.

1963 Older than fortress

Archeologists at Louisbourg discover the foundation of a building older than the Fortress. Seven years before the Fortress was constructed, Louisbourg was settled by French fishermen who had moved from Placentia, Newfoundland. The 1713 foundation is found beneath the Place des Armes or rallying place of the Chateau St. Louis, where research is being carried out to restore a guardhouse.

1964 Milestone passed

Carl Anthony Crawford becomes the first Negro to be appointed to the Sydney Police Force.

1971 Booth Fisheries begins negotiations

The Canadian Food and Allied Workers Union begins negotiations with Booth Fisheries Ltd. of Petit de Grat, following the earlier recognition by Booth that the CFAWU represented the fishermen.

The decision marks a new phase in the bitter period of fish company—fishermen relations in which fishermen had tied up their boats for months in 1970 in an effort to be represented by the British Columbia-based United Fishermen and Allied Workers Union. At that time, as fishermen were not regarded as employees but as co-venturers, voluntary recognition by the fish company was the only way in which fishermen could be represented by the unions and the fish plant extended such recognition only to the CFAWU, a Canadian Labour Congress affiliate.

1973 Micmac to Nashville

Thirty-four-year-old Lee Cremo of Eskasoni has been fiddling for about eighteen years. The three-time Maritime fiddling champion has been invited to participate in the Grand Masters' North American Fiddling Championship in Nashville, Tennessee, on the weekend. He is one of the ten finalists. Devco recently presented Mr. Cremo with a trophy for being the first Micmac ever to be invited to the Grand Ole Oprey.

January 8

1983 Big talkers

There are about 92,000 telephones on Cape Breton with about 60,000 customers. The province, including Cape Breton, has 550,000 telephones. Inverness, Victoria and Cape Breton Counties alone have as many phones as the entire province had in 1925. Until recently, Canadians talked more on the phone than anyone else in the world.

1998 Snowmobile trail

Thirty-eight-year-old Laurie Cranton of Margaree, the Nova Scotia representative in PowerStreak Rendevous '98, takes part in a scheduled 45-day trip starting from St. Anthony, Newfoundland, to Squamish, BC. The snowmobilers will map out a new Trans Canada Snowmobiling Trail. Cranton, a paraplegic from a forestry accident, says that regardless of

Fig. 1.5 Port Hood fishing fleet, c. 1900.

ability, only a snowmobile can take you through deep snow. "Traveling in vast wilderness areas during winter gives you a whole different perspective on nature. From the mountains to the valleys, you get a taste of all different types of scenery and wildlife."

The almost 1,300 kilometres of our Cape Breton trail system are also to be expanded and upgraded.

January 9

1918 Fish story

Statistics to the end of 1917 show that fish marketed in Inverness County are numerous and diversified.

	1917	1983
cod	$196,775	$3,169,000
haddock	154,814	4,000
mackere	1176,610	18,000
lobsters	107,278	4,035,000
herring	34,914	73,000
salmon	22,212	66,000
hake and fillets	29,403	316,000
halibut	7,470	1,000
smelts	3,100	4,000
sole	1,180	44,000
fish oils	4,557	–
oysters	2,760	–
squid	4,800	–
pollock	15,000	–

January 10

1881 Inverness leads

The census of 1880 illustrates the leading role of Inverness County agriculture in Nova Scotia. With 29,843 cattle, 458 oxen, 45,453 sheep, 5,573 pigs, Inverness County has more of these animals than any other county in the province. In addition, during the year the county produced 117,081 lbs. of wool, 649,279 lbs. of butter, 158,000 lbs. of cheese, 147,811 yards of cloth and flannel and 9,549 lbs of flax—all more than any produced in any county of Nova Scotia. (See also March 1, 1821.)

1930 Talkies

Talking movies arrive on Cape Breton, making their debut at New Waterford's Majestic Theatre. *They Had to See Paris,* starring Will Rogers, features "beautiful women, gorgeous gowns, gay scenes, comedy and thrills, life and love." *Movie-tone News* is an added attraction. Admission for matinees is 15 cents for children and 35 cents for adults, while in the evening it's 35 cents for children and 45 cents for adults.

January 11

1831 Courts come closer

Courts are established in the southern and northwestern districts of Cape Breton. Before this, a man would have to go to Sydney—by boat or horse or by foot—if he wanted the title deed to this land, his will probated or any other legal business transacted.

January 12

1910 Smallpox

Last summer, another epidemic of smallpox raced through different districts, but the Boards of Health were able to cope with it and keep it from the more populous areas. However, smallpox and other infectious diseases over the past nine years have cost the county a great deal of money. If people would only allow themselves to be vaccinated, the ratepayers would save money as well as life.

1931 Christie's Restaurant - Sydney

SUNDAY SPECIAL
Full Course
Chicken Dinner .50

January 13

1978 Buckley's Mixture

William Knapp Buckley, formerly of Sydney, internationally known druggist, died recently in Toronto. His red-white-and-blue-labelled Buckley's Cough Mixture is a familiar drug counter item. The mixture was developed by Mr. Buckley when he noticed that a certain old prescription that came with the drugstore he had bought kept being refilled. During the First World War, soldiers in the trenches used the mixture against some of the stresses of war. Carageenin, the extract of Irish moss, was later substituted for the druggist's old standby of gum tragacanth to hold the ingredients in suspension..

January 14

1920 Fire

Central School, Glace Bay, is completely destroyed by fire.

1922 Coal "check-off"

The Dominion Coal Company won't use the UMW check-off system at the Glace Bay Collieries. Instead, dues for the miners' organization will only be collected in the pay offices from the men who are actually mining coal in the pits. This means the company will not recognize as members of the UMW any employees who are engaged in overground work. The men feel this embarrasses them and weakens the union by reducing its membership.

1935 A lot of snow

Snow fell today: 63.5 centimetres. The average for the month of January is 74.5 centimetres.

1990 Last train

Four hundred people gather to protest cuts to passenger rail service. Four men shackle themselves to the engine of the last train, preventing it from starting its final run.

2005 Open road

The Sydney Port Access Road opens. At 2 p.m. traffic begins to move on this five kilometre road which runs from the intersection of Grand Lake Road and Highway 125 to the Sydney waterfront and includes a link with Lingan Road, providing another road in and out of Whitney Pier. Some two to three thousand vehicles a day are expected to use the new road.

January 15

1901 Louisbourg

The town of Louisbourg is incorporated.

1909 Plague

Thirty people in the Baddeck area die of Cholera plague this winter.

1949 TB hospital

The Point Edward Tuberculosis Hospital opens and proves to be a milestone in the treatment of TB in Cape Breton. At the beginning of this century, more than 200 of every 100,000 people died each year of TB. In 1882, the cause of TB was found to be a germ, but it was not until the introduction of the antibiotic streptomyacin in 1947 that treatment became really effective. Before this, TB was treated by long months or years of bed rest at various TB annexes. The opening of the Point Edward Hospital will reduce the long delay of patients waiting for modern treatment.

The death rate continues to drop—to below one in every 100,000—and, although a smaller service continues for a while, on March 31, 1973, the Point Edward Hospital is closed out by Dr. Donald Robb. TB is no longer a dreaded disease, a white plague. It is little more than a minor inconvenience, treatable in most cases by drugs at home while the patient leads a normal life.

January 16

1922 Situation desperate
Residents at a meeting in Glace Bay learn that available funds of No. 11 local are exhausted. Many families are now keeping their children home from school because they have no clothes to wear. The situation is desperate. In a very short time several families may face actual starvation.

1934 Best in the East
Schoolchildren in North Sydney get a half holiday to attend the opening ceremonies of the toboggan slide and ski run on Ferris Hill. To date this is Nova Scotia's only ski run and it's said to be the best toboggan slide east of Montreal. It was built during this Depression by unemployed labourers. Extras include a large arch of spruce boughs at the top and lights that are strung and lit along poles running up the hill. Coffee is available in a log cabin at the top.

1952 Junior College opens
Principal Dr. Malcolm A. MacLellan formally opens Xavier Junior College in Sydney. After the dedication by Most Reverend John R. MacDonald, Bishop of Antigonish, the Inspector of Schools in Cape Breton County, Thomas L. Sullivan, speaks on "The College and the Community." Xavier Junior College has opened in time to take part in the Centennial celebrations of St. FX University next year. The George Street campus will also house the Cape Breton headquarters of the St. FX Extension Department. (See also August 10, 1853.)

1999 Industry on the Northside
Precision Fineblank Components, an automotive fineblanking operation in the Northside Industrial Park, is expending into manufacturing value-added products in March with a General Motors contract. The plant, which employs 187 people, is a division of Tesma International, global supplier of engine transmissions and fueling systems.

2000 Musician dies
World-renowned Cape Breton musician, John Morris Rankin, aged 40, of Judique, is killed in a motor vehicle accident at Whale Cove, on Cape Breton's western shore. Three teenage passengers, including his son Michael, escape with minor injuries. They were on their way to a hockey festival in Cheticamp.

January 17

1923 Beware Reds
Nova Scotia miners are warned that they cannot remain members of the United Mine Workers if they affiliate with the Red International labour Organization of Moscow. "The Russians are out to destroy our Labour movement and substitute their own."

1944 Highlanders into battle
The Cape Breton Highlanders, recently arrived in Italy and one of the two forward patrolling battalions of the 11th Infantry Brigade north of Ortono, on the Adriatic Coast, attack a

hill held by German paratroopers. The Highlanders are caught in a deadly crossfire from German machine guns, and there is too much wind for the effective use of smoke. This is the first battle experience of the Highlanders and that night they—and the Perth Regiment on their left flank—are withdrawn. Two companies of the Highlanders lose thirteen men killed and three officers and thirty men wounded.

Following this baptism of fire the Cape Bretoners fight their way up the Adriatic coast. They later leave Italy and land in France at Marseilles and join the First Canadian Army at Nijmegen. Their last battle of the war is on the Ems Estuary. (See also April 28, 1945.)

1950 Coal blocks canal

The 68-ton coastal packet *Corrine* bound for Canso from North Sydney with a cargo of coal is crushed by ice and has sunk, blocking St. Peter's Canal.

1966 Closure

No. 18 Colliery at New Victoria closes.

January 18

1943 Spirits low

Nova Scotia has liquor rationing and it's the most drastic plan in any province. An individual's weekly purchase is now limited to either two ounces of spirits, two quarts of wine or a dozen quarts of beer.

1968 Mink go West

In what is believed to be the largest shipment of its kind to leave Cape Breton, 225 mink have been sent to a ranch in Saskatchewan. Besides the breeding stock, mink and fox pelts are earning Cape Breton ranches a growing reputation.

1989 "Because it's there"

Forty-seven-year-old heart transplant recipient David Gilholm, makes it to the top of Africa's highest mountain. David, who received his heart transplant at The University Hospital in London, Ontario, reached the summit of 5,889-metre Mount Kilimanjaro without the aid of oxygen and accompanied by two other Canadian transplant recipients. He said in a telephone interview from Tanzania, "It was so windy at the top and with ice pellets flying that when we tried to take out the Canadian flag we couldn't even keep it in our hands." The expedition was, he said, "A lot of work but I really enjoyed it." His wife Deanna, waiting at home said, "The trauma of waiting for word of the trek was the worst." David relaxed before returning to Sydney by exploring some of the jungle of Tanzania.

January 19

1905 Glace Bay ghost

There is one house on a quiet street in Glace Bay that is more than it appears to be. New owners move in with high hopes, only to leave after a few weeks. The peace and quiet is shattered by heavy tramping and unearthly screams coming from the closets, heavy flapping sounds against the windows, and lights that suddenly go out.

1941 International recognition

An Gael, the official voice of Scotland's "An Comunn Gaidhealach" pays tribute to the late Stephen B. MacNeil of Gillis Point, well known Gaelic scholar and piper.

January 20

1921 Ice strike

Twenty ice-cutters, working for the Cape Breton Ice Company at Grand Lake, near Sydney, for a maximum of $2.50 a day each, strike for higher wages, demanding five-and-a-half cents an hour more. The Company has refused their demands and within a short time replaces the strikers with other workers.

1976 College of Cape Breton Press

The new College of Cape Breton Press publishes its first book: *The Proceedings of the Bras d'Or Lakes Aquaculture Conference.* The College's president, Dr. Donald F. Campbell, believes that the College can play an important cultural role in Cape Breton and to this end he has established the Press. Eric MacEwan, Steve MacDonald and later Tim Belliveau as directors of Public Relations are responsible for the policies and publications of the Press.

The material published focuses on Cape Breton. History items include *Cape Breton Historical Essays,* edited by Professors Don MacGillivray and Brian Tennyson, and *The Well-Watered Garden* by Laurie Stanley, a history of the early Presbyterian Church in Cape Breton. Cape Breton architecture is emphasized in Terry Sunderland's book, *Still Standing,* while Cape Breton musicians are featured in Allister MacGillivray's book *The Cape Breton Fiddler. Mining Photographs and Other Pictures,* a co-publication with the Nova Scotia College of Art and Design, brings another facet of Cape Breton to life.

The College Press also publishes a series of record albums, including the three very successful versions of *The Rise and Follies of Cape Breton Island.*

January 21

1884 High child mortality

This is the time of year with the greatest mortality of children as a result of typhoid, scarletina and diphtheria. Last year alone, Judique and Inverness ranked second highest (Lunenburg was first) in child deaths in the province. Inverness County lost 59 children to diphtheria and 2 each to typhoid and scarletina, while Richmond County with 26 deaths due to diphtheria, 2 to typhoid and one to scarletina, reported the fewest deaths in Cape Breton. July is the second worst time of the year for these diseases.

1930 CJCB up front

CJCB, in broadcasting the King's Address from the Naval Disarmament Conference in London, becomes one of twenty-four radio stations taking part in the largest hookup Canada has known.

1997 FIRST HALFWAY HOUSE
Nova Scotia's first halfway house for young offenders opens in Sydney.

January 22

1889 PORT HAWKESBURY
The town of Port Hawkesbury is incorporated.

1897 TIP FOR TRAVELLERS
"It is worth remembering, especially when staying in hotels, that, if the bed clothing is not sufficiently warm, two or three newspapers spread between the blankets will insure a comfortable night."

1917 TRAFFIC HALTED
Heavy snow stops traffic. The S & L daily express takes two days to get from Sydney to Glace Bay, and the tram line has been tied up for eight days. Three snowplows, coupled together, struggle to get up Commercial Street in Glace Bay, leaving behind snow piled to the tops of the store windows.

Fig. 1.6 Traffic halted by heavy snow, n.d. Eastern Light & Power.

January 23

1849 TWO PETITIONS
Mr. Harrington presents two petitions in the House. One is for a canal to be cut across a neck of land at St. Peters to provide "free communication" with the Bras d'Or Lakes. The other petition is for the erection of a breakwater on the south side of Bras d'Or.

January 24

1941 GAELIC BANNED
The Cape Breton Joint Expenditure Board, along with both town and city councils, urge the federal government to lift the ban on the use of Gaelic in the transmission of telegrams.

2005 TAR PONDS COMMITTEE
A new tar ponds liaison committee is announced to come up with the solution to the cleanup of the tar ponds. The tar ponds have been created by the run-off from the coke ovens and various other industrial plants at the steel plant over the years. Many people think the tar ponds are the worst toxic site in Canada, our own polluted Love Canal. Lead and arsenic are above tolerated levels. Health concerns for nearby residents are raised, some houses are evacuated, some families offered re-location.

The coke ovens site is a 68-hectare, former industrial property bounded by residential and industrial lands. From 1901 to 1988, various coke production plants operating on the site provided carbon and fuel for a nearby steel mill. Other industrial plants on the property used by-products from the coking operations to manufacture various commercial products.

In 1986 a promised cleanup was proposed to be finished by the mid-1990s. Various methods are discussed and rejected, including using an incinerator or cementing the ponds over. Millions of dollars are used but little progress is made. In 1996 the Joint Action Group (JAG) is formed to determine a successful process.

Fig. 1.7 Steel plant and tar ponds, 18-Jul-86. Owen Fitzgerald.

January 25

1842 First ship registers

The SS *Industry* is the first ship to register at the Port of Arichat.

1843 Blankets for Indians

Joseph Howe, who hopes to get to Cape Breton himself, reported today in the House of Assembly in Halifax on Indian Affairs. He comments that in 1838 there were about 520 Micmacs on Cape Breton. The government gives "relief only to the old and infirm, the sick or maimed, or to those who had met with some calamity." One hundred pounds a year has been allocated for the use of Indians throughout the province and this is mostly used to buy blankets and coats.

1929 The people's horse

At a meeting to revive light harness racing in Cape Breton, Glace Bay and other communities are urged to buy shares in a "free-for-aller," a horse owned by and raced for the community. The town of Reserve is an early leader with its purchase of "Lambert Todd." Allan Lewis, who started racing in 1904, says, "Buy a share, even investing only $1, in a community horse, and you'll become a race fan, and so get people out to the races, and the game will come back to this part of the country."

2005 Home Depot comes home

North Sydney native Annette Verschuren, president of Home Depot Canada, officially opens the new store in Sydney—on the new Port Access Road by the Bypass/Grand Lake Road intersection. She keeps in close contact with Cape Breton. As well as being a successful businesswoman, last October, she was also installed as Cape Breton University's second Chancellor.

January 26

1744 Strategic Cape Breton

Massachusetts Governor William Shirley tries to sell others on the potential of Canada particularly Cape Breton. Later in July, Governor Shirley calls Louisbourg Harbour "the key of the French and British Northern Colonies." The Harbour, he argues, is strategically placed and it poses a threat to New England if controlled by the French.

1851 "1850 Census"

The Census of 1850 contains dozens of categories including whether residents are male and female, deaf and dumb, blind, lunatic, idiotic, coloured or Indian. The County of Cape Breton, including at this time Victoria County, has 2,179 children attending seventy schools. Religious denominations show Church of England, Roman Catholic, Kirk of Scotland, The Free Church, Presbyterian Church of Nova Scotia, Baptists, Methodists, Congregationalists and Universalists. Richmond County has one Quaker.

January 27

1846 Island potato famine

Mr. McKeageney presents a strong case for the Relief Bill in the House of Assembly. Relief is desperately needed throughout Inverness County to help people affected by the potato blight last summer. Capt. Neil McLellan of Broad Cove is one of the presidents of the Agricultural Societies in the county who submitted reports to Mr. McKeageney. He reports appalling conditions. He tells of the almost total failure of the crop in his district. William McKeen of Mabou reports that fully one-half of the crop has been destroyed, and it is impossible to tell whether or not the potatoes saved will keep. The people in South Lake Ainslie have enough potatoes for only two months, and those in Skye Glen will have no food by St. Patrick's Day.

1934 Cape Bretoners starving

A reporter manages to reach Ingonish by plane, and he sees many people close to starvation. The icebreaker *Montcalm*, laden with food and supplies for some 3,000 people in North Victoria County, will try to smash through solid ice with relief for beleagured fishing villages. Destitute families are stealing sheep from their more fortunate neighbours. Dairy cows are being slaughtered. The stores are empty. Many children, undernourished and scantily dressed, are suffering from frostbite and impetigo. One resident comments, "I don't suppose you would find half the families in this bay could buy a barrel of flour. If there aren't supplies coming within the next two weeks there'll be a lot of corpses, because some can't live." (See also February 10, 1934.)

January 28

1901 Biggest town

Glace Bay is incorporated as a town. It's Canada's biggest town, having more than ten thousand people. Glace Bay qualifies to be a city, but it prefers to be Canada's biggest town.

1950 Major fire
Fire destroys one of the oldest buildings on the steel plant site—the open hearth department's brick warehouse.

1978 Award winner
The Grant Crabtree film, *Song of Seasons*, a film about Cape Breton with a storyline that follows a year on a sheep farm, wins the top award in the Public Relations Category at the Berlin Agriculture Film Festival.

2005 *Fidhel Mhor A'Cheildh*, The Big Fiddle
The newly renovated Marine terminal in Sydney is renamed the Joan Harriss Cruise Pavilion, in honour of the late business leader who did so much to encourage port and cruise ship development. She is also remembered for her efforts in buying and restoring Jost House, one of Sydney's oldest buildings, and for starting walking tours of the historic north end of Sydney. Outside the new Marine Terminal, *Fidhel Mhor A'Cheildh*, the Big Fiddle, is officially named and tuned. An exact model and locally built, it is believed to be the world's largest and it stands from the ground to seventeen metres including the three-metre pedestal. The bow has 144 steel "horsehair" strings.

Fig. 1.8 The Sydney Marine Terminal and giant fiddle greet cruise ships, n.d. Vaughan Merchant.

The Pavilion contains the tourist bureau, a large interpretive centre, craft market, farm market and retail space, a 1,200-seat theatre and a lighthouse.

January 29

1834 Shipping losses
Known shipping losses in 1833 are valued at £20,000 excluding cargoes. 746 people have survived being wrecked off the coasts and have been landed at Sydney.

1929 One female student
The first ground-school class of the Cape Breton Flying Club is held at Central School in Sydney. Students learn the principal parts of the plane and the theory of flight. There is good attendance and intense interest. Among the enthusiastic audience is one young woman.

1951 Post Office cuts

The Post Office reveals that by April, mail deliveries will be down to once a day, excluding businesses, which will continue to receive two mail deliveries a day.

2002 And the Oscar goes to...

Sydney-born Howard John Russell dies today at age 88. A non-professional actor, he is the only person to receive two Academy Awards for the same role. A teenager when his family moved to the Unites States, he enlisted in the U.S. army after Pearl Harbor. In an accident later in the war, Russell lost both his hands, which were replaced with two hooks. While recuperating, he was featured in the film, *Diary of a Sergeant*. This led to his being cast in *The Best Years of Our Lives*, a movie in which he also played a soldier who had lost both hands.

He received an Oscar for Best Supporting Actor and a special Oscar for "bringing hope and courage to his fellow veterans." Years later, in order to help with his wife's medical expenses, Russell sold one of the Oscars. The Academy now won't let that happen.

January 30

1654 Denys granted land by King

Fifty-six year old Nicholas Denys, "La Grande Barbe" (Greatbeard), receives Letters Patent from King Louis XIII of France making him Governor and Lieutenant General over the coasts and islands in the Gulf of St. Lawrence from Cape Canso to Cape Rosiers and over Newfoundland. These are lands he bought a short while ago from the Company of New France. In 1651 he established himself at St. Peters, "an admirable station for the Indian trade and the fishery."

He has been part of a power struggle, but now his forts at St. Peter's and St. Ann's are his, and he can rule securely. The King grants him a monopoly of the fur trade and of the sedentary fishery along the coasts "as far as Virginia." His new power lets him make treaties with the natives and search for gold and silver and other minerals. He also farms, builds boats, cuts timber, builds a road across the isthmus and uses oxen to haul his ships on skids to the Atlantic.

In 1672, his two-volume book, *Geographical Description of the Coasts of North America, from New England* to *the River Saint Lawrence, with the Natural History of the Peoples and Animals of the Country* is published in Paris.

In 1967 a Museum, built in the style of his trading post, opens in St. Peter's. (See also September 29, 1671.)

1929 Consider the people

Rev. J. H. Hamilton, representing the ministers of Sydney, pleads in Ottawa for an eight-hour day at the steel plant. He wants the government to consider the human factor and the fact that Manpower is a part of the success of the Plant. The workers at present work 11 hours by day and 13 hours by night in a two-shift, 24-hour day.

1951 Closure at George's River

The dolomite quarry at George's River closes in a few days, after being in business for fifty years. The dolomite is shipped in crude form to the Sydney Steel Plant where it is crushed and used in the manufacture of steel.

1959 Massive blow

The ferries at Big Harbour will be eliminated when the bridge at Seal Island is completed. The work schedule for the causeway approach to the bridge involves the blasting of a huge slice of Kelly's Mountain to be dumped into the channel. Work is also progressing on the thirteen-mile stretch of highway over Kelly's Mountain. The closing of the ferries is a massive blow to the communities of Big Harbour and Ross Ferry.

January 31

1853 Noted Inverness lawyer

Daniel McNeil is born in Mabou. He becomes a lawyer and a commissioner of the Supreme Court of Nova Scotia. He is elected to the Nova Scotia Legislature in 1886 and is made a member of the Executive Council, without portfolio. He is one of several Cape Breton lawyers, doctors and businessmen who are honoured in the book, *Great Men of Canada,* or *Success by Example,* published in 1895.

1917 Submarine warfare

Germany initiates unrestricted submarine warfare against all ships, including merchant ships. Canada has been using east coast coal-burning patrol boats, and these call in at North Sydney for fuel. Since 1916, British transports have taken on coal at North Sydney for their return voyage. But this year Allied shipping suffers tremendous losses and the government introduces convoys on the most dangerous routes. (See also July 10, 1917.)

1995 Dangerous snares

The Landsburg family of Groves Point on Boularderie find their five-year-old Golden Retriever strangled by a snare on their large property. They are further disturbed to learn that trappers are permitted to set snares on private property without getting permission from the landowner.

On the St. Peter's side of the island, in the St. George's Channel area, deer snares are found. These, however, are illegal. Hunters, who prefer to hunt rather than to trap, as well as members of the Department of Natural Resources, are dismantling the snares when they find them. This latest snare, clothesline wire stretched between two trees, is about one metre square: "Big enough to catch a man," notes conservation officer John Mombourquette.

Winter in Cape Breton

Fig. 1.9 Sons of Temperance sleigh parade, Sydney, n.d. C. H. Woodill.

Fig. 1.10 Eel fishing, Leitches Creek, 1975. Owen Fitzgerald.

Fig. 1.11 Ice fishing, River Ryan, 1991. Paul Prendergast.

Fig. 1.13 Silver thaw in Sydney Mines, n.d.

Fig. 1.12 Pamela Newton

February

"Those Magnificent Men in Their Flying Machines"

"Those magnificent men in their flying machines,
they go up tidly up-up, they go down tidly oun-down.
They enchant all the ladies and steal all the scenes,
With their up tidly up-up and their down tidly oun-down.

Up! Down! Flying around!
Looping the loop and defying the ground!
They're! All! Frightfully keen,
Those magnificent men in their flying machines.

Excerpt from the 1965 movie of the same name, set in 1910

Music by Ron Goodwin; lyrics generally attributed to Ron Goodwin

Fig. 2.1 McCurdy in the Silver Dart, *Baddeck Bay, Feb. 14, 1909.*

February 1

1881 Coxheath copper mine
Over one hundred men are employed at new Coxheath Copper Mine. Archibald McDonald discovered the copper and interested local businessmen and Americans in investing in a mine. John E. Burchell of Sydney is one of the few Cape Bretoners on the Board.

1913 Spring?
The temperature soars to a record high of 59° F.

1967 Fire
The Zellers store in the Sydney Shopping Mall is destroyed by fire.

1967 End of an era
It's the end of an era in the postal service. The last load of mail to be carried by train from Halifax to Sydney is unloaded this morning. From now on the mail will travel by highway. It's a sad occasion for Michael MacNeil who has carried mail between the railway station and the Sydney Post Office as had his father before, starting some fifty years earlier.

1995 Design plans
Sobeys (Atlantic Shopping Centres Ltd.) has purchased the Prince Street Playground across the street from their presently owned Sydney Shopping Centre for $1 million. Design plans call for an additional shopping centre and a multiCinema complex. The playground ball field is to be used for recreation until October. The playground, once a city dump, is on land reclaimed from the Sydney Tar Ponds. The contaminated soil is to be removed.

February 2

Ground Hog Day

1883 Hard Going
A terrible winter—the snow banks are 20 and 25 feet high. The railway hasn't been extended into Cape Breton yet and travellers leaving from Sydney today won't reach the Strait of Canso for 12 days. Travellers make only a half-mile a day on the East Bay Road even though 50 men work 16 hours to burrow a way through the immense drifts.

1921 Prohibition Begins
As of midnight tonight, no liquor can enter Nova Scotia. The appointment of a chief inspector for Cape Breton is expected early in March.

1978 Sydney Mines native top paramedic
Sydney Mines native, Dr. Ronald Stewart, practised medicine along the northern coast of Cape Breton for two years before becoming Medical Director of the Paramedic Rescue Program for the county of Los Angeles, the largest such system in the world. Today he receives a U.S. National Institute of Health scholarship which will enable him to study in Russia.

1995 Traffic lights
Provincial funding is requested to develop controlled access to the K-Mart Plaza. A widening of Welton Street and new traffic lights will help the safe flow of traffic. This follows the traffic lights installed at Ashby Corner in 1993.

February 3

1839 Better harbour
A letter writer to the newspaper *The Nova Scotian* claims that Louisbourg is a better harbour and would make a better capital site than Sydney. Sydney's harbour, the writer argues, is frozen from about mid December and choked with drift ice nearly four months of the year. Louisbourg Harbour used to hold up to 600 vessels in her heyday. "Now, with the exception of a half-dozen miserable houses, not one vestige of the once-flourishing city remains."

1995 Upgraded trail system
Sports enthusiast will welcome the plan to upgrade the trail system—the 700 km of marked and groomed trails from Port Hawkesbury into the Cape Breton Highlands. New trails are to be created and parts of existing trails will be widened and combined, making a loop encompassing communities along the way through Cheticamp to Margaree and Mabou and back to Port Hawkesbury. "The trail system is of substantial economic benefit now," says Bill MacCarthy of the Inverness/Victoria Federation. It's also a lot of fun for hikers, mountain bikers, horseback riders, runners and snowmobilers.

1998 K-Mart slashes stores
To stay competitive, K-Mart Canada begins shutting down money-losing department stores and slashing its workforce. As many as twenty stores must close after the busy Christmas season. The Sydney K-Mart, which opened in 1964, survives the first cut, but it isn't long before it too is closed.

February 4

1861 Improvements needed
The House of Assembly is told in the speech from the throne that Cape Bretoners would be happy to hear of transportation improvements. A steamer crossing the Strait of Canso would be most welcome, and a new road from Plaister Cove (Port Hastings) to Baddeck would cut some 26 miles from the average journey.

1951 Fire at St. Rita's
Fire guts St. Rita's Hospital in Sydney and causes evacuation of the patients.

1970 The *Arrow*
The 11,379-ton Liberian tanker, *Arrow,* goes aground on Cerberus Rock in Chedabucto Bay, five miles from Arichat. About one half of the *Arrow*'s cargo of 3.8 million gallons of bunker oil has escaped to pollute up to 125 miles of shoreline. The main oil slick is about a mile long. Considerable destruction of sea bird life follows. On February 19th, P. O. MacTaggart-Cowan,

the "white knight of Chedabucto Bay," forms a task force to deal with the *Arrow* spill. On April 8th, the one millionth gallon of oil spilled is recovered.

Fig. 2.2 Arrow, *Feb. 4, 1970. Ray Fahey.*

February 5

1848 *Post* take heed

William C. McKinnon, editor of the newspaper, *The Cape Breton Spectator*, is willing to take good oats for arrears in payment of subscriptions.

1901 The bunch of fives

Twenty-five minutes past five on the afternoon of the fifth day of February. The final stages of the first output of iron from the furnaces of the Dominion Iron and Steel Company begin. "In that product is the budding materialization of the hopes and dreams of the gentlemen who have invested their capital in the mighty enterprise, and of the citizens of Sydney who have encouraged its establishment.

"From the early hours of yesterday morning until the first casting was completed, the blast furnace and vicinity were haunted by groups of interested spectators. During the operation of slag-tapping a rush was made toward the banks of the crimson stream that bubbled and swirled as it flowed from the caverns of the throbbing furnace into the cars on the outside of the building; but the spectators were frequently driven back by the sulphurous tempest arising from the molten mass."

Fig. 2.3 N.d. Raytel Photography.

1903 Hockey trophy lost

Despite a daring rescue attempt by a hockey enthusiast, the trophy of the Cape Breton Hockey League is lost when a fire destroys Sutherland Brothers of Sydney—gents' furnishings, boots and shoes. The rest of the Burchell building, including two law offices and a law library, is also destroyed.

February 6

1856 Family disaster

Mrs. John Campbell, two of her children and two visitors, Mary Campbell and Mary MacPherson of Middle Cape, die in a freak accident at the Campbell farm at Big Pond.

Last night the Campbells held a milling frolic at their home. Mary MacPherson and Mary Campbell stayed over to help with some sewing, while Stephen MacDougall stayed to help dry grain for the gristmill. The household retired early tonight. Shortly afterwards the snow careened in a massive slide off the mountain behind the house. Stephen MacDougall's family, wondering where he was, went to the Campbell farm. There was no sign of the buildings. The men were trapped and couldn't help the others.

1901 First iron tapped

The first molten iron is tapped at the Sydney Steel Plant.

1929 Ice driver

Stan Cleary of North Sydney, taking to the ice above Kelly's beach, drives the first car of this season, his Chevrolet, across the ice to Sydney. He doubts that the ice is safe for a heavy car or for that matter safe for any car.

Fig. 2.4 Stan Cleary and his new car, c.1940. Nelson Rice.

1951 North West Arm "Monster"

Rube Chislett of Upper North Sydney gets a surprise when he investigates a log floating just offshore. The log turns out to be a "sea horse" about seven feet long, which disappears as the ice forms in the harbour.

1995 Roads a "total disaster"

Provincial court judge Stan Campbell sentences a young motorist convicted of failing to yield to oncoming traffic on Kings Road. He comments, "The Kings Road area is a total disaster." (See also June 14, 2004)

February 7

1580 Bay of Basques

Basque whalers, who first hunted whales in the 11th century in the Bay of Biscay, are now hunting whales off the west coast of Cape Breton. They use the shelter of the Bay (Cheticamp) as a work area near the whale grounds in the Gulf of St. Lawrence for the "trying" of oil and related tasks. The Basques, who also hunt walruses off the coast, are joined and followed by fishermen from several nations using the area to catch and dry codfish.

February 8

1759 Birth of a bishop
Angus MacEachern, the first Scottish Catholic Bishop of Cape Breton, is born in Scotland.

1899 Bright prospects
"Great excitement over the new iron works. Everybody's going to be rich so it is said."

1904 Two-way ladder
Michael McLean of Baddeck patents an improved firefighting extension ladder that is hailed as a major advance. His ladder incorporates a fire escape apparatus that enables occupants of a building to escape down the ladder while it is being simultaneously used by those fighting the fire.

1979 Clock company in operation
North East Margaree Colonial Clock Company sets up operations.

February 9

1760 Demolition ordered
William Pitt, Britain's War Minister, writes Jeffrey Amherst, Commander-in-Chief in North America. "The King has come to the resolution that the Fortress of Louisbourg, together with all the works and Defences of the Harbour, should be most effectively demolished." Except where necessary to destroy the fortifications, the houses are not to be demolished but, "In the demolition of all works you will particularly have an eye to render as far as possible, the port and harbour of Louisbourg as incommodious and impractible as may be." (See also Nov. 8, 1760.)

1950 Champion Visits
Barbara Ann Scott, former World's amateur and Olympic figure-skating Champion, performs at the Glace Bay Forum, the 9-11th.

1951 No sub net
The Point Edward Naval Base, so important in World War Two, is not included in the new multi-million dollar defence plan announced in Ottawa. A spokesman also discounts reports that the submarine net used in the war will again be spread across the Sydney Harbour entrance.

February 10

1903 Never on Sunday
A committee of the Lord's Day Observance Society visits the General Manager of DISCO and demands to know why steamers are being loaded on a Sunday and why men who exercise conscientious scruples against working on a Sunday are being dismissed. The Gen-

eral Manager comments that, "Work is necessary on Sunday to ensure that steamers are cleared before they can be caught up in ice." When the wharf is erected, no work will be done on Sunday "except when necessary."

1934 Richmond County families near starvation

The warden of Richmond County, J. McIntosh, set out over snow-covered roads to take an appeal to Halifax for food. Conditions, particularly in Petit de Grat, are reported as critical. Hundreds of people are in desperate and immediate need of food. Some families are believed to have been without food for a week. The early freeze-up closed harbours and coves sooner than expected and fishermen have been unable to get their boats to sea. Earlier, the fishing communities had been hit by low prices for fish. Parish priest, Father Boudreau, reports that many fishermen pooled their flour to make bread for the children, but they have now run out of everything. (See also January 27, 1934)

1995 lots of people want jobs

SHL Systemhouse announces they are opening their first data entry and imaging centre in Sydney, which will create 100 jobs. Canada Employment Centre reports that in only two-and-a-half days, more than 800 applications are made.

February 11

1918 What bounty!

A visitor to Cape Breton writes, praising the island, "The people down here are the most fortunate in Canada. The trains are only a few hours behind time (as opposed to 2-3 days). They have all the coal they can use. They have plenty of food and they don't have to work too hard."

1922 Sealing declines

Capt. Matthew Ryan of North Sydney leaves on the *Eva June*, the only vessel which still goes sealing out of Nova Scotia. Years ago a number of vessels rounded Cape Horn and went north to hunt seals in the Pacific. In the early years of this century the South Atlantic replaced the Pacific grounds. Gradually, even these grounds have been considered largely unprofitable.

2002 Anne-Marie MacDonald

Major award-winning playwright, actress and novelist, Anne-Marie MacDonald, appears on TV's Oprah Winfrey Show. Anne-Marie spent many summers on Cape Breton. Among her many awards is the Commonwealth Writers prize for her book *Fall on Your Knees*, portraying a dysfunctional Cape Breton family. The book is now added to the Oprah Book Club list. Anne-Marie's second novel, *The Way the Crow Flies*, is reported to have earned a one-million-dollar advance, making her the highest paid Canadian author for one book.

February 12

1916 Children's crusade

Enlistment in the Armed Forces is voluntary until conscription begins in 1917. Students in Cape Breton, along with others in Nova Scotia, carry home a letter from the commanding officer of the NS Highlanders, the 85th. The children are encouraged to get their big brothers and their fathers to enlist. And they succeed. In twenty-two days, 3,500 men are recruited.

1930 Dominion Number One

Fires at Dominion No. 1 Colliery at Glace Bay are drawn. The pit stopped producing coal in 1927, but its boilers have been kept working to supply No. 1B with steam. Dominion No. 1 was the first mine to be opened in Cape Breton by the Dominion Coal Company. During its 33 years of operation it has produced more than 13 million tons of coal—about twice the annual output of other mines in the province.

1959 Tory roads

Liberal MLAs complain that roads in their ridings are bad and need work. Good roads, they insist, are being built in Cape Breton and Colchester counties, both Conservative areas.

1995 ECMA

Sydney hosts the ECMA (East Coast Music Awards) for the first time. The Awards ceremony takes place in Centre 200, which is transformed from a "hockey ice rink into a futuristic concert hall." For the second year the show, which includes performances as well as award presentations, will be televised by CBC. It "culminates four days of events including artist showcases, a trade show, seminars and a luncheon aimed at the music industry." Aspiring Cape Breton musicians will also have a chance to be heard in performance.

Creignish's nineteen-year-old fiddling and stepdancing Ashley MacIsaac wins for Instrumental Artist and Live Act. The Barra MacNeils win for Best Roots and Traditional Group/Artist, while Rita MacNeil gets the Country Music Award (she's in Nashville recording at the moment). John Allen Cameron, from Glencoe Station, Inverness County, known as "the godfather of Celtic Music," is honoured with a Lifetime Achievement Award.

Twice as many people as last year called in their votes for Entertainer of the Year. Lennie Gallant of P.E.I. wins. He now has a total of six ECMA awards placing him in the record book with Cape Breton's Rankin Family (twelve) and Rita MacNeil (ten). He performs "Man of Steel", and his dedicating it to the workers at the Steel Plant is appreciated.

Sydney hosts the ECMA again in 2000 & in 2005.

February 13

1918 Piggy bank

"Pig clubs" are being used to educate Cape Breton boys in good farming practices. Realizing that the older farmers don't take kindly or quickly to new ideas, the government will encourage the boys. Boys will buy a number of pigs, raise them and keep the money made over the initial costs.

1918 War demand
Baddeck wants a second government mill. Production continues to increase. In 1915 the government mill processed 400 bushels of wheat; in 1916, 3,000 bushels; and last year 12,000 bushels, with the mill running over capacity.

1980 Educator honoured
Dr. Joseph Patrick McCarthy, formerly of Sydney, principal of the NS Teachers College for seventeen years, is honored for his work in teacher education. At a special ceremony in Truro, McCarthy Hall, a new learning resource centre, is named for him. Dr. McCarthy taught at St. Joseph's School and at Sydney Academy.

1987 Treaty rights
Three Whycocmagh Mi'kmaq argue that hunting and fishing regulations don't apply to them because of treaty rights. A provincial court thinks otherwise and this month rules against the Indian treaty rights.

February 14

1754 Love almost conquers all
Chevalier Toulssant-Marie de la Noue, a young officer in his third year of service at Louisbourg, secretly marries Marguerite Guedry, daughter of one of the Acadian families who had been encouraged to settle in Cape Breton. La Noue fell in love with her when he was sent to command the small outpost the government maintained at Baie des Espagnols (Spanish Bay/Sydney Harbour). Shortly after Christmas, la Noue had tried to get Governor Drucour's permission to marry, but he was refused. A young French aristocrat does not marry peasant stock. By the end of January, he had returned to Espagnol to wind up his affairs. Early in February he sent a messenger to the governor resigning his commission and another to Port Dauphin (Englishtown) asking for a priest to visit the sick people in the settlement. And so, the young couple are secretly married. But the groom is soon brought back to Louisbourg to be put into prison until he can be shipped home to France later in September. The marriage is annulled.

1847 The Marriage of Evangeline
The bride is Evangeline, celebrated in Henry Wadsworth Longfellow's poem "*Evangeline. A Tale of Acadie,*" published this year. The groom is Gabriel Lajeunesse. Bride and groom are fictional characters, but the notary is not. Rene LeBlanc was a real notary public in Acadia who, after the expulsion from Grand Pre, came in 1755 with a few families to settle at Caribou Cove (Port Malcolm, Richmond County).

> Then Evangeline lighted the brazen lamp on the table,
> Filled, till it overflowed, the pewter tankard with home-brewed
> Nut-brown ale, that was famed for its strength in the village of Grand Pre;
> While from his pocket the notary drew his papers and inkhorn,
> Wrote with a steady hand the date and the age of the parties,
> Naming the dower of the bride in flocks of sheep and in cattle.
> Orderly all things proceeded, and duly and well were completed,
> And the great seal of the law set like a sun on the margin.

And the notary rising, and blessing the bride and the bridegroom,
Lifted aloft the tankard of ale and drank to their welfare.

1927 Phantom of the Opera

> **Starring LON CHANEY**
> TONIGHT AT KHATTER'S
> "I am a Devil I am a Man
> I am a Saint I am a Ghost
> I am the
> 'Phantom of the Opera'.

February 15

1717 No booze

At Port Dauphin (Englishtown) new recruits are determined to have liquor to help them celebrate the Mardi Gras tomorrow before the beginning of Lent. The commissaire-ordonnateur, Soubras, equally determined not to give them any liquor without being paid for it, threatens a thirsty mob with a pistol and a riot breaks out. Later, the worst offenders are punished on the wooden horse, a narrow piece of wood much like a modern saw horse, which the offender is forced to straddle with his feet, with cannonballs attached, dangling some inches from the ground.

1719 De La Boularderie: colonizer and developer

Louis-Simon Le Poupet, the sieur of Boularderie, is granted priority rights to a concession along the Little Bras d'Or and the Island of Niganiche (Ingonish) for a fishery. He married at Port Royal, Acadia in 1702 and retired later from the French Navy to engage in shipping. In 1714, after helping relieve the starving garrison at Port Toulouse (St. Peter's), La Boularderie proposed to establish a major farming settlement at lie de Verderonne (Boularderie Island) and the eastern shore of La Petite Brador (St. Andrew's Channel).

He tries large-scale coal exports, but even though the coal is burned at the Fortress at Louisbourg and by New Englanders, it is considered too sulphurous for export to France.

La Boularderie builds houses, a good road, a large storehouse, a sawmill—the only one of its kind in the colony—and a flourmill. His ambition is to supply the Fortress with food and coal and with lumber for the fortifications. He dies in debt in June 1738. (See also August 23, 1705.)

1916 Brrr

The record low is reached today: -25°F.

1929 Year's first

Following an old custom, the businessmen of North Sydney present Captain Rhude of the SS *Stanley* with a gold-headed walking cane for being the first captain to bring a foreign ship into port this year.

1969 Record dive

Thirty-year old Leading Seaman Bill Lukeman of Point Edward is assigned as a diver technician with thirteen American aquanauts. One group stays down longer than anyone has before; the other group, Sealab 3, dives deeper. Their tank-car-shaped habitat stays 600 feet under the Pacific off the California coast. Mr. Lukeman keeps his interest in diving, and today he operates submarines in the offshore "oil patch."

1973 Gentlemen?

Dr. Michael Laffin, MLA Cape Breton County, receives a fourteen-day suspension from the House for striking Paul MacEwan, MLA Cape Breton Nova, during a session of the House.

1982 Archie Neil's Cape Breton

Archie Neil's Cape Breton goes national on CBC radio at 2:04 p.m. The half-hour show, hosted by Archie Neil Chisholm of Margaree Forks, has been on local radio for three years and features the "best" of violin and piano music as well as songs and stories of Cape Breton.

1995 Family business busted

Seven people, including brothers, sisters, in-laws, uncles and a babysitter, are sentenced on charges of conspiracy to traffic in cocaine. The New Waterford "family" has been selling $100 bags of cocaine.

February 16

1905 Big snow

Residents of Cape Breton are in the middle of the severest storm of this "Year of the Big Snow."

1929 *The Girls From Happyland*

The Strand Theatre of New Waterford, with seats for 650, formally opens. The 18 x 14-foot mirroroide screen is the same as the screen at the Casino Theatre in Sydney. The Strand will produce road shows, tabloid shows and motion pictures. Opening day feature film is *The Girls From Happyland*.

1929 Big winners

Even though the ice is not in the best condition, today's Sydney Harbour harness racing is a success. The free-for-all is won by Hector, and his owners, Nicholson and Anderson, receive a silver cup donated by Brown's Jewelry. Second prize is a rug, and third prize is three bushels of oats and a bag of potatoes.

1929 Surprise find

A liquor cache is discovered hidden beneath a false drawer when an inspector searches the bureau in his room at the Victoria Hotel.

February 17

1845 Judge needed
Cape Bretoners petition the House in Halifax for a permanent judge to reside on the island.

1870 Free ride
Heavy rains following a blizzard are blamed for an unusual accident today in Creignish. A huge mass of snow crashed down a hill, struck a house, and carried it and Donald MacEachern, his wife Elizabeth and their five small children down the hill. At the shoreline the family, the baby still asleep, spilled out, while the house continued out onto the ice. Only Mrs. MacEachern is injured in the ride.

February 18

1907 Power politics
The Cape Breton Electric Company turns electric power on to a transmission line which connects Sydney and North Sydney. North Sydney has had electricity for some years now but it isn't until this fall that street lights are turned on, burning from dusk to 1 a.m. except when the moonlight makes them unnecessary.

1952 Hung up
Three U.S. Airmen on a flight to Newfoundland run into very bad weather over Cape Breton and are forced to abandon their plane and parachute to safety. They all land safely: one near the Cape Breton Hospital, another at the tracks on Keltic Drive, and the third is rescued from his landing suspended upside down in the telegraph wires in front of the Tracey home in Sydney River.

1963 Fish plant
A new Grade One fish plant at Alder Point, designed to process all types of fish, provides needed employment in the area.

1987 The boy from Cape Breton
Jimmy Burns, 52, leaves his home town, New Waterford, to fly to Vancouver to begin his cross country run to raise money for Alzheimer's research. He arrives home in August to a hero's welcome and a testimonial dinner.

February 19

1829 Early labour problem
Hugh MacMillan of Plaister Cove (now Port Hastings) requests higher payment for carrying the mail on his ferry across the gut of Canso. He's getting £56 a year. "Not enough," he argues, "to keep the ferry fit for men and cattle."

The first ferry route, in 1819, was from MacMillan's Point to Cape Porcupine. Getting across the Strait of Canso remains a problem until the construction of the Causeway (in 1955).

1929 "Mecca for tourists"

At a meeting of the executive council of the Cape Breton Tourist Association, Judge Walter Crowe and the Venerable Archdeacon Draper of Louisbourg argue that "the restoration of the fortress ruins at Louisbourg ... will make Louisbourg the greatest Mecca for Tourists on the North American continent."

February 20

1939 Burny Banks

The entrance to the Old Burnt Mine near Port Morien is deliberately destroyed to discourage bootlegging. The entrance is in the 75-foot cliffs on the Atlantic, and bootleggers carry the coal up the slopes in bags. Also known as the Burning Bank or the Burny Banks, the Burnt Mine was mined earlier by the Louisbourg French. Bootleg mining was carried out during the strikes of 1909, 1923, 1925 and during the Depression, becoming a regular business in the 30s.

1999 *Pit Pony*

Following the success of last year's movie, *The Pit Pony*, a half-hour series of the same name goes on air on CBC-TV. Based on a favourite Canadian children's book, *The Pit Pony* is the story of small town life on Cape Breton and the families of the men and boys who work in the coal mines. Last fall, the movie won Gemini Awards for Best Original Music Score, Best Production Design, and Best Writing in a Dramatic Program. The TV series is being shot at the Soundscape facility, Sydport, Point Edward, and involves a number of Cape Bretoners both as actors and crew.

Fig. 2.5 Pit horses on vacation above ground, c.1930. Shedden Photo.

2005 *Sunburn*

Big Pond's Gordie Sampson sweeps the awards ceremonies by winning five awards: FACTOR album of the year "*Sunburn*." The album's first single and title track win Single of the Year and Pop Recording of the Year; the 4th straight Studio of the Year; Male Artist of the Year and his fifth straight SOCAN Songwriter Award.

Natalie MacMaster is named Female Artist of the Year, and her album *Blueprint* wins Roots/Traditional Solo Recording. J. P. Cormier's newest CD, *X8* (a mandolin collection) wins for Bluegrass Recording and Instrumental Recording. Rita MacNeil is presented with the Dr. Helen Creighton Lifetime Achievement Award.

Celtic Colours International Festival is named Event of the Year. (See also October 10, 1997.)

February 21

1785 First official act

The new British Colony of Cape Breton holds its first Council Meeting at the mines (Sydney Mines) where Lt. Governor Des Barres is spending the winter.

1859 Harbour tragedy

The ice gives way under St. George's minister, W. Y. Porter, as he crosses the Harbour to North Sydney. He manages to haul himself ashore, but he freezes to death before he can be rescued.

1905 Women an endangered species?

A New York doctor, speaking on the health of Canadian women, remarks that Healthy Canadian women are so rare as to be almost extinct. An ad in today's *Sydney Daily Post* has the answer to Canada's problem. It recommends Lydia E. Pinkham's Vegetable Compound for a woman's health.

1918 The home front

Farmers are anxious to show increased production on the land as their part of the war effort, in exchange for their exemption from military service. Visiting agricultural officials are full of praise for Cape Breton farmers and their hospitality. "One would never think it was Lent, from the way they fed us. There is an old story of Cape Breton, and that is that it is a country where the teapot is ever brewing, and we found it to be true." Cape Breton also has some huge men. Mr. MacDonald says that he is tall himself, "but when I got alongside of that man Finlayson down there at Framboise, I felt like a pygmy."

1929 YMCA burns

The YMCA in Sydney is destroyed by fire. Built in 1907, it was one of the oldest buildings in the city. The basement held a kitchen and large dining room. The first floor housed Menzie's Music Store and Harry Grant's Haberdashery, while the second floor was occupied by the recreation rooms and business offices of the "Y." The gymnasium and showers were on the top floor.

February 22

1909 Swan dive drome

No. 5, Cygnet II, Dr. Alexander Graham Bell's new tetrahedral air ship with J.A.D. McCurdy at the controls, makes three attempts to fly over the ice off Baddeck. Made of about 5,000 tetrahydral cells, the Cygnet is the first machine of its type to attempt flight with a man and a motor. The Cygnet is pushed

Fig. 2.6 Bell's "kite," n.d.

on runners along the ice, but the velocity isn't great enough. On the third attempt the ten-foot propeller shears and breaks into three pieces. Dr. Bell writes that the "engine will be transferred to the Silver Dart and a flight attempted tomorrow."

1967 Supreme Court appointment

J. L. Dubinsky, a Glace Bay lawyer, is appointed to the Supreme Court. He is the first Jew in the Atlantic Provinces to be appointed to the Court.

2005 PCBs to Alberta

One of the last shipments of SYSCO's PCB-laden transformers is headed to Swan Hills, Alberta, to be incinerated.

February 23

1909 Red-letter day for Bell

The morning is crisp and sunny as neighbours and others assemble in sleighs and on skates on the ice of the Bras d'Or Lakes at Baddeck. John A. D. McCurdy, a native of Baddeck, takes his seat in the *Silver Dart*, a plane he has designed. He "flexed all the controls and then gave the signal for the start of the motor." In a minute or two the mechanics let go and the machine bounded forward and took to the air after a short run of about 150 feet. "I felt perfectly at home and rose to an altitude of 60 feet, levelled out and flew for about three quarters of a mile and then descended." And so begins heavier-than-air machine flight in the British Empire.

McCurdy continues his story. "Dr. Graham Bell was standing up in the red sleigh and I shall never forget the pleasure and animation showing in his face as he said, 'This has been wonderful. But there will be no more flights today, my boy.' History may have been made so let's have nothing mar the achievement. Put the machine away till tomorrow when you can fly to your heart's content'."

A copious note-taker, Dr. Bell's only entry today is "Red letter day. McCurdy flew over Baddeck Bay in the *Silver Dart* about 1/2 mile."

1959 *Silver Dart* remembered

Fiftieth-anniversary celebrations honouring Canada's first pilot and the birth of Canadian aviation, take place in Baddeck. J. A. D. McCurdy, bundled in a raccoon coat, is conveyed to the main platform in the sleigh from which Alexander Graham Bell witnessed his historic flight fifty years ago. During a re-enactment of the event, the *Silver Dart II*, piloted by RCAF Wing Commander Paul Hartman, bucks a treacherous crosswind as the wind catches the plane and hurls it sideways to the ice.

1984 *Silver Dart* remembered again

Prince Michael of Kent is an honoured guest at the 75th Anniversary celebrations at Baddeck. Gordon MacRae of Baddeck has masterminded the building of a second replica of the *Silver Dart*, presently housed in the Masonic Hall. In the fall, this replica is displayed at the Farnborough Air Show in England.

2005 Kidston Island Lighthouse

Baddeck may take over ownership of the Kidston Island Lighthouse. Established in 1875, it remains a symbol of the village.

Fig. 2.7 Kidston lighthouse, n.d.

February 24

1896 You think Celsius is confusing

Changes in the weather code
Dense fog becomes chill; light fog becomes chilly.
Dense haze becomes chip; light haze becomes chippy.
Dense mist becomes crisp; light smoke becomes crispy.
These words will be used instead of fog, haze or smoke.

1905 Feed supply critical

A critical situation at snow-struck Gabarus is relieved by the arrival of the schooner *Basil M. Gelhart* out of Halifax with a cargo of hay, flour, meal and general merchandise. With hay costing only $18 a ton earlier in the winter, many people along the coast decided to over-winter more livestock. Both livestock and people are now running out of food.

1909 Airplane two

The second flight of the *Silver Dart* at Baddeck is more spectacular and longer than the first. This time Baddeck Bay is circled, with several turns, a distance of 41/2 miles, at varying elevations.

1950 Boer War veteran

William Airey, North Sydney native, the only local veteran of the Boer War still living, is honoured by the North Sydney branch of the Canadian Legion on the 50th anniversary of the Canadian victory over the Boers in Parrsburg, South Africa.

February 25

1828 Contempt?

The Lord's Day Act states that "No person shall use, or suffer to be used, any game, play, sport, or pastime on the Lord's Day." A Sydney man, charged with skating on a Sunday, complains about his fine. He sets out on another Sunday, is caught and found guilty a second time. This time he is fined 10 shillings, to be used by the poor. In his letter to the editor of the newspaper, *The Nova Scotian*, he refers to the judge as a "Just ass of the Peace."

1950 Moonshiners sleep in shifts

An intensive drive by the RCMP has so filled up the Cape Breton County Jail with moonshiners that the prisoners are compelled to eat and sleep in shifts.

1970 Native crafts revival

A couple from the Whycocomagh Reserve are conducting workshops on making handcrafts: basket-weaving, bead, leather and quill work, birchbark technique, axe handle carving and furniture building. Nearby woods supply the rock maple, white and black ash, spruce, yellow birch, white maple, alder and poplar. Moose and deer hides are cut, sewn into everything from moccasins to key cases. Birchbark gets transformed into canoes, photo albums, teepees, coaster and drums, while sweetgrass becomes bindings and baskets. This is believed to be the first program of its kind to be conducted on an Indian Reserve in Atlantic Canada.

2005 Cape Breton University

University College of Cape Breton is now Cape Breton University, its fifth incarnation since Xavier Junior College opened in 1951.

February 26

1929 CJCB on the air

CJCB goes on the air officially from the dining hall of the Isle Royale Hotel. Frederick Philip Grove, noted Canadian author and educationalist, speaks on "Why I am a Canadian." Listener interest is intense and widespread, with one enthusiastic supporter calling from Framingham, Massachusetts.

1929 Eelgrass exported

Eelgrass, found in abundance around our coastline, has long been a source of inconvenience for the fisherman because it clogs nets and fouls boat propellers. Through the years, eel grass has been useful, however, as rural Cape Bretoners use it as banking for their homes in the winter.

Other uses are now reported for eel grass. "Fireproof, non-verminous, and sound absorbent," it is being woven into mats for use in many public buildings being built in England.

1930 Sydney homes quarantined

Fifty-four houses in Sydney are quarantined because of an outbreak of scarletina.

1981 Line needed

CN has decided not to abandon its Inverness line. The Evans Coal Company at St. Rose, the only remaining privately owned coal mine on Cape Breton, is expanding and rail transportation is necessary to this expansion.

1984 Loud voice?

Yvonne LeBlanc, reading the weather on CJCB radio is heard in Milan, Italy.

2005 Prize-winning photographer
Katheryn Gordon, wife of Cape Breton photographer Warren Gordon, is named Maritime Professional Photographer of the Year for the second time. One of the judges comments, "She had a beautiful set of prints, a magnificent entry. She pretty much stole the show. There really wasn't anybody in her class at this competition."

February 27

1851 End of line
A public meeting is held to discuss making Sydney a packet station and one of the terminals for the proposed railway.

1905 That's entertainment
Plays at Sydney's Lyceum Theatre this month:

Feb. 13th: *In His Power*—scene is Paris at the time of the Franco-Prussian War.

Feb. 14th: The latest English comedy, *The Marriage of Kitty*; *Peggy O'Grady* from *The Isle of Spice* and the Japanese hit *One Little Soldier Man* will be among the latest hit songs heard. Other performances include *My Geraldine*, a thrilling Irish drama.

Lecture and musical evening, including a lecture on the Rise and Growth of Representative Government, *In Mizzoura, The Master of Woodbarrow, Brown's in Town* and that "thrilling, sensational drama," *Lost in New York.*

1922 Company store
Company Store - Dominion Coal Company:
Sirloin steak and roasts - 22 cents lb.
Butter - 40 cents lb.
Sugar - 8 cents lb.
Best hard wheat flour in wood - 9.50 bbl.
Extra fancy molasses - 75 cents gal.
Salt beef - 14 cents lb.
Tea - 50 cents lb.
Overalls - 1.50 pair
Pit boots - 2.75 pair

1929 Landmark goes
Built some 70 years ago, one of North Sydney's oldest landmarks, the Belmont Hotel, is destroyed by fire. The second-floor balcony was the scene of many political speeches and the announcements of election results.

1939 Vogue opens
It is a gala opening. "First-nighters thronged the street in front of the new institution of entertainment long before the opening hour and several police had to be on hand to keep the throngs in check." CJCB broadcasts the opening. Several guests are in evening dress. They marvel at the lavish Art Deco interior, the Roman Travertine marble on the floors, a water fountain, lounges, the deep-piled carpet, the velvet drapes.

The *Post* reporter continues to marvel: "The auditorium will cause wonderment and rapture. The decorative features represent an artistic sense and taste in the fullest degree. Soft hues of the Neon lighting sparkle off the walls and there is a rhapsody of swank and smartness about it all that places the patron in a high receptive mood for the presentation of the picture." Opening night movie is *Sweethearts* with Jeanette MacDonald and Nelson Eddy.

The Vogue closed in April 1999.

February 28

1781 Desperate struggle

Ensign Prenties and five other survivors of the ill-fated *St. Lawrence*, which foundered last December 5th off the west coast of Cape Breton, have been in the area of St. Ann's Harbour for ten days now. They are exhausted and have been existing on boiled kelp and melted candles, which have made them violently ill.

Two Indians out hunting arrive, help them with food and build a roaring fire. The Indians return later with an old woman who remembers the survivors of another shipwreck, *L'Auguste* off Cape North some twenty years earlier. The Indian who is translating had rescued the Captain of *L'Auguste*.

The present survivors of the "*St. Lawrence*" are taken further into the Harbour to the Indian camp at Goose Cove. If, after they were shipwrecked last December, the men had turned south instead of north, they would have reached Canso within two days and been spared their extreme hardships. (See also Dec. 5, 1780.)

1801 Duel

An officer of the regiment stationed in Sydney and his good friend, a member of the government of Cape Breton, have a heated quarrel on the Esplanade this spring. Compelled by the fashion of the times to settle their dispute with a duel the two meet with their seconds at a point near where the Central School now stands. They are handed pistols, pace out thirty feet and each turns to face and fire at the other.

Both their shirtfronts are spattered red and the horrified duellists fall to the ground— to the amusement of their seconds who, instead of charging the flintlock pistols with shot, have loaded them with powder and cranberries.

1883 What's in a name?

The memory of the Red Man
How can it pass away
While their names of music linger
On each mount and stream and bay.

Richard Huntington, Grand Mira

There are Indian names such as Whycocomagh, meaning "Head of the Waters," or "End of the Bay" or, even more picturesque, "Beside the Flowing Wavetops;" Baddeck, "Place with an Island Nearby;" Eskasoni, "Green Boughs;" Washabuckt, "Placid Waters;" Shenacadie, "The Cranberry Patch;" Benacadie, "The Humble Place;" and Poulamon, "Tom Cod."

There are many French names as well: D'Escousse, Grand Etang, Main-a-Dieu, Framboise, Cheticamp ...

And Gaelic: Estmere, Ben Eoin, (Jonathan's Mountain) and perhaps Gabarus, which some think is a Gallicized corruption of "Cabot's Cross," indicating the place where Cabot landed. Who knows for sure? There are many names that kept alive for the early settlers memories of their former homes: New Waterford, Barra Glen, Iona, Inverness, Mull River, Skir Dhu, Loch Lomond, Dunvegan. Then there are others: Nyanza, named after Lake Nyanza in Africa, Ottawa Brook, for the preoccupation of the people there for talking politics, and Soldiers Cove, which used to be called "Laugh at the Yankees."

1924 First radio in Margaree Valley

John F. Hart's new radio can pick up programs only on American stations, some from as far away as Florida. The early radios need either an aerial strung between two 45-foot poles 100 feet apart or a 2-wire outdoor antenna.

1930 Logue wins

More than 3,000 people watch Dick Logue, driving a Buick Master Six Roadster, set a new speed record for racing on the Sydney Harbour ice. Logue wins the McAdam Trophy for the second year. In a 2.5-mile race from a point off the quarantine station at Point Edward to a point near the Atlantic Engineering Works in Sydney, he covers the distance in one minute, 25 seconds, at an average speed of 106 miles an hour. Bert Sampson in his Nash comes in second, while Charlie Libbus, driving Joe Khattar's Velie, is handicapped by the loss of a studded tire and comes in third. Gordon Elman follows in his Chev.

Bob McGowan, Cup winner in 1928, is unable to start the race because his new Graham Paige Six is giving him some trouble. But the next day in an inpromptu race over the same course, Dick Logue beats Bob McGowan anyway.

1952 C-47 crashes at Sydney River

A C-47 crashes into the woods off Kings Road in Sydney River. For seventeen of the eighteen men who bail out, it is their first experience in parachuting. Several of the men land near the home of Mr. & Mrs. Malcolm MacDonald and are attracted by the lights inside the house. The two-year-old MacDonald child is teething, and Mrs. MacDonald is up and about.

March

Dear Sydney

Sydney, dear Sydney, why not sing of thee?
Who nestling on the brink of thine own river,
Hath never raised ambitious eyes, or thought
Of what fate had in store within her quiver.

In thy seclusion, in thy quiet life,
Thou dids't not think that fame would reach thy shore;
But by the financiers' enchanted hand,
Thou art waked from lethargy and shall not slumber more ...

Contentment hath no place and such is life;
Thy greed for gold hath now attacked thy town;
And now that Whitney comes to make thee rich;
You feel that fate for thee will never frown.

So be it. I will also hope with thee.
And trust the future'll bring no cause for fears;
And may thy risen star keep bright and strong,
High in the zenith, where it now appears.

George Sims – 1900

Fig. 3.1 Dominion Iron and Steel Co., 1903. Nation Publishing Co.

Orando Cheap Breatainn

Fonn: 'S e Cheap Breatainn tir mo ghraidh,

Tir nan craobh 's nam beanntan ard';
"S e Ceap Breatainn tir mo ghraidh,
Tir is aillidh leinn air thalamh.

Anns a' gheamhradh, am an fhuachd;
Am nam bainnsean, am nan luadh;
Chluinnte gillean air cleith-luaidh;
"S gruagaich 'le guth' cruaidh 'g an leanaid.

'N uair bhiodh am-fucadh ullamh, reidh,
Chuirt' an fhidheall sin air ghleus;
Dhannsamaid air urlar reidh,
Gur e "Cabar Feidh" bu mhath leinn.
Chite cailleach ghasda, choir,
Tighinn mu'n cuairt a thomhas a' chlo;
An cromadh aice air a dorn
'S cha robh doigh ac' air a mealladh.

Dan Alex MacDonald

Song to Cape Breton

Chorus: Cape Breton is the place I love

A place with trees and high mountains.
Cape Breton is the place I love
A place that is the finest in the land.

Winter is the time for cold
and the time of weddings and milling.
You would hear young men at a milling table
And maidens with a hard voice following them.

When the milling would be over and done,
the violin would be brought up and tuned.
We would dance on a smooth floor;
And "Cabar Feidh" was the tune we would like.
We would see a kind old lady
come to measure the cloth
with a measure on her hand
And they had no way of fooling her.

translation: John Dan MacNeil

Fig. 3.2 Milling frolic, 1993. Owen Fitzgerald.

March 1

1821 Agricultural society
An agricultural society is established in Mabou to promote better agriculture on the Island. Within a short while, Inverness County becomes a provincial leader in agriculture. (See also January 10, 1881.)

1899 First freight
A load of fish from a wrecked boat is the first freight ever carried from Port Hood to Port Hastings on the new Inverness-Richmond Railway.

1923 The hard way
This winter the Oxford Paper and Pulp Company at Murray (near North River Bridge) employed some 700 men and ran ten logging camps. Over the winter the men, with the help of 150 horses and using axes and crosscut saws, cut 58,000 cords of wood. By 1931, the depression in the pulp market ends the operations at the plant and wages to the choppers of $5–10 a day, plus good accommodation, ends with it.

Fig. 3.3 Cape North Men at a Maine lumber camp, c.1900.

1925 Church union opposed
Cape Bretoners finish voting on Church union. They are trying to determine whether or not the Presbyterian, Methodist and Congregationalist Churches should join into one body called the United Church of Canada. The Little Narrows Presbyterian congregation is one of the two congregations in Canada that fail to record even one vote in favour of union.

1986 Arson
The day before it is to re-open, Skipper's Landing Restaurant in North Sydney has two suspected fire bombings. Last August, under previous ownership, it also suffered an arson attack. "The bright spot," say new owners Lorna Dolmont and her husband Mike, "is we had so much kindness from people offering to help."

Centre 200
Mayor Manning MacDonald announces that close to $6 million of the estimated $12-13 million has either been spent or committed on the construction of Centre 200.

1993 Gaelic is alive and well
The Gaelic College announces a summer series of weekend immersion courses in Gaelic as well as a week-long session during August. Gaelic is alive and well throughout the island with adult language classes and traditional singing. *Feists* "festivals" are spreading to Glendale and Christmas Island. In Iona, Rosmairi MacCormack, host of CBC's *Island Echoes,* runs a

children's pre-school Gaelic play group and Marjorie Beaton teaches Gaelic in high school in Mabou.

March 2

1933 Liquid gold

Cape Breton's largest liquor seizure in two years is made today at Dominion. The illegal treasure of ninety-four five-gallon kegs of Black Diamond Rum was hidden in a subterranean vault. Valued at more than $7,000, the rum is worth $15,048 at retail prices.

1965 Power flows

About 3:30 this afternoon, Premier G. I. Smith, chairman of the Nova Scotia Power Commission, closes a switch at the Seaboard Thermal Generating Station near New Waterford and sends Cape Breton electric energy flowing into the interprovincial grid. Our power is being used in Pictou and Guysborough counties as well as in Maine and Quebec.

1992 Firewood

An unofficial survey by the Department of Natural Resources reveals that firewood sales on Cape Breton are a $1 million industry. With the bulk being cut in Cape Breton County, the tally of 10,000-12,000 cords of hardwood sold each year may, in fact, be more than 15,000 cords.

March 3

1929 Black diptheria

The diptheria outbreak at Dominion No. 6 is, according to Dr. Archibald, "the worst type of black diphtheria" he's ever seen.

1949 Doctor dies

Dr. James Adams Proudfoot, Inverness County coroner and health officer, dies. The doctor was a former Member of the NS Legislature for Inverness County. In the Royal Medical Corps during WWII, he served in Egypt and Cairo and later Camp Hill Hospital. His work during the 1917 Halifax explosion brought added recognition.

1973 Mine sealed

Fire at No. 12 Colliery in New Waterford results in the death of miner Earl Leadbetter and mining executive Donald MacFadgen. The mine is sealed.

March 4

1992 Resignation

Vince MacLean resigns from the leadership of the provincial Liberal Party following an acrimonious annual meeting on Saturday at which he had been unable to garner sufficient support for his leadership.

1993 VLTs

Convenience store owners want video lottery terminals (VLTs) reinstated in their outlets. Since their removal, sales are down, full-time staff is reduced and security affected. Storeowner Harold MacIsaac, says "the VLTs are designed for recreation, not gambling, and for the most part, are treated in that manner." Will VLTs being only accessible where liquor is sold create a problem for alcoholics or gambling addicts or both?

March 5

1920 Crackdown

Sydney City Council passes laws regarding motor vehicles. Vehicles will not be allowed to pass a stopped tramcar or to make U-turns on Charlotte Street between Townsend and Dorchester Streets. They must stop and move over for engines, and signals must be given when turning. Vehicles aren't permitted to be left standing in the street unattended or unlocked with no brakes on.

1984 New press

The new press rolls at *The Cape Breton Post*. The first edition is run on the new Goss Urbanite eight-unit, high-speed, offset press in the *Post*'s newly built plant and office building at the corner of Dorchester and George Streets in Sydney.

The *Cape Breton Post* has its beginnings in two separate weeklies. In 1906 the Liberal *Record*, started twelve years earlier as a weekly, became a daily newspaper. At the same time, the Conservative *Post* was published as a weekly between 1896 and 1900, when it too became a daily. Each weekly continued to be published, under a different name, for some years. In 1929, the *Post* issued an evening edition and, in 1934, the *Post* merged with the *Record* to become the Independent *Post Record* and later, in 1956, the *Cape Breton Post*.

March 6

1918 Help for horses - 1,309th day of war

Local horsemen plan a special event on the ice of Sydney Harbour as a fundraiser for an unusual but very important organization. The Blue Cross has been organized to relieve and care for horses wounded in the war. Thousands of good stock are shot and maimed as they haul ambulances, draw guns to their positions and aid the Allies. Local horsemen hope to attract many fans and entries from all over Cape Breton. Events include an exhibition race, a race of champion stallions, and a free-for-all trot.

1967 Hair today ... Gone tomorrow

Two students of Woodill Jr. High School in Sydney are sent home when they fail to have their hair cut.

They have been warned a number of times. According to principal, John MacKeigan, "Long hair is all right for girls, but for boys it's nothing but an improper influence on other members of the class."

March 7

1920 Aground

The Dominion coal carrier SS *Cape Breton* goes ashore on an isolated section of Scatarie Island. Heavy seas and thick ice hamper the rescue attempts by the steamer *Kyle*.

1951 Lyceum

The Lyceum is destroyed by fire (see also May 23, 1904). Early in April of this year St. FX University starts reconstruction and classes begin in September for the new Xavier Junior College.

1967 Heavy water

Heavy water is scheduled to be in production by May 1st. The Deuterium of Canada Ltd.'s heavy water plant at Glace Bay is undergoing the first stage of start-up testing prior to actual production. The process, an air water test, will be completed before any hydrogen sulphide gas in introduced.

1970 Eclipse

Heavy overcast skies add to the darkness of today's total eclipse of the sun.

2004 Sister Peggy Butts

Sister Peggy Butts, local educator and social activist, dies aged 79. She was appointed a senator in 1997 and resigned two years later at the regular senator retirement age. During her years as senator she donated her government salary to the poor and she continued to lived in a convent, rather than rent an apartment.

2005 "Set for life"

Thirty-three year-old Jennifer Woodsworth of Albert Bridge celebrates her birthday a few days after her real birthday. Her brother gives her a Scratch n' Win Set for Life Lottery ticket he just bought. It's her lucky day. She wins the $675,000 prize which she is going to take as $1,000 a week for the next twenty-five years.

March 8

1902 Seam exposed

Prospecting for coal at the head of Lingan Bay has exposed a good seam 4 feet 6 inches thick containing more coal than any other seam owned by the Dominion Coal Company.

1902 Steel at Sydney Mines

A blast furnace will be erected at a point between the Queen pit and Big Pond in Sydney Mines. It is hoped that before the summer is over, pig iron will be exported from Sydney Mines as well as from Sydney. North Sydney's offer to establish the furnace in that town has been declined by the Nova Scotia Steel and Coal Company, because the coal and coke required to make steel are already produced at Sydney Mines.

1918 Anthrax - 1,311th day of war

A Belgian worker in Sydney has died of anthrax, a disease of animals, particularly sheep, transmissible to man.

This dread disease is very rare in Canada. The Belgian isn't the first Cape Bretoner to have died from it. Lieutenant-Colonel R. C. McLeod, officer commanding the St. FX hospital unit, is believed to have become afflicted with anthrax while using a shaving brush in the headquarters of a unit in England about a year ago.

1920 Elegant prize

This is the first day of the *Post*'s $10,000 contest. In an attempt to encourage new prepaid subscribers, to collect back payments for subscriptions, and to test the initiative of local boys and girls, the *Post* is offering an elegant touring car, a "six-cylinder McLaughlin equipped with spare tire and bumper and trimmed with genuine hand-buffed leather." Second prize is a Chevrolet touring car. Pianos are also included in the prize list. The *Post* costs 3 cents an issue.

March 9

1992 Debating champs

Over the weekend Cory MacDonald and Laura Penny of the Sydney Academy Debating Club win the North American High School Debating Championships at McGill University in Montreal. This follows the Academy Cub's third provincial title recently won at the Halifax High School Debating Tournament.

1993 Flower show

Cape Breton flower arrangers, Lillian MacLeod, of the Middle River Garden Club, and Pam Newton, of the Westmount Garden Club, join summer resident of Belle Cote, Fran Eggers, in competitions at the New England Flower Show in Boston for the third consecutive year. All are winners with Lillian and Fran taking first prize blue ribbons.

March 10

1826 Apples for the teacher

Under the new School Bill, money is available for school construction and "Reading, Writing and the elementary rules of Arithmetic taught therein." When this system is adopted, no person will be able to teach school unless he/she has passed an examination and received a license. Yearly salaries can be as high as £50 and part of this may be paid in produce. A school may be kept open during a whole year if a district contains at least thirty families. If a district isn't large enough to support a school, it may be joined with another.

The costs of building the schoolhouse, its annual repairs, teacher's salary and any other expenses will be collected from the residents of the district.

2005 Baby Day

It's Baby Day at the McConnell Library. A new program starts for babies 0-18 months and their parents or caregivers. "The one-hour program includes rhymes, stories, puppets and songs as well as play sessions with toys, board books and lots of chat."

2005 New image

"Come To Life," a new image for Nova Scotia, is unveiled by Tory Premier John Hamm. The jingle, sung by Sydney Mines folksinger Bruce Guthro, accompanies a symbol of a tri-coloured wave. The province is moving away from fiddles and fishermen to an "urban, mellow way of life."

"Today is about celebrating Nova Scotia and its people.... Ultimately, coming to Nova Scotia is about coming to a place where ideas can take hold and grow, and where you can be happy and fulfilled."

March 11

1790 Moose poaching

Word has reached the Council that poaching gangs are at work again slaughtering moose and caribou in northern Cape Breton. Led by guides, an expedition of an officer and thirty men of the 21st Regiment sets out with snowshoes, toboggans and other articles, including copies of the ordinance passed by Council on December 21, 1789, regarding the killing of moose and caribou. The toboggans can only be used on the ice of the bays, and the soldiers, unused to snowshoes, are having problems with their feet. Some become sick and several have to be left in the care of the few inhabitants of St. Ann's and Niganiche (Ingonish).

Those who plod on as far as Cape North with orders to destroy all the huts of the poachers are unable to carry out their mission. The hunters hide in the woods, leaving their wives and children in the huts. The soldiers, who will not turn them out, return to Sydney with promises that the families will leave as soon as weather permits. (See also Jan. 1, 1790.)

1918 Votes For women -1,314th Day of War

Sydney City Council supports the government's plans to allow married women to vote. Before this, only spinsters and widows over 21, British subjects who possess the required property qualifications could vote. The number of women in this category in Sydney is small. In last week's election, for example, out of 3,500 who voted, probably fewer than 200 were women. Women will be able to vote in the 1919 civic election.

1983 Protecting heritage

The Lyceum building in Sydney becomes a Nova Scotia Heritage property. Also protected under the new Heritage Properties Act are Cossitt House, St. George's Church, St. Patrick's Church Museum in Sydney, the Marconi property at Birch Grove, the old Sydney Mines Post Office, the Gilbert H. Grosvenor Hall in Baddeck, the MacRae-Bitterman House at Middle River and the MacAskill House in St. Peters.

Fig. 3.4 Sydney Mines Post Office, c.1909. McCoy Printing Co.

2005 Too much
Volunteer organizations are hard hit by rising liability insurance rates. Police-run boys and girls clubs find their rates could get as high as $3,000 a year. Groups using schools after hours are only a few of the other organizations facing "the risk that some volunteer will misbehave, but that's the world we live in," comments a *Post* writer. Royal Canadian Legion liability extends to being responsible for irresponsible drinking.

March 12

1918 Too many pilots? 1,315th day of war
At a meeting of harbour pilots in Sydney, various items are discussed, including pension funds and the fact that there may be too many pilots for this harbour. Any strange ships entering will now be allowed to proceed to a berth without being fired on, but then they will be investigated. The news from Halifax Harbour is that the people there are beginning to recover their nerve after last December's explosion and temporary structures are being built in the city.

1931 First hockey broadcast
The final hockey match for the Commercial championship between the *Post* and *"Merchant's Seals"* is broadcast over CJCB radio and becomes the first radio broadcast of hockey in the area. Allan MacDonald gives the play-by-play description and between periods, Tommy Robertson outlines the history and activities of the Commercial Hockey League.

1950 Surprise!
Mrs. Effie Bennett of Upper Prince Street gets more than she bargained for when she purchased a half ton of coal from the Dominion Coal Company's depot on George Street. Getting up early this morning, before her eight children were up, to kindle the kitchen stove fire, she discovers a stick of dynamite in her load of coal.

1992 Ski hopefuls
Two young Cape Bretoners, fourteen-year-old Amanda Williams of Neil's Harbour and Avery MacDonald of Ben Eoin are part of the three-member Nova Scotian team competing at this week's National Juvenile Ski Championships being held at Quebec's Mont Tremblant in the Laurentian Mountains.

March 13

1521 First Portugese
Joam Alvares Fagundez, Portugese sailor, receives a grant of the lands of Cape Breton, Nova Scotia and probably Newfoundland from the King of Portugal. Fagundez wants to found a colony and it's believed that Portugese fishermen will spend the winter at what is now Ingonish, but no permanent settlement will be made. They will also use the area at what is now St. Peters as a fishing base (from 1521-1537), calling it San Pedro.

1988 Beware of coyotes

An additional problem with this year's spring lambing is the recent arrival to the island of destructive coyotes.

March 14

1933 Builds own airplane

With commercial pilot Ralph Peters of Westmount at the controls, 23-year old Donald McEachern flies his two-passenger monoplane over Sydney Harbour. Having only sporadic work at the steel plant, McEachern wanted something to do, so he built a plane in his workshop on Inglis Street, Sydney, with materials purchased from a local building supply firm.

1950 *World's Greatest Love Story*

World's Greatest Love Story, the story of Samson and Delilah, produced by Cecil B. DeMille and starring Hedy Lamarr and Victor Mature is playing at the Paramount. Matinees: Children, 35 cents; Adults 75 cents. Evenings: Children 35 cents; Adults $1.00.

March 15

1979 *Kurdistan* cracks

The British oil tanker *Kurdistan*, en route from Port Hawkesbury to Sept Isles, Quebec, earlier this afternoon was proceeding slowly through the heavy ice in the Cabot Strait. Forty-six nautical miles northeast of Sydney between Cape Breton and Newfoundland, the crack in her hull widens and the *Kurdistan* splits in half, spilling out part of her cargo of 29,662 tons of Bunker C oil. Bunker C is heavy black oil that congeals in cold water. It's more difficult to clean up than crude oil and it decomposes more slowly. It was Bunker C that fouled the shoreline of Chedabucto Bay in Canada's first and only major oil spill to date, as a result of the sinking of the *Arrow*. (See also Feb. 4, 1970.)

The crew is rescued from lifeboats and transported to Sydney by the Canadian Coast Guard Icebreaker *Sir William Alexander*. The captain will be airlifted off the stern section at daybreak.

Fig. 3.5 Women shovelling "gunk" from the Kurdistan, *13-Apr-79. Owen Fitzgerald.*

1986 Jobs

Most of the 4,000 jobs to be created by the NS Training and Employment Program and Challenge '86 will be targeted for Cape Breton, according to Development Minister Roland Thornhill.

2005 New residential centre

The new state of the art residential centre for adolescents-at-risk between the ages of twelve and sixteen officially opens. Comhla Cruinn, Gaelic for "coming together," is located in

Sydney. Operated by Children's Aid, it will offer the young teens the comforts of home while giving them the counselling they need.

March 16

1948 Millionaires

The Sydney Millionaires hockey team wins the Maritime Senior Hockey championship against the Moncton Hawks at Sydney Forum. Back in 1941, the team came within one game of winning the Allan Cup, losing to the Regina Rangers in a series of games that were all played in western Canada. On Sept. 20, 1980, the team is inducted into the NS Sports Hall of Fame.

1950 Not guilty of murder

Donald Jack McLean, former mayor of Sydney, is found not guilty of murdering Joseph MacKinnon, the city registrar, in a hit-and-run death on December 18, 1949. He is convicted on the lesser charge of manslaughter and sentenced to three years imprisonment by the Supreme Court petit jury.

March 17

1748 St. Patrick's Day

The Irish are in Louisbourg. They are fishermen, soldiers, servants and stonemasons, and girls taken from a British ship seized by the French off New York. Catholic Irish couples from Newfoundland come over to be married and have their children baptized. Many immigrate for other religious reasons, as a reaction against Protestantism in the British Colonies of Nova Scotia and Newfoundland. It is reported that a few Irish are in Main-a-Dieu before 1750.

After the French leave Louisbourg, still more Irish come from Newfoundland. The cheapest passenger rates from Ireland across the Atlantic are to Newfoundland, and so many Irish come to North America via this route. They include Maurice Kavanagh, whose grandson becomes the first Catholic allowed to sit in the House of Assembly without taking an oath against his faith.

An economic depression following the Napoleonic Wars and a scarcity of fish force even more Irish to leave Newfoundland after 1815, but Cape Breton, itself suffering from crop failures, is unable to feed them. (See also April 7, 1815.)

A few Irish land accidentally in Cape Breton because of shipwrecks or desertions. Patrick O'Connor, for example, escapes from a British ship in Halifax, walks to the Strait of Canso, swims across and finds a home in the Margaree Valley. The Irish in Cape Breton tend to settle close together in villages clustered around coves, like Rocky Bay, Ingonish, Main-a-Dieu and Irish Cove.

1828 Contracts called

Contracts are called for supplying 2,300 chaldrons of Sydney coal for the use of the troops at Halifax. A quantity of fresh beef of "the best quality" is also needed, as well as 70 chaldrons of Sydney coal for use at Sydney. (One chaldron equals 36 bushels.)

1908 First Scouts

William Glover, an Englishman who came to the area to work in the North Atlantic Coal Company, starts the first Boy Scout troop in Canada with eleven boys in Port Morien. At first they meet at his home and later at the Blockhouse School. At this time there is no set program and the boys do a lot of hiking and other nature-related activities, following the Scout Founder Lord Baden Powell's words that "Scouting is mainly a great adventure played out of doors."

Fig. 3.6 Boy Scouts, 1910.

1917 Harbour race

About 3,000 fans watch Allie Lewis, a veteran horseman from Reserve, drive John Hill's grey mare Tonita C to a win at the light harness meet on Sydney Harbour today. Instead of money, blankets, bags of oats and whips are given as prizes.

Fig. 3.7 Harness racing on North Harbour, c. 1947.

March 18

1848 Situation desperate

A petition is sent to the Lieutenant-Governor of Nova Scotia from Rev. Norman McLeod and other settlers in St. Ann's asking for help. A visitor to the district comments: "The situation of the people here both in the Back and Front Settlements owing to the want of provisions and seed is really fearful. Not one person in every five hundred has seed of any kind to put in the ground and unless seed is, by some means, secured, the certainty of a general Famine next winter must be admitted on all hands. Not only has the seed been used for the purpose of sustaining life, but cows, calves, and even the working cattle have been slaughtered for the same purpose. Many are now therefore without either cattle or sheep or the means of obtaining seed or food so that it is certain that if something is not instantly done, deaths from starvation will take place." (See also Oct. 28, 1851.)

1913 Women and children nervous

A vote is passed at a meeting of the local women's council to ask Sydney City Council to insist on improvement of the ferry service between Sydney and North Sydney. The boats now used by the Cape Breton Electric Company are "the cause of much inconvenience and nervousness to the women and children passengers."

March 19

1967 Sunday coal

The retail depot in Sydney remains open all day filling emergency orders, marking today as the first Sunday for DOSCO coal deliveries. A coal shortage was caused after three consecutive storms hit the local area.

1969 *America Hurrah*

The Nova Scotia Regional Dominion Drama Festival is held for the first time in Cape Breton. Four productions are scheduled for presentation at the Eastern Institute of Technology. Xavier College's *America Hurrah* by Jean-Claude van Itallie, directed by Harry and LizAnn Boardmore starts the festival tonight. Tomorrow night St. Mary's University will do *Laura*, followed by St. FX's *The Bacchae*, and *Blues for Mr. Charlie*, presented by the Acadia Drama Society and the Inglewood Players of Bridgewater.

America Hurrah is chosen to represent the Atlantic Provinces at the National Festival in Kelowna, BC. The College's technical crew captures the top award for lighting and Alec Allison wins the Most Promising Young Actor award. The excellent production is a big turning point and Island interest in drama continues to grow.

Later, The St. Ann's Players is one of the groups involved in the revival of drama around the Island. The University College of Cape Breton establishes its own Spring Festival of Plays and, by the end of 1984, produces more than 200, including several original works.

March 20

1739 Major supplement

A soldier and his dog from the garrison at Louisbourg return from a hunting trip to Spanish Bay (Sydney Harbour) with thirteen partridges. The soldiers are encouraged to supplement their food allotment by hunting and fishing. They fish cod, shoot seals on the ice, gather strawberries, herbs for soups and spruce boughs for spruce beer. Powder is allocated for hunting and molasses to make the beer. Regular expeditions are made to the woods for spruce boughs. Even the well-to-do drink spruce beer when their other beverages run low. During the summer of 1744, large quantities of beer are brewed for the garrison and for the British prisoners taken at Canso and quartered at Louisbourg.

1907 Novelist born

Hugh Maclennan is born in Glace Bay. Describing himself as a "Scotsman, a Presbyterian and a Nova Scotian," Maclennan becomes one of Canada's foremost writers. His novel *Each Man's Son* is set in Glace Bay and Broughton. Parts of the story are based on his own childhood.

1983 Woman ordained

Margaret Ann Collins is ordained an Anglican priest in Port Morien. Rev. Collins, the fourth woman to be ordained in the Diocese of Nova Scotia, is the first in Cape Breton.

March 21

1918 Million logs to England

A strange "ship," a raft of almost a million logs, is anchored off North Sydney. The story began last year when Ivan Bayley of North Sydney responded to an advertisement from England. Logs were in desperate need in the coal mines as coal fuelled the Royal Navy. Logs had been delivered to Britain across the North Sea from Scandinavia, and Bayley reasoned that they could be delivered in the same way across the Atlantic. Bayley planned a huge raft of logs, shaped like a cigar, with deck quarters, and a motor. There would also be a six-inch gun on deck, presumably to repel potential German submarines.

Bayley and others from North Sydney went to Bonne Bay, Newfoundland, and cut 8,000 cords of hemlock, spruce, oak, pine and juniper and laced them together into a great raft with steel rope, iron rods and chains. Then they set sail. Near Cape Ray a storm struck and logs began to break away. The tug hauling them has brought the forward section of the raft to North Sydney Marine Railway. Within a week shipwrights will have it secured again. Once more the tug and her raft set sail for England. They are never seen again.

1962 Gift from Cheshires

A brass bell, presented to the 2nd Battalion Nova Scotia Highlanders (Cape Breton) is used at tonight's Regimental Dinner at the Sydney Garrison Officers' Mess. The bell is a gift from the 22nd (Cheshire) Regiment. The Cheshires had landed with Wolfe at Kennington Cove near Louisbourg in 1758, and Louisbourg became the Regiment's first battle honour. The 2nd Battalion is the closest Regiment and has become affiliated now with the 22nd in England. According to Regimental tradition, the ringing of the brass bell costs the offender a round of drinks.

March 22

1971 Municipal services to Membertou

Northern and Indian Affairs Minister Jean Chretien is in Sydney to formally sign an agreement between the city and Membertou Reserve to provide municipal services to the reserve. This is the first agreement of its kind in Canada.

March 23

1672 The "Noble Savage"?

Nicholas Denys' newly published two-volume *Geographical Description of the Coasts of North America* includes descriptions of the Micmac Indians he found on Cape Breton. "The law which they observed in old times was this—to do to another only that which they wished to be done to them. They had no worship. All lived in good friendship and understanding. They refused nothing to one another. If one wigwam or family had not provisions enough, the neighbours supplied them, although they had only that which was necessary for themselves. And in all other things it was the same. They lived pure lives; the wives were faithful to their husbands, and the girls very chaste. They were not subject to diseases, and know nothing of fevers. If any accident happened to them, by falling, by burning, or in cutting wood, (the latter happening) through lack of good axes, theirs being unsteady through failure to cut well, they did not need a physician. They had knowledge of herbs, of which they made use and straightway grew well."

1922 Rockabye

George "Rockabye" Ross is born at West Bay Road. In 1967 he wins the Canadian Middleweight title from Len Wadsworth of Ontario. He also boxes for the British European Middleweight Championship in England against Randy Turpin, who wins in a TKO.

1992 Big Ben murder

At 4 a.m. this morning the body of the night clerk is discovered at Big Ben's Convenience store in Sydney. Forty-seven-year-old Marie Lorraine Dupe has been brutally murdered, stabbed more than forty times. Marie and her husband Douglas moved to Cape Breton three years ago for an easier way of life and to escape big city crime. Her murderer is not found until years later, when modern DNA tests on a cigarette butt left at the scene leads to the capture of Ernest Gordon Strowbridge. He pleads guilty to second degree murder and in May 2003 is sentenced to life imprisonment. Because he was seventeen years old at the time of the murder, he is eligible for parole in seven years. The case is featured on television's A&E's *Cold Case Files* in June 2003.

March 24

1735 Banished

For her part in a robbery, Judith Pansart La Bretonnaire, is banished from the colony at Louisbourg, not a common punishment, and her property sold at public auction. As with other public auctions, it was publicized by a huissier and a drummer reading and posting notices around town. This morning, walking and drumming around the town again to the quay, they attract a good crowd to bid for Judith's seven goats, four kids and some poultry.

1902 Marconi sites station

Marconi selects Table Head, about a half mile from Dominion No. 2 colliery and directly in the vicinity of the old Hub mine, for his wireless telegraph station. Four towers are to be built in a square 210 feet apart and 220 feet high connected by wire cables. The station here will be more powerful than the one in Poldhu, England.

1903 The bachelors

Residents of North Sydney wonder whether or not the town is in for a rash of weddings when five well-known bachelors are seen buying coal scuttles, eggs and butter and hiring housemaids and cooks. But the five bachelors are just moving into their own home, over the stores of C. W. Lovett, W. J. Christie and A. D. Morse. They are listed in the phone book as "The Bachelors."

1911 Ship wrecked

The SS *Bruce*, on a voyage from Port aux Basques to North Sydney, in snow and high winds, finds Sydney Harbour crammed with drift ice. In attempting to reach Louisbourg, she crashes on the rocks off Main-a-Dieu. There is only one casualty, a man who falls overboard as he helps with the lifeboats. The women and children find shelter in fishing huts. The freezing survivors are rescued and taken to shelter in Louisbourg. Despite their miraculous survival, many passengers refuse to leave for Sydney until they find out what is going to happen to their luggage, still on board the wrecked ship.

Fig. 3.8 The SS Bruce *under steam, postmarked April 1907.*

1979 Fiddler dies

Fiddler Angus Chisholm of Margaree Forks dies, aged 70. He started playing the fiddle at the age of eight with a violin bought from a horse trader for $15, and he played by ear until he was fourteen. His fiddle-playing virtuosity is particularly remembered from small concerts and private homes, where his bowing and fingering and his playing of clogs was admired. It was said that he won so many competitions that he was barred from entering any more. He was one of the first Cape Bretoners to make a 78 rpm recording. Before he moved to Boston, where he played with other Cape Bretoners including John Campbell, Joe Cormier and Bill Lamey, he was a schoolteacher and a warden at the Highlands National Park. He died in Boston and was buried in Margaree Forks.

March 25

1888 Sally Anns parade

Led by a big drum and tambourine, the recently formed unit at the Salvation Army holds its first parade today in North Sydney.

1903 Passport to Sydney Mines

Four hundred workers living in North Sydney but working in Sydney Mines are turned back when their train reaches the town line this morning. Last night's Board of Health meeting resolved that medical certificates must be produced by everyone going into Sydney Mines. This attempt to isolate contagious diseases from spreading is causing great annoyance. Stipendiary Archibald probably never sets foot in Sydney Mines, but he lives just inside the town's boundaries and is forced to produce a certificate every time he wants to go home to lunch.

March 26

1927 Glace Bay disaster

The worst fire in Glace Bay's history destroys seven large blocks of the town's business section, putting sixteen firms out of business.

1930 New ferry
The Baddeck-Iona ferry begins operations.

1937 New press
Since its installation on April 1, 1913, the Hoe Unique Press at the *Post Record* has turned out more than 75,000,000 newspapers on about 5,000 tons of paper. But a new 60-ton press will soon run off its first newspaper. The biggest single press in the Maritimes, the 32-page Quad Hoe Press will be able to roll 30,000 16-page papers an hour against the average run of 5,500 on the present press. The base and sides have already been swung into place. The press rests on foot wide concrete pillars and is cradled over a concrete pit five feet deep and twenty-nine feet long. Three railway cars are used to transport the press here from New York.

1940 CCF victory
Clairie Gillis wins the federal constituency of Cape Breton South for the CCF. He is the only CCF candidate elected this side of Winnipeg.

1983 Cape Breton journalists cited
Two journalists from Cape Breton win top awards in the 1982 National Newspaper Awards. Blaine MacDonald, formerly of Sydney, now with the Hamilton *Spectator* becomes the nation's top cartoonist, while Joan Fraser, of Boularderie, wins the top award for editorials. She is with the *Montreal Gazette*.

March 27

1907 Latest fashion
The Easter millinery opening at Miss Marr's attracts women from Sydney, Glace Bay and across the harbour. Trimmings have moved from the underbrims to the top of the hat, allowing for a trailing effect. Wings and gulls are popular, but the favourite trimming of the season is flowers. The latest novelty is grasses of various kinds and these are placed to give a soft trailing effect to drooping brim hats. Colours range from champagne, tan and pearl to burnt gold and "a lovely Copenhagen blue." Other novelties include a large ball-headed pin tinted, pearl Dresden, enamel and gunmetal to hold the hat on the head or simply to be used as a decoration.

Fig. 3.9 Women shopping at Vooghts, North Sydney, cir. 1914.

1969 Expansion

Nova Scotia Pulp Ltd., established at Point Tupper in 1962, announces an expansion program creating the equivalent of 1,000 jobs. The newsprint operation is to be increased by an addition of 160,000 tons and an increase in the output of bleached sulphite pulp. Crown lands will be more intensively and productively managed and the private woodlot owner will find a market for low-grade material.

1978 Wreck Cove

The first electrical energy is produced at the Wreck Cove Hydroelectric Station of the Nova Scotia Power Corporation. The Station is designed to produce 290 million kilowatt hours annually and displace about a half a million barrels of imported oil. Over 2.5 million cubic feet of earth and rock were moved to construct eleven major dams. Nearly 900 men were employed to construct a total of 19 dykes and dams, canals and 5 major tunnels. The drainage area collects water from 216 square kilometres. Total cost of the project is $150 million.

March 28

1966 Chief dies

Ben Christmas, long time chief at Membertou Reserve, dies.

1969 Caribou fly in from Quebec

Earlier this month, twenty-three caribou from Quebec were trussed in slings, blindfolded and flown to Sydney on a DC-3. They were then released in the Cape Breton Highlands National Park and will be joined by more later this year.

Years ago, caribou were plentiful on Cape Breton. But they were an easy animal to kill for garrison food at Louisbourg and Sydney, winter meat supply for the Indians and fishermen, and supplies for the ships. By the turn of this century, the caribou had virtually disappeared except on the highlands of Cape Breton. Their decline benefited the white-tailed deer, who were beginning to come to Cape Breton.

March 29

1811 Early census

A census shows that there are 1,703 predominately French people living in the area of Arichat, River Bourgeois and St. Peters. There are 93 over sixty years old, 775 between the ages of fourteen and sixty, and 835 children. The area boasts 105 vessels, 21 horses, 800 head of cattle and 1,301 sheep.

1911 Lake Ainslie oil hoax?

"We have received most encouraging reports of the prospects of reaching oil in paying quantities at Lake Ainslie." This article in the Port Hood *Greetings* starts people investing in the Lake Ainslie Oil Company. However, a fourteen-year-old telegraph messenger, so one story goes, while delivering a message to the site, sees men dump a barrel of oil *into* the drill hole. A short time later, samples of the "new" oil are found to be of very high quality oil indeed. (See also Oct. 10, 1906.)

March 30

1907 Stranded, or down and out in the land of opportunity

Stranded English immigrants appear at City Hall in Sydney looking for help. All of them have the same hard luck story. They had been encouraged to leave their homes and jobs by an agent who painted a rosy picture of opportunities in Canada.

The men were invited to London where they heard more glowing speeches and decided to take advantage of the offer. All they needed was 5 pounds 10 shillings ($27.50) for their passage and one pound ($5) to buy food on the way over. In Halifax they would be met and put on a train for Winnipeg where they would immediately start work. But no one met them in Halifax, and, after roaming around for a few days, they were given money for tickets to Sydney where they might find employment. They are here now with no money, no food and no lodgings.

1911 Sydney promoter

An article in *The Financial News* of London, England, calls Sydney "The Shipping Centre of Canada." Mr. A. C. Ross, who for years represented the North Riding of Sydney in the Federal Parliament, is the largest real estate owner in Sydney. He is in England promoting his city. He claims "Sydney as a coal and steel centre is nearer to every place of importance in the world than any other centre."

1922 End for *Pawnee*

The old ferry boat *Pawnee* is sold to Joseph Salter & Sons, who will tow her hull across Sydney Harbour to be used as a floating warehouse at his wharf in North Sydney. Built about 30 years ago in an American Shipyard near New York, the *Pawnee* was in the service of the Cape Breton Electric Company and the old Sydney Ferry Company between Sydney and North Sydney until 1913, when she was condemned. Her place has been filled since then by the *Electronic*.

1965 First mobile reading instruction centre

The first mobile reading instruction centre in North America is now in operation at Park Jr. High School in Sydney. Cape Breton school officials and teachers will be introduced to mechanical devices for testing and improving reading abilities.

1985 Brutal murder

Former Sysco president Derek Haysom and his wife Nancy are found brutally stabbed to death as they sit down to dinner in their home in Virginia. Their daughter Elizabeth and her boyfriend are suspected, chased by Interpol from Europe to Bangkok and finally caught when they were shoplifting at a Marks and Spencers store in England. The couple are brought back to the United States, tried and found guilty. In October 1987, Elizabeth is sentenced to 90 years as an accessory to murder.

Interviewed for the Associated Baptist Press in 2004 at Fluvanna Correctional Center for Women in Troy, Virginia, and now a member of the handbell choir in the prison, she says, "weekly handbell practices, led by a local minister, are a blessing…. I can't think of anything else for which I have such an exuberant expectation, month after month."

March 31

1856 Dangerous drivers

Although Baddeckers for years have used the Bras d'Or as their highway, they are now using the newly constructed streets and roads. The Municipal Council, concerned for safety on the roads, has passed a by-law that states that any person riding or driving a horse at full speed on a public street or highway shall be fined not less than $1 or more than $4 for each offence.

1898 Oldest man remembers

At 103 years old, Angus Campbell of Middle River, Cape Breton's oldest living man, recalls his early pioneer days in the Gaelic language weekly *MacTalla*. Born in Applecross, Ross County, Scotland, Angus came to North America in 1803 on the Polly with his family and about five hundred other passengers, landing at Belfast, PEI, after a five-week crossing, during which many on board died of fever.

His mother was drowned while crossing the Bay to deliver a tub of butter to pay the shoemaker. When he was nine years old, he and his family crossed to Middle River in a boat they built themselves. At that time there were only five houses in Baddeck and about fifteen families in Victoria County. Trees grew down to the water's edge. Potatoes were planted among the ashes and stumps of the trees cut and burned to clear the land. Five people were drowned because there were only trees and no bridges over the river. There were no roads. Supplies were brought from Sydney or Arichat by open boat.

1951 Busy airport

Twenty-seven transatlantic planes are among the 225 airplanes from almost every major airline in the world, including TCA, BOAC, Pan American, Trans World, Swiss Air, KLM, SAS, Air France and TWA, serviced at Sydney Airport this month. A total of 5,000 passengers pass through the airport. Aero Caterers serve 2,800 meals while Shell and Imperial Oil dispatch some 160,000 gallons of gas.

1959 End of era

Thirteen telegraph offices around Cape Breton have been made uneconomical and unnecessary by the availability of commercial telephone service and will close today. Offices at Arichat, Baddeck, Big Bras d'Or, Breton Cove, Cheticamp, Englishtown, Grand Etang, Ingonish Ferry, Lower L'Ardoise, St. Peters, Margaree Forks and River Bennett will become part of history. The offices in Fourchu and Gabarus will be kept open as there is no other form of communication system there. One of the full-time government offices recently took in 20 cents in one month.

1961 My kingdom for a butt

The CN ferry *William Carson* with its Captain, Mike Tobin, 95-man crew and 71 passengers, batters her way through to open waters, landing at Mulgrave, exactly one week after leaving Port aux Basques. The ice pack is the thickest in years, with the ice pan extending 30 feet below the surface. Cigarettes ran out on the third day and many passengers and crew emptied out ashtrays to salvage butts. They welcomed the cigarettes and baby food airlifted out Wednesday by the Eastern Flying Service. The kitchen staff baked bread, and three passengers in the main lounge played a marathon 702 games of gin rummy to pass the time.

April

Bay of St. Ann's

Oh, the ocean is a fortune for the people by the sea.
They go out in their own boats to feed their families.
And they sail to meet the sunrise
These men who leave the land
On the Bay of St. Ann's.

And they rise up in the darkness and they sail to meet the light.
They go out in their own boats to meet the end of the night.
And they sail to meet the sunrise
These men who leave the land
On the Bay of St. Ann's.

Leon Dubinsky

Fig. 4.1 Fishermen with nets, n.d.

April 1

1734 Light shines

The light first shines from the lantern of the recently completed lighthouse on the eastern side of Louisbourg Harbour. Started in 1731, this is the first fireproof concrete building in North America. Coal from the nearby Port Morien area is burned in an iron pot set on a tripod in the lantern. The light shining from the top of a tapering sixty-foot tower can be seen twelve miles out to sea. Fire in 1736 destroys part of the cupola, but a fireproof lantern, using oil and with glass screening, is installed.

1890 Whitney consolidates

Henry Whitney of Boston becomes the first president of the Dominion Coal Company, formed today by the consolidation of nine independent mining operations. Mines incorporated into the Companv include the Glace Bay Mine, Bridgeport, Caledonia and the International Mine. Mr. Whitney will search for American markets for coal, ruined when Confederation ended Reciprocity.

During the next few years, railway lines are relocated or linked up to provide means of shipping coal through Sydney or Louisbourg. The founding of the S & L Railway results from the merging of the various mine-owned lines to give the area a first-class railroad. Some of the first mines of the Dominion Coal Company are in the area of what later becomes Glace Bay. The town's real existence as a community begins with the consolidation of the mines and their systematic development. (See also Oct. 20, 1826)

1932 Mounties get their work

The Provincial Police Force is absorbed into the RCMP service. The chief work of the Provincial Police has been to check the contraband liquor trade and operate the highway patrol. The RCMP are also taking on the work of the Federal Customs Excise Enforcement Officers.

1942 Gas rationing begins

Gasoline rationing begins as a war measure. The initial ration book entitles a non-essential automobile from 60 to 70 units depending on the size and horsepower of the car. Each unit represents 5 gallons of gas. Butter rationing begins on December 21st.

1965 First court

Nova Scotia's first family court, a pilot project to determine the feasibility of establishing similar courts in other areas, is established in the county of Cape Breton.

April 2

1824 First Counties

Cape Breton is divided into three districts.

1873 Barber advertises

One of North Sydney's first barber shops advertises, "A good clean shave guaranteed if money paid right down. Paper collars always on hand." This same shop offers shaves for 5 cents and haircuts for 10 cents. Shaving mugs, with the regular customers' names written on the outside in gold and with brushes standing inside, line the shelves of the shop.

1907 School for kids

Compulsory education for children between the ages of eight and sixteen comes to the Sydney area. Only children between fourteen and sixteen who are actually working will be exempt.

1944 First power saws

Bobby Stevens of Northside East Bay becomes the owner of the second power saw in Cape Breton. It's a Precision from Toronto and it weighs 65 pounds with the gas in it. Mr. Fraser of Baddeck had the first saw on the Island. His weighs 105 pounds.

1986 YMCA

The Sydney Young Men's Christian Association (YMCA), incorporated in 1886, celebrates its 100th year of activities. Initially it found accommodations for new arrivals who came to work at the new Steel Plant. That activity is quite different from today's schedule of athletic events, aquatics, fitness, racquet sports, pre-school and summer camps.

April 3

1823 First Catholic MLA

Laurence Kavanagh, prominent St. Peter's merchant, elected as one of the two members of the House from Cape Breton, is allowed to take his seat as the first Catholic in the Provincial Legislature. He does not have to swear his faith away, or take an oath against Popery. Catholic emancipation comes to Nova Scotia before Great Britain. Kavanagh is known as "The Emancipator."

1905 Expensive trip

Residents of Englishtown and North River visit Sydney in thirty sleighs today and on the trip home lose three horses through the ice of St. Ann's Bay.

1926 Situation desperate

An Ingonish resident reaches North Sydney with reports of the terrible conditions in the fishing villages along the North Shore of Victoria County. The winter's supplies are almost exhausted and although the inhabitants have the money (after a successful season last year), no supplies are available because of impenetrable ice conditions and impossible roads. For several weeks some families have been subsisting on a diet of fish and any small game they can trap or hunt.

1990 Monument works

Four generations of Steeles have operated the Monuments Works of North Sydney since its beginning in 1896. New equipment and modernized cutting and polishing operations continue to make it a viable business. It's had its ups and downs over the years as the appeal for marble and granite in building construction declines or becomes fashionable. Granite tiles for home decoration are "in" at the moment. Now the company works mostly with monument stone. The most popular stone is European black and Canadian grey granite.

April 4

1753 "Popular" early lotteries

Officials attempt to control the public lotteries in Louisbourg. But public lotteries, *"blanques,"* are entertainment and the tickets are inexpensive. Everyone can take part. Prizes include liquor, supplies and personal belongings. Influential members of Louisbourg society can afford to support state-sponsored lotteries in France which offer more valuable prizes.

1940 Historic park

Proclaimed a National Historic Site in 1928, the Fortress Louisbourg is designated as a National Historic Park.

1966 *Chameau* treasure recovered

Their secret is revealed. Last fall, three Cape Breton skin divers, Alex Storm, Dave MacEachern and Harvey Macleod, discovered treasure aboard the sunken 18th-century French pay ship *Le Chameau*, fifteen miles off Louisbourg. Gold and silver coins are among what is believed to be the richest treasure ever recovered in Canadian coastal waters. The divers were bothered by strong tidal currents, sharks, dogfish and seals. (See also August 26,1725.)

Fig. 4.2 Reconstruction at Louisbourg, n.d.

April 5

1940 Northerners want more

Residents of northern Cape Breton want better transportation services in the Spring. They argue that if the *Aspy* overwintered in North Sydney instead of Sydney, she could start her trips earlier. Last month, for example, the boat could have made several trips with much needed hay, food and other supplies. A larger and faster boat with better passenger accommodations is required. Two trips a week are not enough.

1940 Cheers!

Cape Breton County residents drink a lot. The eight Liquor Commission stores operating in the county sold a total of $1,411,291 worth of assorted liquors and beer in the past year. This is only $90,216 less than the four stores operating in Halifax. In New Aberdeen, the sale of beer exceeds that of hard liquors, and in Dominion they drank more beer than hard liquors and wines combined.

1984 Fire in No. 26

Fire, which broke out at No. 26 Colliery, Glace Bay, spreads rapidly. The blaze is believed to have started around the Number 7 belt drive. Dayshift workers, 320 in number, escape from the mine. One man, 42-year old fan operator Ronald MacDonald, fails to reach the surface. In an effort to extinguish the fire, part of the mine has been sealed off.

1990 Cape Breton Oilers

Cape Breton Oilers win the opening game of the playoffs at Centre 200. This is the club's second season here and during the past year it has come from being the worst team in the American Hockey League to being in second place. Personnel changes in goaltending and defence and the hiring of Norm Ferguson as assistant coach have made the team stronger. Supporters of Mayor Manning MacDonald now say "he deserves to take a bow for overcoming all odds in bringing the Oilers to Cape Breton. He stood fast against criticism that the city couldn't afford Centre 200." In early March 1996, the Oilers are told that by the end of May they will be moved to Hamilton, Ontario.

April 6

1888 Entrepreneur extraordinaire

William Penn Hussey, entrepreneur extraordinaire and coal wholesaler in Massachusetts, plans to develop the coal field at Broad Cove, in western Cape Breton. There is no harbour, no railroad and no market, but he has purchased a property for $62,500 and set out to develop it. An enormous man, he rides a large white horse, dresses as a cowboy, carries a pair of six-guns and wears a six-gallon hat. Nevertheless, he is apparently shrewd and is able to attract wealthy capitalists from Britain, France and Switzerland. One, a gentleman from Switzerland, looked to the shore of Cape Breton from his boat to where Hussey had had the walls of rock facing the sea painted black. The European, impressed with the volume of coal, promised support and development of the Broad Cove Mine began.

Hussey purchases more land, builds a narrow-gauge railway from the pits to the proposed harbour and opens a channel to the sea at MacIssac's Pond. Cottages are built, coal seams mined and a pier constructed.

1904 Formerly Broad Cove

Inverness is officially incorporated as a town. Known as Broad Cove until 1903, Inverness received its present name from a suggestion by Sir William Young, its first MLA. Broad Cove began to expand with the arrival of William Penn Hussey. Row upon row of miners' cottages, stores and halls stand where pastures used to be. The Inverness Railway and Coal Company now operates three mines.

April 7

1815 Volcano erupts

Halfway around the world from Cape Breton, the volcano Tambora erupts on the Indonesian island of Sumbawa and throws great clouds of volcanic ash into the air. Solar energy is reflected away from the earth and abnormal weather conditions result. Cape Bretoners, along with others living on the eastern seaboard, have an excessively cold summer: blossoms die on the trees, snow falls and crops fail, causing great hardships.

1884 Railroad on Cape Breton

Word is received from Ottawa that the railroad will be extended into Cape Breton, The road is to be built along the Central Route with a bridge at Grand Narrows. Engineers will arrive as soon as the snow is off the ground. (See also June 4, 1888.)

1918 Soldiers of the Soil - 1,343rd Day of War

Soldiers of the Soil committees will enrol boys for farm service throughout the summer months. Several thousand Canadian boys worked on farms last year and it is hoped that the 25,000 boys needed for this summer will be found. Two thousand are needed in Nova Scotia, and 150 on Cape Breton. Boys from fifteen to nineteen years old are wanted, but younger boys are encouraged to work on farms of relatives or friends.

1935 Fire at the Ex

The main building at the Cape Breton Exhibition grounds on Kings Road in Sydney is destroyed by fire. Once thronged by thousands of Exhibition fans, the buildings have been unused since the Island Exhibition Commission abandoned their annual fair and show a few years ago. (See also September 4, 1936.)

April 8

1933 Spruce Gum to England

The students of Cains Mountain school in Victoria County send gifts to students at an English school. One of the gifts is spruce gum, gathered from the spruce trees on the Mountain. Spruce gum, little round lumps on the trees, is bark-coloured and turns an orange colour when chewed.

April 9

1714 First Governor

Philippe Pasteur de Costebelle is appointed the first governor of Isle Royale (Cape Breton). On September 25th, he will leave Placentia, Newfoundland for Louisbourg.

1884 Smugglers at Broad Cove Marsh

Dr. Cameron, MP for Inverness County, complains about the amount of smuggling in his riding, and that most of it is in "ardent spirits." Apparently, the most active smugglers are to be found at Broad Cove Marsh, but there is also a need for revenue officers at West Bay, Mabou, Whycocomagh and Judique.

While the MP may have had cause for concern at revenue losses from smuggling, Inverness County's exports are considerable—more than double the imports. The county exports fish, cattle, butter, beef, mutton, sheep and horses and annually produces hundreds of thousands of bushels of wheat, oats, hay and potatoes. Inverness County is the biggest exporter on Cape Breton, and Cape Breton contributes nearly one quarter of all the exports from the Province.

1895 Hart Storm

An unusual April storm, known in Baddeck for years to come as the "Hart Storm," leaves drifts up to fifteen feet high. Baddeck merchant A. I. Hart, accompanied by thirty local men, set out early this morning to get two carloads of hay from the Alba railroad siding, twenty-four miles away. About seventeen miles of the route is over the ice of St. Patrick's Channel, but spring thaws have weakened the ice, and each man drives a single horse sleigh capable of carrying only one-half ton. Mr. Hart's powerful black horse, Charlie, leads the way.

As they load, hail begins to fall and "the horses got restless. Some would lie down in an attempt to get clear of the hail." By the time they reach Little Narrows, 15-18 inches of new snow has fallen and the men stay there the night. Because the horses now have to take turns breaking the road, most of the hay is left at Little Narrows. By six that evening the expedition reaches home safely.

2005 Canadian Idol

Canadian Idol auditions are held at Centre 200 in Sydney. One of the 10 finalists in the 2003 contest, Richie Wilcox of New Waterford, is returning to his home town to conduct summer theatre workshops.

April 10

1716 First in

The first merchant ship of the season arrives at Louisbourg.

Fig. 4.3 Survivors of settlers who sailed on the Highland Lass, *c.1890.*

1852 Arrival

Rev. Norman McLeod and his followers from St. Ann's arrive in Australia. On January 7, 1854, MacLeod and a few families sail for New Zealand to join other Cape Breton families from the *Margaret* and the *Highland Lass*, a second emigrant ship from Cape Breton, which had left in September 1853, having discovered that Australia was not their promised land. (See also October 28, 1851, May 17, 1852.)

1885 First town

Today, North Sydney becomes the first town on Cape Breton to be incorporated. From the early settlement of North Sydney and Sydney, the seat of government has been across the harbour, and this becomes increasingly inconvenient for those on the Northside. By 1841, the Northside districts, with their steady increase of wealth and population, formed a separate township. One of their responsibilities is the maintenance of their own poor.

Fig. 4.4 Driving party, upper North Sydney, 1902.

1970 Tie up vessels

Trawler fishermen employed by Acadian Fisheries at Canso and Mulgrave and Booth Fisheries at Petit de Grat tie up their vessels in an effort to force the companies to recognize their union. Under the Trade Union Act, trawler fishermen are not defined as "employees." (See also January 7, 1971)

April 11

1929 Angus "Ferry"

Angus "Ferry" MacNeil of Grand Narrows starts work this month on the ferry. The crew consists of Angus and the Captain, on call twenty-four hours a day, seven days a week. As engineer of the *Grandona,* built by Casey Baldwin (of Alexander Graham Bell's Aerial Experiment Association fame), Angus earns $75 per month and helps ferry 1,400 cars over the Straits at Grand Narrows in his first year. In 1983, over 100,000 cars are ferried across. Angus becomes Captain and serves for forty years and ten months on the Grand Narrows ferry.

Back in 1847, Sandy Hector MacNeil and his brother Donald ferried people and up to 1,200 head of cattle a year across the Straits by scow, with two sets of oars and a sail.

1988 "Cape Breton Island – Nova Scotia's Masterpiece"

A new tourism logo is revealed on a 60-foot-long mural which is part of SeaSell 88, a marketing promotional tour to New England. "Cape Breton Island—Nova Scotia's Masterpiece—Put Yourself in the Picture."

April 12

1849 Helps Inverness
Crop failures last summer cause great hardships this winter. As soon as the ice broke this spring, William MacKeen, one of Inverness' first MLA's went to Pictou, loaded up his boat with flour and meal and returned to Port Hood to distribute them freely to the people. Returning to Pictou, MacKeen bought £700 worth of provisions on credit and brought them back to Mabou. He further extended his credit to buy bread in Halifax to sell on credit to the starving people.

April 13

1907 First Class?
Residents of Sydney Mines complain about mail delivery from Sydney. Mail takes twenty-four hours to reach them from Sydney. A letter leaves Sydney early in the morning and reaches Florence by 9 o'clock. Sydney Mines is only about one-and-a-half miles away, but the letters aren't delivered until the following morning.

1963 *Mass For Shut-Ins*
This Lent, *Mass for Shut-Ins* is broadcast from the CJCB-TV studio in Sydney. Father A. J. Macleod, and later other priests from the region, including Father Bedford Doucette, the Chaplain of UCCB, says Mass for a studio congregation and for the many Catholics at home unable to attend their regular church services.

1989 No more jets
Canadian Airlines announces this month that they are discontinuing jet service to Cape Breton.

April 14

1958 "Not only in Canada, you say?"
The *Post* helps promote Tea for Canada Week, April 14-19. Tea relieves tension and gives the drinker a sense of well-being. Besides being the world's least expensive drink, with the exception of water, tea is the most popular drink. For hundreds of years, it has been the favourite of people from Japan and Tibet to Britain and Canada. Canada is among the largest tea consumers in the world. Canadian soldiers in Britain during the First World War brought home the custom of afternoon tea.

1996 Unemployment
According to Human Resources and Development Canada, the average rate of unemployment in Cape Breton is 23.2 per cent. This is significantly higher than the Nova Scotia average of 12.6 per cent. The unofficial percentage in industrial Cape Breton is 40 per cent or higher. It's expected to get even worse as Devco is closed out.

April 15

1788 Gift, not bribe

Colonel Graham reports to the council. Last winter, with relations between France and England deteriorating once again, Cape Breton's second governor, Macarmick, became concerned about the potential threat of renewed French interest in Cape Breton. But unless threatened with imminent attack, he was to do nothing that could be interpreted as a potentially hostile act.

Macarmick sends a few ships to spy on any movement of troops to St. Pierre et Miquelon. One of them, carrying Colonel Graham, is icebound at St. Pierre and forced to spend the winter there. When the ship returns to Sydney, Colonel Graham brings with him two cases of Bordeaux wine, sent from the Commandant of St. Pierre to Macarmick. The Council decides that the wine is a gift, not a bribe, and Macarmick is allowed to accept it.

1907 Long day's journey

In a talk to the "Boys of Old Sydney," Archdeacon Smith reminisces about his arrival from Mahone Bay in 1872. He travelled from Halifax to Pictou and by steamer to Port Hood, then by stage coach thirty miles to Whycocomagh where he caught the steamer *Neptune* to Sydney.

1950 "Finest ballroom in the east"

The Venetian Gardens on the Esplanade in Sydney is advertised as the "finest ballroom in the east." Used later for boxing matches and bingo games, the Venetian Gardens is demolished in June 1984.

April 16

1747 "Worst spot on globe"

Charles Knowles, British governor of Cape Breton from 1746-47, doesn't like his posting at Louisbourg. In a letter to England, he writes "... in general I can only say it is the worst spot upon the Globe ... for my part I have struggled hard to weather the winter, which I've done, thank God, though was not above three times out of my room for five months."

1788 Soldiers and settlers

Governor Macarmick begins building roads—one between Sydney and Conway Harbour (Arichat) and St. Peter's and one, a narrow portage road, to East Bay. Soldiers do some of the work; settlers help in return for the high wages or provisions.

1915 TNT - 254th day of war

By-products from the coke ovens of the Dominion Iron and Steel Company are used for the manufacture of the high explosive, tri-nitro-toluene (TNT). This is in addition to the manufacture of several tons of cordite and powder for shell supply contracts.

1927 Rare find at Number 2

Miners blasting down an overcast in No. 2 Colliery find a fossil of a young alligator in the rock. About two feet long and eight inches wide, this is one of the most interesting fossils ever found in the mines. Fossils of ferns are common, but a baby alligator is remarkable. The fossil was about two miles out under the sea under a covering of 1,350 feet of clay and rock and 350 feet of the Atlantic Ocean.

April 17

1927 Iona church burns

Easter Sunday—the Church at Iona, erected 25 years ago, is destroyed by fire. A new one will be built of cut stone on the same commanding site overlooking the Bras d'Or.

1958 Robbery on the Halifax Express

Early today, on the Halifax-Sydney Express, an armed masked man entered the mail car at Port Hawkesbury, locked the two mail sorters in a washroom and ransacked the mail. The robbery is discovered when the Bras d'Or mailman got no response to his knocks. This is the first train robbery in Cape Breton's history. Mounties have set up roadblocks.

1977 Veteran newsman dies

Joe MacSween of Ironville dies in Ottawa. A reporter with the Canadian Press since 1946, MacSween had received three National Newspaper Award citations. He worked at CP bureaus across Canada, as well as those in New York and London.

1982 Buchanan to Privy Council

Premier John MacLennan Buchanan, formerly of Sydney, is made a member of Her Majesty's Privy Council for his part in negotiations for Patriation of the Canadian Constitution. Premier Buchanan was first elected to the Nova Scotia Legislature in 1967 and was appointed Minister of Public Works and Fisheries. In 1971, he became leader of Nova Scotia's Progressive Conservative Party. He was elected Premier in 1978 and was re-elected in 1981 and 1984.

April 18

1785 St. George's Church

The Anglican Church's development in Cape Breton starts in the new settlement at Sydney. Today, Frederick Amelia, the infant son of Benjamin Lovell, garrison chaplain to the 33rd Regiment stationed in Sydney, is one of the first children to be baptized here. In 1786, Reverend Ranna Cossitt, St. George's first rector, arrives from the States and helps finish building the church. Most of the stones used in the construction are from the ruins at Fortress Louisbourg.

Fig. 4.5 St. George's Church, Sydney, circa 1933.

One of the church's prized possessions is to be "Nelson's Chair," a Chippendale donated to the church by the visiting officers of Nelson's flagship in 1805 for the use of the bishop.

1787 Boat building

This year, the Sydney Shipping Register is started, covering the entire Island. In 1790, the first seagoing vessel in the Sydney area, the 101-ton *Nancy*, a tubby brig with the figurehead of a woman, is built by Philip Ingoville. But most boat building takes place at Arichat, spreading within a few years to Bras d'Or, Cheticamp and other parts of Cape Breton, and between 1800 and 1810, forty schooners and twenty-seven shallops are built. Water trade and transportation expand and in 1864, for example, 364 sailing vessels are owned and sailed by the men of Arichat and West Arichat.

The boats, their builders and the men who sailed them are celebrated in *Cape Breton Ships and Men,* by Capt. John P. Parker of North Sydney.

April 19

1759 "Noxious vapours"

John Knox comments in a letter to Scotland on the almost perpetual fogs around Louisbourg. While some people believe them to be "the steamy breath of the vast quantities of fish and sea animals," he feels the climate is healthy and attributes this to "the myraids of venemous reptiles and insects that absorb the noxious vapours."

1826 The Royal gout subsiding

"We are happy to learn that the King's health has improved, and that the gout is subsided," reports the *Nova Scotian* newspaper.

1926 Johnny Miles wins

Eighteen-year old Johnny Miles of Sydney Mines, running his first marathon, sets a new record as he wins the Boston Marathon. His time of 2 hours, 25 minutes, 40 2/5 seconds is nearly four seconds under the old world record. He wins the Boston Marathon again in 1929.

Fig. 4.6 Johnny Miles, c. 1920.

April 20

1912 Fiddler born

Donald Angus Beaton is born in Mabou. His first public appearance is at Glencoe Mills at the age of twelve. The composer of *The Mabou Jig* and other pieces makes part of his living blacksmithing with his father. He is a master of the difficult technique of bow "triplets" (or "cuts") and the use of "flying speccato," the art of bouncing the bow to achieve several distinct notes without reversing bow directions.

1936 Northern Lights

The Aurora Borealis covers the whole Northern and Northwestern sky tonight in the Sydney area.

1970 *Patrick Morris* sinks

The CN rail ferry *Patrick Morris,* assisting in the search for the eight crew members of the herring seiner *Enterprise,* founders in a vicious gale. The ten-million-dollar ferry, battered by fifty-foot waves, sinks off northern Cape Breton shortly after dawn. Forty-seven crew members are rescued, but the captain of the *Patrick Morris,* Roland Penney, 54, is lost along with three engineering officers and the eight fishermen from the herring seiner.

The *Patrick Morris* had spotted bodies from the fishing boat and was positioned to take them aboard, but with winds averaging 50 mph and gusting to 70 mph, she apparently took a huge wave through her stern doors. She sent out an SOS, but 35 minutes later goes down in 200 feet of water.

April 21

1972 Church burns

A fire discovered shortly after midnight completely destroys L'Eglise des Sainte-Agnes Gardiens in L'Ardoise. In December 1976, the new church is completed and blessed.

1989 No more heavy water

Atomic Energy Canada is to dismantle the Heavy Water Plants at Glace Bay and Point Tupper soon.

April 22

1926 "Jimmy The Dep" upsets new man

Today is search day at No. 4 Colliery, New Waterford. Deputies are obliged every week to search all the men entering the mine to see that they have no matches, pipes or anything which might be able to cause an explosion. The miners accept the procedure as a fact of life. But today, a new pit labourer, a stranger to the area, gets upset when Jimmy the Dep (James McPherson) starts his search. A scuffle ensues that provides everyone else with a good laugh. "Jimmy got real mad, and with a neck and crotch hold, he turned the stranger upside down and put him down headfirst." The man's "piece can" breaks open and his lunch spills out. Both men finally calm down.

1929 Risks high for Cape Breton drivers

Insurance company statistics show that Sydney has the highest loss ratio from car accidents in all Canada. Many prominent companies have left the Island. Automobile insurance will cost 45 per cent more than last year, and insurance companies are considering making Cape Breton a separate district with a very much higher increase in insurance rates.

April 23

1907 Women wild about cigarettes

North Sydney ladies have come down on cigarettes. It upsets them to see children, particularly, with "the deadly cigarette between their lips" soliciting lights from passersby. The women hope to prosecute anyone who sells cigarettes to minors. They caution that the last person to be taken before the courts for breaking the law regarding the sale of cigarettes to minors was fined $20.

April 24

1889 Town is born

Sydney Mines is incorporated as a town.

1903 Explosion

An explosion at Reserve Mines causes the death of four miners, three of whom are Newfoundlanders, and serious injuries to another miner.

1905 Delayed operation

Eighty-four-year-old boat builder, Alexander Mac Kinnon of Gabarus, arrives in Louisbourg to have his hand operated upon. About forty years earlier while in a boat off Gabarus Harbour shooting sea fowl, Mr. MacKinnon was hit in the palm by a stray bullet from the gun of someone in another boat. Just recently the pain increased.

1919 Nine acts

The Gaelic play *Domhnull-Nam-Trioblaid*, a play in nine acts about the life of the Gael in olden times, is showing at the Lyceum in Sydney. Admission is 50 cents and 75 cents, plus 3 cents war tax.

Fig. 4.7 Cotter's Saturday Night, *c. 1937.*

1934 Unique program

CJCB radio's *Cotter's Saturday Night* is praised today by J. F. Willis, Director of Broadcasting for the Maritimes. It is a unique Canadian program, in fact unique on the North American continent. "I don't know of any other programme that compares with it in originality," he comments. The program helps the tourist industry by describing in great detail spots around Cape Breton.

April 25

1918 Soldiers honour Scouts - 1,361st day of war
To commemorate the work done by Scouts in France during the war, returned soldiers and sailors today present a Union Jack to the troop in Sydney with the greatest number of King's Scouts, the First Sydney Troop. The moulded spearhead staff was made by wounded soldiers in the Military Hospitals here and the silk red-white-and-blue cord and tassels were woven by sailors in port.

1927 Shipping service
The Dominion Steamship Co. Ltd. of Halifax starts a passenger service sailing from Halifax to Cape Breton every ten days. The *Dominion Halsyd* will call at St. Peter's, Johnston's Harbour, Grand Narrows, Iona, Little Narrows, Whycocomagh, Nyanza, Baddeck, North Sydney and Sydney, returning via communities on the south coast.

April 26

1918 No loafing – 1,362nd day of war
It is announced that "every male person between the ages of sixteen and sixty residing in Canada must hereafter be engaged in some useful occupation. Any person violating the new law, shall be liable to a fine not exceeding $100, or six months in the county jail with hard labour, or on the county farm." Idleness and loafing will not be tolerated when the country so urgently needs human energy for the war effort.

1923 Emigration
Two hundred and twelve men and women have left Sydney this past month for the United States. Most of the young men are going to Pittsburgh, Detroit and other industrial centres.

1959 *The Student Prince*
Rotary Club of Sydney presents *The Student Prince* with the largest male chorus ever assembled on Cape Breton.

April 27

1933 Horsepower
The following ad by an enterprising Sydney auto firm appears in the *Sydney Post Record.* "We will accept a number of good, sound horses as part payment for new or used automobiles and trucks."

1959 Cutback
Because of a lack of patronage, CNR ends its sleeping car services between Sydney and Montreal.

1959 Wagon Wheel

The old Coal Company's Hotel in Reserve Mines is demolished. It was built in 1906 to house boarders when coal mining was in full swing in the community. For the past few years it has been operated as a dine and dance place, the "Wagon Wheel."

April 28

1828 Thou shalt not fish

A Cape Breton fisherman complains about the Lord's Day Act. If the fishermen do not set their nets out over night, they will be idle the next day. This is a financial loss to the families. But it's also considered "wicked," and the fishermen are even being fined for putting out the nets after dark on Sunday nights. Mondays are "spent in idleness; and by some, I am sorry to say, in drunkenness also."

1909 Strike

The UMW establishes a local branch in Inverness, and 526 of 618 miners have joined. But the Company continues to collect dues for the Provincial Workers Association. On May 8th, a group of men hurl a package that includes the cancellation of the PWA dues from their paychecks into the manager's office. The Company also has a "closed shop" policy, refusing to let UMW members work underground. On July 9th a strike starts. By August 17th the mayor appoints five special constables. By the fall, troops brought in to quell any disturbance are camped under large canvas tents on the field parallel to MacIssac's Pond, but they aren't really needed. The strike of 1909 lasts from July 9, 1909, to April 28, 1910. Some miners return to work during the strike, which is not as effective as hoped. The strike ends with a compromise favourable to the Inverness Railway and Coal Company.

1911 Well laid out

In a lecture on the history of Sydney, Mr. E. T. McKeen comments that "one of the standing jokes that used to be cracked against Sydney was that "it was well laid out, but that anything had to be dead before it could be laid out. This jibe is now, and always was, a jealous one."

1945 Last battle for Highlanders

At 10 p.m., the Cape Breton Highlanders, who had relieved the Perths the evening before, attack Delfzijl on the Ems Estuary in Germany. Progress is slow because of mines and wire, but after vigorous attacks on the railway station and four large enemy bunkers, the Germans retreat across the Estuary. The Cape Bretoners suffer 68 casualties in this, their last battle of the War, and they capture from the SS Headquarters an eagle and swastika wall emblem, which is to decorate the wall of the Officers' Mess at Victoria Park in Sydney.

1972 Senator Al Graham

Al Graham is appointed to the Senate. He has had an outstanding career in a wide variety of roles from the political scene to broadcasting. At forty-two, he is one of Canada's youngest Senators.

April 29

1865 Price on their heads

A small schooner sails into Sydney Harbour with four Confederate Army soldiers on board. They are on their way to Halifax, from where they hope to escape to Europe. They have learned from a newspaper that the Civil War is over, but that a price still remains on their heads for their part in a recent raid on St. Albans, Vermont. By chance, a British steamer arrives in the Harbour and the Confederates have booked as passengers.

1953 St. Rita Hospital opens

St. Rita Hospital is officially opened by Bishop John R. MacDonald. It operates as such until November 1989, when it is amalgamated as the Sydney Community Health Center with Sydney City Hospital and the Cape Breton Hospital. When the new regional hospital opens in 1995, the older facilities are closed and soon torn down.

1981 Gaelic poet

Malcolm Gillis, well known as a Gaelic poet, singer, composer, fiddler and bagpipe player from Southwest Margaree, is featured today in a national TV program on CTV, *The Celtic Peoples in Canada*, researched and hosted by Prof.essor Norman MacDonald of UCCB. Gillis died in 1929.

April 30

1920 Death rate appalling

The Public Health Inspector for Nova Scotia comments that Sydney needs a health organization. The mortality rate for children under the age of one year is appalling—432 deaths from 1914-1917 could have been prevented.

1991 Beached whale

Cape Bretoners invade quiet Rocky Bay to see the large dead sperm whale beached on their shore. The whale, over 30 feet long, weighs over 45 tons. About a mile down the shore another whale is beached. They may have died because they couldn't find an air hole, and they suffocated under the ice. Local fishermen tow the carcasses off the shoreline. The whales cause much excitement and some problems for the local residents, who are used to quiet.

May

New England Bravery

(To the tune of "Chevy Chase")

Come all New England's gallant lads and lend me an Ear,
And of your Brethren's Mighty Acts I will in short declare
Brave Pepprell with three Thousand Men (perhaps some hundreds more)
Did land the very first of May, upon Cape Breton Shore;
And tho' opposed by Morepang, with full two hundred Men,
A handful of our gallant Lads, did drive them back again....

Written in 1745 by a New Englander

"A View of the Landing the New England Forces in ye Expedition against CAPE BRETON, 1745

"When after a Siege of 40 days the town and fortress of LOUISBOURG and the important Territories thereto belonging were recover'd to the British Enpire. The brave & Active Commodore Warren, since made Knight of the Bath & Vice Admiral of ye White, commanded the British Squadron in this glorious Expedition. The Hon. Will'm Pepperell Esq. (since Knighted), went a Volunteer & Commanded the New England Men who bravely offer'd their services and went as private Soldiers in this hazardous but very glorious enterprise.

Fig. 5.1 Depiction of landing of New England forces, 1745.

May 1

1852 Daily stage

DAILY STAGE
Three times a day each way a
DAILY STAGE
will operate between the store of
Messrs. Archibald and Co.
At the North Bar (North Sydney)
and their store in Sydney Mines

1918 Price not critical - 1,367th day of war

The enlistment of miners in the services causes a shortage in the work force, but production has to be increased says a speaker to the Mining Society in Cape Breton. "The price of coal is not a deciding factor in days of fuel scarcity. The important thing, the paramount necessity, is to produce coal; to produce it as cheaply as possible, but above all and beyond all other considerations, to produce."

1920 Maternity unit opened

The Sisters of Saint Martha open a small maternity unit in the Ross house on Kings Road near Wentworth Park which served as a convalescent hospital for soldiers. Renamed the Ross Memorial Hospital, it soon expands, changes its name to St Rita Hospital in 1929, and eventually will be relocated to a new and larger building further along Kings Road. (See also April 29, 1953.)

Fig. 5.2 Ross Memorial Hospital, c.1930.

1942 Trans Canada Airlines

A new plane service between Moncton, Sydney and St. John's is inaugurated, as a Trans Canada Airlines ten-passenger Lockheed 1408 lands at Sydney Airport. TCA will become Air Canada in 1965.

In the first month of operation, TCA operates one flight east and west through Sydney daily, for twenty passengers per flight. In 1967—on its 25th anniversary—there will be 624 seats on eight daily flights. In 1984, DC9s carry one hundred passengers on each of the two daily flights, three on weekends in summer.

1967 Heavy water

Premier Robert Stanfield officially opens the Deuterium of Canada Ltd. heavy water plant at Glace Bay, the world's first commercial heavy water plant. Guests at the opening include Dr. Harold C. Urey, who was awarded the Nobel Prize in 1934 for the discovery of Deuterium Oxide.

Heavy water is processed from ordinary water and used as a moderator to slow and control the fission of uranium in reactors. It is central to Canada's program to develop electrical power through nuclear energy. By October 1, 1970, when the first heavy water is produced in Canadian General Electric's plant in Point Tupper, the plant at Glace Bay is not yet in production. It has already cost the federal government 120 million dollars and is running four years behind schedule. In 1964, the Nova Scotia government had hired Jerome Spevak. He had convinced them that Deuterium Oxide (heavy water) could be more cheaply produced from sea water than fresh water. The Glace Bay plant, however, suffers from major corrosion problems and the system undergoes major modification. It isn't until the summer of 1976 that the first barrel of heavy water is produced here.

In 1980, a greenhouse, heated by hot water effluent from the plant, begins producing tomatoes and cucumbers for the Cape Breton market. This waste heat greenhouse is a joint project of Devco, the Nova Scotia Department of Agriculture and Atomic Energy of Canada Ltd.

1977 Cape Bretoners in Edinburgh

Cape Breton musicians are well received as they perform in Edinburgh, Scotland, at the International Gathering of the Clans. Performers include fiddlers Buddy MacMaster and Winnie Chafe, pianist Doug MacPhee, piper Danny MacIntyre and stepdancers Father Eugene Morris and Margaret Dunn.

1996 New owners for the *Post*

The *Cape Breton Post* is one of six Atlantic Canadian newspapers scheduled to be purchased from the Thompson Newspaper chain by Hollinger Inc.

2005 Gaelic online

An online course in Gaelic for beginners is now available. The course, *"Beul an Tobair,"* consists of twelve lessons and has been granted full university accreditation by Cape Breton University and by the Nova Scotia Department of Education as meeting the criteria for the Grade 10 Gaelic curriculum.

May 2

1784 Colony of Cape Breton established

The Colony of Cape Breton is officially established by an Order-in-Council.

1904 New spirit

In a new spirit of confidence, the Cape Breton Iron and Steel Company is organized to manufacture iron, steel and brass castings of all kinds, and also to do general jobbing, specializing in marine work.

1920 Largest in Empire

Cape Breton iron and coal deposits on the Atlantic combine with the financial resources of Great Britain. The new British Empire Steel Corporation (BESCO), incorporating the Dominion Steel Corporation, Canada Steamship Lines Ltd., and Nova Scotia Steel and Coal Ltd., will be the largest consolidation in the British Empire, and second only to the U.S. Steel Corporation. (See also Dec. 31, 1967)

1965 The we-don't-have-winters-like-we-used-to department
A new winter record is set in Cape Breton. Since November first, a total of 222.5 inches of snow has fallen, breaking all records dating back to 1874. By the end of the winter, Cape Bretoners will have shovelled through 240.8 inches of snow.

1990 Clean coal
Louis Comeau, president of the Nova Scotia Power Corporation, defends the decision to build a $300 million coal-fired power station at Point Aconi. He said he's tired of getting flak from environmentalists about carbon dioxide emissions. "For the first time in all the history of Nova Scotia," he says, "we've got a power plant that has the latest technology to clean coal."

May 3

1990 Justice delayed
The retirement of two Cape Breton judges, Charles O'Connell and George LeVatte, prompts fear of a serious backlog in court cases to be heard.

1744 War
News of the war between France and England reaches Louisbourg.

1984 Heritage churches
Three ethnic churches in Whitney Pier, Sydney, are declared Provincial Heritage Properties. St. Philip's is the only African Orthodox Church in Canada. Formally opened in July, 1928, it is used by West Indian immigrants and their descendents. St. Mary's Polish Church, completed in 1918, is the only Polish Church east of Montreal. The Holy Ghost Ukrainian Catholic Church was originally built in 1913. Destroyed by fire, it was rebuilt in 1933. Celebrating the Byzantine Rite, it is the only church of its kind east of Montreal. (See also March 11, 1983.)

May 4

1824 First Catholic judge
John Hugh MacDonald is born in South River, Antigonish County. In 1859 he is elected provincial representative for Inverness and goes with Joseph Howe to England to oppose Confederation. Elected to the House of Commons in 1872, he becomes a member of the Queen's Council and president of the Privy Council. He is chosen Minister of Militia and Defence in Sir John A. MacDonald's government. November 5, 1873, he resigns to become the first Catholic judge of the Nova Scotia Supreme Court. He dies February 28, 1899.

1913 North Sydney burns
Fire in North Sydney destroys 41 businesses. From the ferry wharf on the waterside of Commercial St. to the Marine slip, and from Archibald Avenue to Caledonia St. on the other side, nothing remains. The fire levels much the same area as the 1881 fire did. (See also Dec. 12, 1881.)

1991 Arctic fox
An arctic fox spotted near the Fortress Louisbourg may have travelled here on heavy northern pack ice drifting down from Labrador.

May 5

1783 For sale
J. F. W. DesBarres' Atlantic Neptune charts of Nova Scotia are advertised for sale.

1937 The Hindenberg: They almost had the disaster here
The German dirigible airship, the *Hindenberg*, on its first transatlantic voyage of the year, passes over Cape Breton. Spectators watch it fly low over the railroad tracks, and it seems that the *Hindenberg* just misses hitting the Grand Narrows bridge. "Big Gordie" MacNeil of Grand Narrows is the Major in charge of "A" Company and the Bridge is in his territory. "Big Gordie," a veteran of the First World War, as the company commander has all the stores in his barn. He races for a Lewis gun and a pan of ammunition. Luckily, his Colonel, Willie G. MacRae, is over visiting from Baddeck. He knows that in every five bullets there is a tracer which would cause fire and that the *Hindenberg* is filled with hydrogen. The Colonel is able to intervene before there is a disaster.

The *Hindenberg* sails on, cheered by thousands in Times Square, New York City, before trying to dock at Lakehurst, New Jersey. It bursts into flames and crashes, killing thirty seven people.

1945 End of war
All German forces in Holland and northwest Germany surrender, and hostilities officially cease in this area at 8 a.m. this morning.

The North Nova Scotia Regiment, which includes many Cape Bretoners, have fought their way through Normandy and France, across Belgium and Holland, and have recently completed fighting across the Ems River and through the town of Leer in Germany.

The Cape Breton Highlanders have fought up the Adriatic coast of Italy, later joined the First Canadian Army at Nijmegan, and on April 30th, see their last action of the war at Delzijl on the bank of the Ems Estuary in the Netherlands.

The Cape Breton contribution to the Allied victory was not confined to service in the North Novas or the Cape Breton Highlanders. Cape Bretoners served in other infantry regiments, with service and support units and with the Navy, the Air Force and the Merchant Marine.

May 6

1931 White plague
The Minister of Health holds a meeting to determine ways of controlling the "white plague," tuberculosis, in Cape Breton. Each district can either erect a TB annex or provide additional facilities in their respective hospitals. (See also January 15, 1949.)

1935 Silver Jubilee

Cape Bretoners turn out to celebrate the 25th anniversary of the ascension to the Throne of King George V. Nineteen Sydney residents, from all walks of life, are presented with Silver Jubilee medals.

1968 More responsibility

Indians of Eskasoni want officials of the Indian Affairs Department off the Reserve. Two days later, the Department agrees to allow the Indians to take on more responsibility for their own affairs.

May 7

1745 The British are coming

A naval assault, which will result in the fall of Louisbourg, is expected at any moment. Louisbourg's Governor, Du Chambon, has sent for all male inhabitants of the surrounding countryside from as far away as Niganiche (Ingonish) to come to the Fortress. Women and children are expected to hide in the woods near their homes if the British attack. Many go with Madame Boularderie to the Baddeck Region.

1840 Class of 1840

William Ayre reports that he has 47 scholars in his school at Broad Cove. Hired first in 1834 with a salary of $80 a year, Mr. Ayre started teaching before the schoolhouse was built. The Class of 1840 has six students in their early 20s, the eldest is 22-year old Hugh MacDonald, and the youngest, 8-year old Eliza Sutherland. This is the first advanced school in Inverness County. These early schools were hewn logs with a moss, clay and plaster mixture used to fill the cracks. Inside furnishings included a large wood stove, a drinking-water pail which had to be filled from the brook, a painted hardwood blackboard, slates, wooden desks, homemade ink and quill pens.

1980 Terry Fox

Terry Fox arrives in North Sydney from Port aux Basques. Terry, who lost his leg to cancer when he was 18, has started running across Canada to raise money for cancer. He records in his journal about his time on Cape Breton: "Twenty-six miles is now my daily minimum. It is beautiful, quiet, peaceful country. I love it." Near Thunder Bay on September 1st when he is two-thirds of the way home he is forced to stop his race. He dies June 28, 1981, one month before his 23rd birthday. Canadians are determined to finish his race. A Terry Fox Run to raise money for cancer research is held annually in communities across the country.

1987 Loonie

The new one-dollar "loonie," partly made of old tin cans, is officially minted. The gold coin gets its nickname "loonie" because of the imprint of a loon on one side.

1992 Murder at McDonald's

It's the early hours of the morning in the McDonald's restaurant on Kings Road, Sydney River. Night manager Donna Warren counts the coming day's register "floats." Co-worker Arlene MacNeil waits for her to finish her shift. Jimmy Fagan arrives early and finds Neil Burroughs already at work preparing for the breakfast crew. An unexpected robbery turns ugly. Donna, Jim and Neil are brutally murdered, and Arlene is badly wounded and left permanently disabled. Employee Derek Wood, thought to be lucky to escape, turns out to be one of the killers. He and his two friends, Darren Muise and Freeman MacNeil, are finally caught, brought to respective trials, convicted and sentenced to life in prison. The restaurant operates at the site for some years before relocating down the road.

May 8

1834 Lighthouse needed

The barque *Astrea*, crammed with 251 Irish immigrants bound for Quebec, strikes the rocks off Little Lorraine and sinks. A carpenter, a seaman and a surgeon are the only survivors. Dr. Jerome O'Sullivan walks for more than two hours before finding a house. There the woman of the house "put me to bed, and gave me some hot tea, and also applied hot irons to my feet."

In June, the magistrate in Sydney writes the government, informing them of the several vessels wrecked this past spring, of the 400 destitute and starving survivors on the community's hands, and of the 121 bodies recovered and buried. Local fishermen have clothed the naked bodies of the *Astrea's* passengers before burial.

By June of 1835, another ship, loaded with Irish immigrants is wrecked off Scaterie, but this time all are saved. The government appoints a Superintendent of Shipwrecks for the northeast and southeast shores of Cape Breton. The British government will erect lighthouses on St. Paul's Island and on Scatarie, if Canada and the three Maritime Provinces will share the cost of construction.

1914 Early feminists

The *Sydney Daily Post* reprints an article from the May issue of *Harper's Magazine* about women and education: "The old education trained women to serve, to please, to charm, to comfort, to endure ... an education designed to qualify women to sustain an accepted relation to society and to men.

"The new education for girls has no quarrels with men, but ... its aim is to turn out girls so far developed mentally, and so trained and instructed, that they can make their own choices in the world."

1914 Killer hanged

Following the most controversial trial in Cape Breton's history, American Frank Haynes goes to the gallows in Sydney for the murder of Ben Atkinson, racehorse owner and operator of the Minto Hotel on Charlotte Street.

1966 Two kinds of Canadians

Sydney Rotary honours Cape Breton native sons. President Ken MacLennan reads a message from Prime Minister Lester Pearson: "I have heard it said there are only two kinds of Canadians: Cape Bretoners and those who wish they were Cape Bretoners."

Native sons honoured include Dr. Walter MacKenzie, president of the American College of Surgeons and Dean of Medicine at the University of Alberta; Rod Kerr, chairman of the board of Railway Commissioners; Allan MacEachen, Federal Minister of Health and Welfare; Rod MacInnis, vice-president of Air Canada; Hon. H. P. McKeen, Lt. Governor of Nova Scotia; Nathan Cohen, Drama Critic, Toronto Star; Danny Gallivan, sportscaster; Air

Vice Marshal Maurice Lipton, Deputy Chief of Staff for Operations, NORAD; Dr. Murray Ross, president of York University; Claude Richardson, QC, prominent Montreal barrister; W. K. Buckley; and Dr. Malcolm MacLellan, president of St. FX.

May 9

1906 Fruit salad

Agriculture officials visit the government fruit-growing station at the Lewis farm in Coxheath. Of the 200-hundred trees, there are 20 varieties of apples, 10 varieties of plums and 50 pears, cherries and quinces. The attempts to grow peaches here have been unsuccessful.

1931 Pioneer flight

Two Cape Breton flying club aircraft, piloted by "Bricky" Stevenson (with Norman Denison as passenger) and Don MacPherson (Fred Mitchell as passenger), fly to Halifax on a good-will flight. Carrying copies of the *Cape Breton Post* and a loaf of bread from Eastern Bakeries for Mayor Mitchell, the planes take 4:45 hours to fly to Halifax.

1932 Fish story

Residents of Dominion No. 6 and Glace Bay come with bags, wheelbarrows, hand barrows and cars to collect their supply of fresh spring herring. Thousands of herring have been driven on shore by the drift ice. Not far off shore the "fishermen" can see porpoises or small whales.

1951 Cape Bretoners to Korea

Forty-five Cape Bretoners, fifteen of whom served in World War Two, leave tonight for Halifax to join the new 25th Infantry Brigade, headed for Korea.

May 10

1930 Inventive cleric

Whitney Pier's Rev. Mr. Shumsky's new invention is now on sale in Canada and the U.S. The hydrolator can be installed on any make of car. It quickens starting and the pickup, saves oil because it eliminates the use of the choke and the warming up of the motor except in extremely cold weather. Guaranteed to give more than 25 per cent more mileage per gallon of gas, it's manufactured by the International Combustion Atomizer Ltd. in the Pier.

1972 Too much

May's average snowfall is only 5.3 centimetres. Today's snowfall is 24.9 centimetres.

1991 Safety glasses

The safety committee of Lingan Local, UMWA, reports that employees now must wear safety glasses, but not in non-work areas such as travelling by rake in and out of the mine. The committee also suggests the use of hearing protection in certain areas.

May 11

1745 Americans land
This morning, New England troops start disembarking at Freshwater Cove, near Gabarus Bay. The Royal Battery at Louisbourg is abandoned by the French.

1817 Smugglers
An official "blind eye" is usually turned when Cape Bretoners smuggle various goods; it increases the Island's trade. But New Englanders have been smuggling Cape Breton gypsum, evading the customs collectors. Now that the rum duty has been suspended, Cape Breton's Gov. Ainslie has been adding to His Majesty's coffers with a tax for digging gypsum and by establishing a customs officer at Port Hawkesbury to handle the increased gypsum trade.

In the States, gypsum has been in demand as a fertilizer and general soil conditioner ever since Benjamin Franklin returned from France and interested farmers in using it New Englanders exchange manufactured goods for gypsum right in the gut of Canso.

1978 Micmac centre
A new Micmac library and resource centre, the first of its kind in the Atlantic Provinces, opens at the Membertou Reserve.

1978 *Sior Flur a Chas*
Today is Community Involvement Day of the 25th Anniversary Celebrations at the Canadian Forces Station, Radar Base, Sydney. Besides dealing with radar transmission, the Base supports the Recruiting Centre, local military units, and the Army, Navy and Air cadets in Cape Breton. The Base crest, with deer, spruce and water, is the only unit crest in the Armed Forces containing Gaelic, *Sior Flur a Chas*, "Ever Vigilant."

1987 Coal award
A. Roy MacLean, Devco's director of mine engineering, wins "the Canadian Institute of Mining and Metallurgy's annual coal award for his contribution to mechanization of mining methods, exploration, safety and research and for his dedication to the Mining Society of Nova Scotia." "He began his career in coal mining with the Dominion Coal Company in 1951, working his way through the ranks."

May 12

1745 New Englanders advance
A detachment of New Englanders, which landed yesterday, advances to the Northeast Harbour at Louisbourg. Houses and storehouses at the head of the harbour are burned. Vessels are sunk. The supply of oil at the lighthouse is removed.

1937 "Gus" Edwards
Harold "Gus" Edwards of New Aberdeen leads the Canadian Military contingent to the Coronation of King George VI. Gus Edwards was born in England but brought to the Glace

Bay area as a boy when his father emigrated. In 1915, having earlier enlisted in the Royal Canadian Navy, he transferred to the Royal Naval Air Service. He was later taken prisoner in Germany but following repatriation, went to South Russia and flew in support of White Russian General Deniken's forces opposing the Bolsheviks. Returning to Canada in 1920, he joined and rapidly rose in the RCAF to Air Marshall and was Commander-in-Chief of Royal Canadian Air Forces Overseas. He dies on Feb. 23, 1952.

1954 First patients

St. Elizabeth Hospital in North Sydney receives its first patients, transferred from the Hamilton Memorial Hospital which has served the town for many years.

1995 New hospital

The new Cape Breton Regional Hospital opens after a decade of fundraising.

May 13

1745 Battery falls

The Royal Battery at the Fortress Louisbourg is occupied by a small group of New Englanders without firing a shot. (See also May 11, 1745 and June 17,1745.)

1934 Rod-riders invade

Reports that economic conditions are improving in the industrial area bring in a flood of hobos. RCMP and CNR police are unable to keep up with the "rod riders," who are arriving from across the continent in search of work.

1957 New tartan

Black for the wealth of our coal mines,
Grey for our Cape Breton Steel
Green for our lofty mountains
Our valleys and our fields.

Gold for the golden sunsets,
Shining bright on the lakes of Bras d'Or
To show us God's hand has lingered
To bless Cape Breton's shores.

The Cape Breton tartan, inspired by Lillian Walsh and her poem, is created by weaver Mrs. Wilson Grant and publicly displayed today for the first time on CJCB-TV.

May 14

1745 New Englanders use French guns

Several of the guns at the Royal Battery, having been improperly spiked by the withdrawing French, are used by the New Englanders against the town of Louisbourg.

1911 Monster steamers

The new steamer *Themis,* launched this spring for the ore trade of the Nova Scotia Steel and Coal Company, arrives in North Sydney with 10,000 tons of iron ore in her holds. *Themis* and her sister ship *Tellus* are the two largest ocean going ore or coal carriers afloat and are said to be the two largest purely cargo-carrying steamers yet launched. Fifteen years ago, the steamer that carried over 3,000 tons was considered a "monster."

1938 Cape Breton goes international

Celtic Ceilidh, Cape Breton's Gaelic radio show, a resumption of the popular "Celtic Forum" staged last January as a test program, will be broadcast from Sydney at 5:30 p.m. every Saturday night throughout Canada and parts of the United States.

1954 Sydney International Airport

Trans Canada Air Lines' first scheduled transatlantic flight with a Super Constellation lands at Sydney Airport en route to London. Flying with 58 passengers and 9 crew aboard, the plane flew from Montreal in 2 hours and 42 minutes, and the flight to London will take just over 9 hours more.

1955 Crossing the causeway

Reginald Hayes, vice-president of CNR, cuts the ribbon across the tracks at the 7,000-foot Canso Causeway. And a few minutes later, at 4:00 p.m., the first regular passenger train, a Halifax-Sydney express with two additional cars filled with officials, crosses over the new Causeway. The historic crossing is made in seven minutes, about fifty minutes less than the time it took to cross on the rail ferry.

Meanwhile...

While there is rejoicing at the Causeway, a few miles downstream, sadness surrounds Capt. George Hadley as he brings the train ferry "Scotia" into her berth at Point Tupper for the last time. Many of his crew have sailed with him for twenty-three years. More than two hundred men will be affected by the changeover.

1984 Fibreglass caskets

The doors open at the Wagmatcook Reserve for employees to be trained in a new fibreglass manufacturing company. This company, believed to be the first in Canada, will manufacture caskets, which look exactly like wooden ones, but last longer.

1996 Bike helmets necessary

Bike accidents have long been a major cause of head injuries. Now bicycle riders who don't wear helmets not only risk head injuries but also a $25 fine and the police seizure of their bicycles for 30 days. Parents are responsible for children under sixteen years of age.
In 1900 the police are concerned with bicyclists riding at nights without carrying lanterns.

May 15

1904 Sea Wolf

Jack London's book, *The Sea Wolf* is published this year. Its hero, Alexander MacLean, was born in East Bay and raised on a farm there. He and his brother Daniel left for the West Coast when he was twenty-two and very shortly acquired a notorious reputation right across the

Pacific for poaching seals, carrying cargoes of illegal liquor and high explosives, fur stealing and piracy. He was sought by police from the United States, Canada, Britain, France, Australia, Japan and Russia.

But even during these wild times he managed to make two trips back home to Cape Breton. He was nicknamed the "Sea Wolf" and before he died in 1914, he had done time in jail in Russia, had been sheriff of the then "wide open" town of Nome, Alaska, and had achieved immortality in Jack London's book.

1943 Girls leave

This month, more than one thousand Cape Breton girls will leave by train from Sydney. Some will go to the aircraft factory in Quebec, while about five hundred will work at the Cockshutt Aircraft Factory in Malton, Ontario.

1954 Open again

No. 26 Colliery, Glace Bay, closed since a disastrous fire several months ago, opens again. Bootleg coal operators are warned that gases will be removed to the surface through No. 1A Colliery. (See also April 15, 1984.)

1987 New food court

A new five-store fast food court is opened at the Sydney Shopping Centre. Manager Don Shaw, who leaves here, after six years, for a new managerial position at Market Square, Saint John, NB, is responsible for the Sydney centre becoming the top shopping centre of the eight owned by the Sobey family. In the six years since he arrived, the centre's "multi-million dollar sales have doubled, and several of the forty stores and services record their own success stories."

May 16

1746 Winter of the bloody flux

A British soldier complains that "Louisbourg is worse than any place in the known world. Nothing but fog rains severe Death and everything thats bad and Disagreeable." This past winter has been the "Winter of the Bloody Flux," with about 900 New Englanders dying from the "bloody flux" (dysentery). Sickness, the cold and damp, lack of fresh food and poor sanitation have all combined to do more damage than the French soldiers had done.

1937 Largest elm

An elm tree, believed to be the largest in Eastern Canada, with a circumference of twenty feet, is located on the property of the new Normaway Inn in Margaree Valley. The tree is no longer there.

May 17

1852 *Highland Lass* sails

The *Highland Lass* becomes the second Cape Breton ship to leave for Australia. A 179-ton brig, smaller than Reverend Norman McLeod's *Margaret*, the *Highland Lass* was built by her owners Duncan and Murdoch McKenzie of Baddeck. Unlike the *Margaret*, whose passengers hailed from St. Ann's, the *Highland Lass* has passengers from Boularderie, Middle River, Baddeck, Sydney Mines and Sydney as well.

The journey is plagued by bad luck. Chicken pox breaks out, most of the bread spoils and heavy rains make open fires for cooking impossible. Captain Jordan is relieved of his command because of drunkenness and inaccurate navigation. Landing in Australia, they discover that living conditions there are not as expected. The two Cape Breton ships are sold and another bought to take them to a new home in New Zealand in September 1853. One woman settler is reported to say, "In Nova Scotia there was snow, in Australia there are snakes, and in New Zealand there are the Maoris. They'll be the least trouble."

1916 Never again

The Nova Scotia Legislature passes a Resolution sent to the town of North Sydney that "all buildings hereafter to be erected on either side of Commercial St. within the town of North Sydney, extending westerly from the ICR (Intercolonial, later CNR) crossing to Peppett St. shall be constructed of brick, concrete or stone." North Sydney's downtown area has twice been destroyed by a major fire. (See also May 4, 1913 and Dec. 12, 1881.)

1964 Cock fighting

RCMP seize seventeen cocks in a raid at River Ryan. Cock fighting "has been condemned as a cruel and bloody sport. It is strictly illegal. Cape Breton is the centre of cock-fighting in Eastern Canada."

People are charged, valuable birds seized and destroyed and a week or two later, the action starts again in another place. The cocks, both equipped with long, needle-like steel spurs on their heels, fight until one of them is dead. Some cocks are imported from the U.S. and cost as much as $3,000, but this can be won back in bets if he wins. Facilities include a fence to enclose the pit and a few rows of bleachers. Some matches are very businesslike, others are livelier with moonshine adding to the carnival air.

2005 Great double axle

Howie Centre's Alix Breski is named Nova Scotia's top female figure skater. The sixteen-year-old is also nominated for the province's female athlete of the year. In March, she performs for the Stars on Ice show at Centre 200 in Sydney.

May 18

1785 The founding of Sydney

Lt. Gov. J. F. W. DesBarres lands at the north end of the peninsula with high hopes and his plans for a carefully laid out capital. British settlers arrived last fall on the *Blenheim* and spent the winter at the Mines (Sydney Mines), where DesBarres joined them later in the winter. The stores were landed at what is now Point Edward.

Fig. 5.3 Founding of Sydney, 1785. Lt. William Booth.

A group of Associated Loyalists, led by Abraham Cuyler, a

former mayor of Albany, New York, after sheltering as best it could in what was left of Louisbourg, follows DesBarres to Sydney and helps build the town. The town is named after Thomas Townshend, Secretary of State for the Colonies, who had recently been given the title Lord Sydney. "Pittsburgh" was one of the names considered for the town, in honour of William Pitt, about to become Prime Minister of Britain.

1971 Al MacNeil

Coach Al MacNeil, from Sydney, the first Nova Scotian to coach a Stanley Cup winner, leads his Montreal Canadians to the Stanley Cup. July 1st will be Al MacNeil Day in Sydney. He's inducted into the Nova Scotia Sports Hall of Fame.

1980 Weight record

Eric LeBlanc, of Sydney, lifts a 1,140 lb (517 kg) total in three lifts to set a new Canadian weightlifting record for his division.

1991 Air Cadets celebrate

Air Cadets celebrate the 50th anniversary of Air Cadets in Canada. After a street parade and a wing parade at Centre 200, two local squadrons—29 Kiwanis Squadron Sydney and 45 Air Marshall Edwards Squadron Glace Bay—are presented with their 50-year banners.

May 19

1846 Once and for all?

The question of the separation of Cape Breton from Nova Scotia is argued before the Judicial Committee of the Privy Council, and it is decided that "the inhabitants of Cape Breton are not by law entitled to the Constitution purported to be granted to them by the Letters Patent of 1784. The Cape Breton Question is now settled!"

1886 Forty years later

A public meeting is held concerning self-government for Cape Breton. A large, representative crowd is enthusiastic about separation. One of the chief supporters is Newton MacKay, Federal Member of Parliament from 1872-1878. But on the way home from tonight's meeting, Mr. MacKay drops dead of a heart attack on the street. (See also July 19, 1844.)

1920 Concrete boat

Canada's first concrete boat, the *Permanicia,* is launched at North Sydney this morning. Schoolchildren have the day off so they can watch. More than twenty carloads of sightseers from Glace Bay, along with people from the area and several "moving picture operators" come to see the launching. The boat expects to be ready for its freight and passenger service to Newfoundland in about six weeks time.

2005 Bright kid

On ATV's *Live at Five* telecast, five-year-old Matthew Sawchuck of North Sydney talks about his appearance on the *Ellen DeGeneres Show*. Matthew's primary school teacher comments on the boy's "intense search for knowledge." Matthew, who is fascinated by and is knowledgeable about, human anatomy, says "I'm glad the body I'm in is so famous."

May 20

1820 Arrival

Norman McDonald sails his boat, the first of seven to come, his passengers, their few possessions and livestock into St. Ann's Bay. The Reverend Norman McLeod will arrive shortly afterwards. A stern, charismatic, self-made preacher, Reverend Norman left Scotland in July, 1817 and arrived in Pictou only to find it too worldly. "I know not the comparison of Pictou in the whole land for shamelessness and daring wickedness." Plans to emigrate to Ohio were changed when on a reconnaissance voyage, they encountered St. Ann's Bay in September 1819. The handful of settlers on the south shore of the Bay greet the newcomers. Those in Pictou are glad to see Reverend Norman leave. (See also October 28, 1851 and April 10, 1852.)

1909 *Aspy*

The new steamship *Aspy*, built in Shelburne for the North Shore Steamship Company of Sydney, is launched this afternoon. The *Aspy* will carry freight and passengers between Sydney, North Sydney, St. Ann's, Ingonish, Aspy Bay and Bay St. Lawrence. At 124 feet long, 25 feet wide, 9 feet deep, the "Aspy" has a freight capacity of about 1,400 barrels and sleeping accommodations for 35 or 40 passengers. The awning deck, extending from side to side, forms a "spacious promenade." The boat will be lit with electricity and carry a powerful searchlight.

Fig. 5.4 The Aspy *at South Haven wharf, n.d.*

1930 Tram car tracks go

Work begins taking up the tram car tracks and removing the overhead wires and crossbars in North Sydney. Glace Bay and Sydney are also scheduled to start dismantling the tram system.

1967 Mod lives on

Rev. A. W. R. MacKenzie, founder of the Gaelic College at St. Ann's, dies of a heart attack while planning this year's Mod.

2005 Chinese early settlers in Cape Breton?

Sydney native Paul Chiasson hopes he has found evidence of 15th-century Chinese settlement on Kelly's Mountain.

May 21

1843 Familiar tale

Mail delivery in Cape Breton is "deplorably inefficient and irregular." While it takes an experienced traveller one day to walk to Baddeck, and four more hours to reach Middle River, it takes the mail sometimes ten days on the road between Sydney and Baddeck and another six days to get to Middle River. This is because by the time the Sydney courier reaches Boularderie, the Boularderie courier has already left for Baddeck and the mail lies at Boularderie until he gets back six days later. After reaching Baddeck, it again waits for perhaps another six days before being taken to Middle River. The same confusion occurs when the mail is sent the other way.

May 22

1971 Rankin family hot to trot

Donald Rankin and three of his sons, Sonny, Joey and Callie, all of the Frenchvale Road, Balls Creek, establish a record at the Cape Breton Sports Centre. All take part as drivers in the pre-holiday meet. According to veteran followers of the sport, it marks the first time ever for four members of one family to appear as drivers in a single meet.

2004 $10 million

Ferne Hawley, 43, of New Waterford wins $10 million with her winning Lotto 649 ticket. She's just lost her job at a local hardware store. Her luck has changed. But has it? She suffers a heart attack, brought on, she believes, by the pressure of people asking her for money. (They even line up at her door.) She says, "Now I just tear up the letters, and if anyone calls, I tell them they need to talk to my husband.

"You know, the second I got home (from travelling to Moncton, NB, to pick up her winnings), I told Tom I wished I could give it all back."

May 23

1832 Newspaper

The *Cape Breton Herald,* a new newspaper for the Island, is published in Sydney by "A Society of (Tory) Gentlemen." Edited by N. H. Martin, Esq., of St. Peters, it lasts for only six months.

1904 Lyceum opens

The Lyceum, Sydney's new cultural centre, opens. *Between Love and Duty,* based on incidents of the American Civil War, is the principal feature of the opening night program. Other items include ragtime songs, dances, singing, an orchestra and a ventriloquist.

Local jewellers have opera glasses in stock. Gowns and dress materials are brought into the city for the gala opening. Tickets for each performance are 25-75 cents.

Passion plays and vaudeville are popular, as are "moving pictures" called Lyceumographs. Between reels, trained dogs, horses or monkeys perform along with magicians, singers and acrobats. Many concerts, plays and sporting events are held over the years. World War II troop entertainment helps keep it going and later the Von Trapp family appears after their escape from Austria. Singer Mario Lanza gives his last performance before going into movies. (See also March 7, 1951.)

Fig. 5.5 Lyceum, cir. 1905. Walter Hall.

1934 New Glace Bay theatre

Destroyed by fire ten weeks ago, the new Russell Theatre opens tonight in Glace Bay with *Going Hollywood*. Upholstered seats are provided for the comfort of the public.

1950 Gracie Fields

Singer comedienne, Gracie Fields, performs at the Glace Bay Miners Forum.

2004 Victorian secrets

On the Lyceum's lower level, the Centre for Heritage and Science celebrates with a special exhibit, "Victorian Secrets," historic reproduction by Pam Newton. Outfits include nightwear, undergarments, corsets, petticoats, hoops and bustles and the clothes that go over them, as well as a line of Victorian bathing suits.

May 24

1819 Queen Victoria's birthday

Victoria is born. Her birthday will be celebrated throughout Canada. In Cape Breton it is the weekend that people plant their potatoes. It is also regarded as the first weekend that townspeople visit their relatives in the country and country residents remove their long johns.

1904 Stir in North Sydney

J. R. Maxwell and A. R. MacKay, Sydney's first automobile dealers, drive their Oldsmobile Roadster, which costs $675, to North Sydney. The appearance of the first car in North Sydney causes a stir in the town and at the Trotting Park, where the owners have come for the holiday races. It will be another four years before North Sydney's first automobile, owned by carriage builder, Archie MacDonald, goes for its "first spin."

1914 Too many potholes

By 1914, only fourteen cars are owned in North Sydney and roads are in very poor condition. It's rare to reach Sydney without a flat tire. Car owners get together each Victoria Day to work on the roads. Even wives are commandeered to help haul gravel to fill up the pot holes.

1921 Cricket
The first game of cricket this season is played between the Jubilee team of Sydney Mines and a mixed eleven on the grounds near the Colliery.

May 25

1842 Cape Breton flourishes
This past week, nine square-rigged vessels and six others, laden with coal for various ports, help show that Cape Breton is not feeling the economic depression others are experiencing.

1893 Specialist, at last?
J. W. Ross, advertising in the North Sydney "Herald," announces that his shop, the one with the plate glass windows on Commercial Street, is the first store in Cape Breton to sell only shoes. There's another shoeman in the town, but he sells boots, lawn shoes, genuine English bluchers (strong leather half boots or high shoes), children's spring heels, English and American kid, goat, calf and cordova footwear and enamelled shoes.

May 26

1942 Army food
"Big Angus" MacPhail is known as "the man the Army couldn't stop from putting on weight." Born in Lake Ainslie, Big Angus is six and a half feet tall. Weighing 202 pounds when he joined the Army in 1932, he's now up to 390 pounds.

1967 Barren Road families flee
A big storm hits the coast. Hurricane winds accompanied by rain and snow, cause many families, including six on the Barren Road, to evacuate their homes when flood waters reach their kitchens.

1983 Trade zone
An International Trade Zone is announced for Sydport at Point Edward. This zone is intended to allow companies to manufacture goods for the international market in Sydport. Sydport is Cape Breton's major industrial park.

May 27

1795 Privateers active
William Macarmick, Governor for seven years, leaves Sydney. During the War with France, he prepared to defend the town and arranged to evacuate the population to St. Peter's.

While crossing the Atlantic to England, Macarmick's wife and two daughters were taken prisoner by the French and sent to Canso. Macarmick requested that they be released among the first exchange of prisoners. Two years earlier, the governor had formally quarrelled with Chief Justice Richard Gibbons. Gibbons was on his way home to England to present his case when he too was captured by French privateers and put in prison. He died there.

1795 This is Sydney

There are 27 inhabited dwellings in Sydney, 17 uninhabited, 27 in ruins and 14 public buildings. Population is about 150-160.

May 28

1892 *MacTalla*

The world's first Gaelic newspaper, *MacTalla*, is published weekly in Sydney by Jonathan G. MacKinnon of Dunakin near Whycocomagh. *MacTalla* carries local and world news, as well as history, proverbs, Greek mythology and correspondence. It was published for the last time on June 24, 1904.

Eighty-seven years later, during Inverness's 75th anniversary celebrations in 1979, Rev. Roderick MacLeod, publisher of the first Gaelic newspaper in Scotland (1977), pays tribute to Jonathan G. MacKinnon at a graveside memorial service at Stewartdale Cemetery near Dunakin.

1899 Dogs for the Yukon

The Yukon Gold Rush brings a great demand for pack dogs and hundreds of these dogs are bought in Newfoundland. Arriving by boat in North Sydney, the dogs are led by local boys to the train station for their journey westwards.

1920 Gaelic society

The Gaelic Society is organized in Sydney.

1932 Unique steel plant

Julian Kennedy, internationally known steel engineer and inventor, dies in Pittsburgh, Pennsylvania. He was the designer of the Sydney Steel Plant for its first owner, H. Whitney. By concentrating all the units used for the manufacture of steel into one complex, Kennedy's design was unique and it made the local steel plant the first of its kind in North America.

1971 Tainted justice

Black teenager, Sandy Seale, is stabbed to death in Wentworth Park. Sixteen-year old Micmac Donald Marshall Jr. is arrested, tried and imprisoned for life.

He spends eleven years in prison before his case is re-opened and he is found not guilty. Roy Ebsary of Sydney is charged, convicted and sentenced to three years. In 1987 a Royal Commission is set up to investigate the Marshall case. It finds that Donald Marshall has been a victim of prejudice and that evidence exonerating him was suppressed. Far-reaching recommendations are made for changes in the province's criminal justice system.

May 29

1720 First stone laid

The first stone of the new barracks at Louisbourg is laid by Gov. Saint-Ovide and the *commissaire ordonnateur*, de Mezy. The idea of building barracks is a fairly new one as usually the troops are billeted in private homes.

1784 First Lieutenant Governor
Governor Parr of Nova Scotia is notified by Lord Sydney that "a Lieutenant-Governor with a suitable civil establishment would be placed upon the Island of Cape Breton." Since the capture of Louisbourg in 1758, Cape Breton has been joined with Nova Scotia, New Brunswick and Prince Edward Island.

1788 First Protestant minister
Rev. Ranna Cossit, Cape Breton's first permanent Protestant minister, his wife and their seven children move into their new home in Sydney. In the spring of 1785, Rev. Cossit was sent here from New Hampshire by the Society for the Propogation of the Gospel, which was relocating its ministers. Rev. Cossit becomes involved in bitter local political conflicts until he leaves Sydney in 1800.

His house, on Charlotte Street, is believed to be the oldest in Sydney. A property of the Nova Scotia Museum, it is operated by the Old Sydney Society. July 11, 1983, it becomes protected under the Nova Scotia Heritage Properties Act.

1828 Doctor uses rum for anaesthetic
Nova Scotia's first medical act, "to exclude ignorant and unskilled persons from the practice of physic and surgery," is passed. About 1830, Dr. Inglis of the Sydney Garrison performs Cape Breton's first surgical operation on Mr. MacVicar of Clark's Road for a strangulated hernia. MacVicar is drugged with laudanum and rum and strapped down with ropes on a barn door. His operation is a success.

Cape Breton's first hospital is the Marine Hospital in Sydney. Two mottoes hang on walls of the convalescent ward. One reads, "All Men Must Die," while the other reads "Prepare to Meet Your Maker."

1951 Dial phones
The dial telephone system becomes official tonight in North Sydney as Mayor A. Charles Thompson makes the first call to Halifax.

1968 Fire at Point Edward
Forest fires at Point Edward sweep through 500 acres of timberland. The fire, running along a two-mile front on one side of the CNR tracks, threatens several homes.

1968 Major Fire
The worst fire in Cape Breton since the 1947 fire at Pleasant Bay blazes out of control in the Wreck Cove area. (See also May 30, 1968.)

1978 World record, for breeding
A New Zealand white rabbit, belonging to Joseph Filek of Sydney, has had a litter of twenty-four. This is the largest rabbit litter known, and it gets the rabbit and Mr. Filex into the Guiness Book of World Records.

1982 Heritage societies
Jim St. Clair of Mull River, Mabou, becomes the president of the Federation of Nova Scotia Heritage Societies. The Old Sydney Society, formed in 1966, was the first of the now thirty-one Heritage Societies on Cape Breton. The words of Joseph Howe express the feelings of all the groups. "A wise nation preserves its records, gathers up its monuments, decorates the

tombs of its illustrious dead, repairs its great public structures and fosters national pride and love of country, by perpetual reference to the sacrifices and glories of the past."

May 30

1968 Smokey burns

Four homes and several barns have been destroyed so far in the fire raging out of control at Cape Smokey. Forty other homes have been evacuated. The fire, which started yesterday, quickly ignited a twelve-mile area stretching to the top of Cape Smokey, one of the Island's most scenic areas. It will not be until June 3rd that rain gives tired firefighters their first real breather in their six-day battle; 2,000 acres of woodland are destroyed.

May 31

1847 Starvation

A little girl in Mira dies of starvation. More deaths are anticipated because of the lack of food. There is not a barrel of flour to be had in Sydney or anywhere else here. (Europe is suffering from a lack of food as well.)

1851 Inflation

The *Banshee*, a paddle wheeler built at Big Bras d'Or, starts her run from Sydney to North Sydney for 15 pence each way. She will also make a weekly trip to Baddeck. In 1901, she will charge 25 cents return on either of the two daily trips across the Harbour.

1902 "South African Jack"

The Boer War ends and Captain John "South African Jack" MacNeil of McKinnon Harbour is one of many soldiers offered grants of land by the government of South Africa. He meets a group of Dukhobors and discovers that living with them are two more Cape Bretoners, a MacKeigan from Marion Bridge and a MacKinnon from Whycocomagh, who had been shipwrecked years before.

1967 Kincenter Opens

The Kincenter, a sheltered workshop providing training and recreational facilities for the mentally retarded, is officially opened in Sydney.

Fig. 5.6 (North Sydney) "Town boys" off to the Boer War.

June

Tribute to the Clans

In the winter when it snows or when bitter storm wind blows
And the night has pushed the hours of light away,
People talk and sometimes sing of the memories that cling
And the songs are edged with sadness drear and grey.

Chorus:

Come ye now it's tartans bold
Belted kilts and sporans old;
And lightly step with lively toe and heel.
Hear the wild beat in you say to the sound of violins
And the drums and pipes will echo what you feel.

Charlie MacKenzie
Music: Stewart MacNeil

Fig. 6.1 Unidentified Scot, c. 1900.

Early Railway in Cape Breton

Fig. 6.2 Trestle near Pt. Edward, 1912.

Fig. 6.3 Track repair crew, n.d.

Fig. 6.4 Locomotive C. G. Swan, *c. 1886.*

June 1

1787 Missionary priest arrives
A Dominican priest, Pere Ledru, is the first missionary to visit Cheticamp. There are too few missionaries around at this time, and this could be a problem for couples who want to get married. Rather than make couples wait, possibly for years, the church permits a couple to sign a marriage bond before witnesses and allows them to live together as though they are married until a missionary visits the community.

1843 Julia Noble
Julia Noble, wife of pioneer doctor John Noble, dies. She is the first person buried in the present Stewartdale Cemetery near Whycocomagh. A midwife helping her doctor husband, she had a number of babies named after her. Julia is celebrated in a Gaelic song, and the Straits of Julia (Sheelagh in Gaelic) at Little Narrows are named for her.

1931 Depression
Total wage earners ten years of age and over in Nova Scotia: 117,781 with 19.33 % of the population out of work.

	Total Wage Earners	Out of Work
Sydney	5,950	1,431
North Sydney	1,288	316
Glace Bay	5,445	725
Sydney Mines	1,833	1,179
New Waterford	2,240	1,406

Total per cent of people out of work in the industrial area is 30.17 %.

1943 Base opens
The Point Edward Naval Base officially opens. Started in 1941, the Base will be fully operational as a repairing and refitting centre for the Royal Canadian Navy by late summer 1944. After the War, the Base is used as a centre for storing and decommissioning.

1967 *Cabot* goes west
At 7:55 this morning, crowds, bands and a bagpiper gather at the railway station to see the departure of the *Cabot*, CN's newest passenger train and the first passenger service to go directly between Sydney and Montreal. Three diesel locomotives will pull the fourteen coaches, sleepers, lounge and dining car.

1986 "Sidewalks are for walkers"
According to Police Chief Richard Walsh, skateboards are "a nightmare on the sidewalk and Russian roulette on the streets." He also wants the sidewalks cleared of freewheeling cyclists and roller skaters. "Sidewalks are for walkers not wheels."

June 2

1755 Smallpox
Smallpox breaks out at Louisbourg and is spreading rapidly.

1907 First draeger

The first draeger rescue equipment is installed at Dominion No. 2 Colliery.

1952 "Big Alex"

"Big Alex" MacDonald of Sydney dies. He was one of Cape Breton's greatest all-round athletes. A member of the Sydney Millionaires hockey team and the Glace Bay Miners hockey team, he also played football during World War I with the 10th Siege Battery and helped win the Eastern Canada Championship. In the 30s "Big Alex" played softball, sometimes called the Depression sport.

1976 Steel ferry

A new highway ferry, named after Cape Breton's legendary giant, the *Angus MacAskill*, goes into service at the St. Ann's crossing at Englishtown this summer. It replaces the *A. Sterling MacMillan*, the oldest ferry in the Department of Highways' fleet, which was built in 1954.

The new ferry will carry fifteen vehicles across in five minutes, as opposed to the *MacMillan*'s five cars in fifteen minutes. It's operated hydraulically, but the cable is twenty-five feet underwater and won't interfere with the fishing fleet.

1986 Fatal accident

An accident at the Sysco boiler plant leaves one man, Robert Whalen, dead and another, Ed Surrette, in intensive care. Four other workers are also injured. The men were working on a valve at the auxiliary steam boiler, which is fuelled by gas combination including carbon monoxide and carbon dioxide.

June 3

1766 Tennis anyone?

Lord William Campbell, new Governor of Nova Scotia, and Major Milward, of the 59th Regiment, take on Lord Campbell's new secretary, Capt. William Owen and Capt. Williams at Louisbourg in what is believed to be Canada's first tennis match. Unfortunately, Capt. Owen is accidentally struck on the left eye by his partner's racket and is blinded.

1786 Halifax keeps settlers

John Andrews, a captain bringing supplies to Cape Breton from Rhode Island, writes Gov. DesBarres that Halifax is keeping settlers away from Cape Breton. His vessel had been seized and families aboard prevented from coming on to Cape Breton: "I find that every art and means is made use of here to prevent the settlement of your government."

1842 Cranky judge

One of the judges of the Supreme Court is angry over his latest trip to Cape Breton. He found there was no accommodation prepared for him. He threatens to move the courthouse from Sydney.

June 4

1888 Barra Lodge

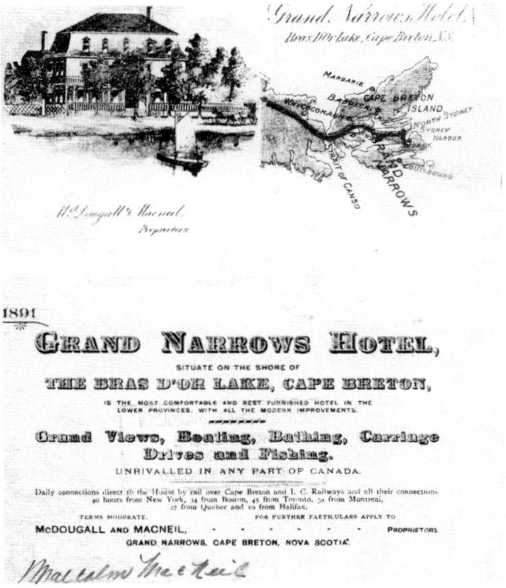

Fig. 6.5 Postcard of the Barra Lodge, 1891.

"One of Eastern Canada's most prestigious hotels," the Barra Lodge in Grand Narrows, is opened for the summer season. The Lodge is the only building east of Halifax to have central heating and hot and cold running water.

H. F. MacDougall, also is the local MP and one of the proprietors, has been successful in his lobby to have the railway come through the Central Route of Cape Breton via Grand Narrows. Construction on the Lodge began when the legislation was proclaimed in Ottawa.

Barra Lodge is to become a popular resort, entertaining both travellers and more permanent guests from as far away as Hong Kong and Tasmania. On one occasion, Helen Keller stays and swims the Barra Straits. The Prince of Wales (later King Edward VII) also stays at the Lodge. The Lodge closes in the summer of 1932. It reopens as a Bed & Breakfast in 1999.

June 5

1901 Death at the Steel Plant

Twenty-four-year-old Thomas Moxham, superintendent, is killed in an accident at the steel plant. Around 4 p.m. he is near the locomotives pushing dump carts heavy with rock fill. He slips trying to board, falls beneath the wheels and is killed instantly. Thomas is General Manager Arthur Moxham's son and the news is sent to him in New York City, where he is conferring with Henry Whitney and other directors.

Close to two hundred men march toward the Moxham house (castle) to pay their respects to the family. Mayor Crowe, three ministers, a priest, friends, company executives and servants gather at the house. Arthur boards a special train home from New York.

Local legend has it that on hearing the news of his death, his pregnant wife "Honey" falls down the stairs. She dies two months later, and her child is stillborn. It is a triple tragedy for the Moxhams, who soon afterwards leave Sydney.

1998 Fossilized forest "the best"

That's what geologists are saying about the fossil forest along the shoreline at Cranberry Head, Sydney Mines. A walk along the shoreline shows several layers of fossilized trees, bark, trunks and crowns of trees exposed on the cliff face. Dr John Calder, a geologist with Mines and Energy Resources, accompanies visiting geologists from England, Australia and the United States as they examine the site. "There is no better example in the world of a fossil forest of the coal age." The visitors "have been blown away by the grandeur of this fossil forest, it is the best."

The site was first studied by Richard Brown, the general manager of the General Mining Association, in 1843. But coal has been mined from the area for years before that. In 1999 a temporary exhibit is set up in Sydney Mines and an interpretive centre, named after Richard Brown, is planned to be opened the following year.

2004 Cape Breton Bordeaux

No, it's not wine. It's a rare type of marble being quarried by MacLeod Resources Ltd of River Denys. Production is increasing with customers in Italy, France and Russia. New equipment will aid the company to cut, shape, wash and polish marble blocks which had previously been sent to Italy for upgrading.

June 6

1929 Flight of the *Bluenose*

Hundreds of Cape Bretoners watch the final miles in the flight of the *Bluenose* as it heads for Sydney Airport, where thousands are on hand to greet her arrival from Los Angeles. "Rolly" Archibald of North Sydney, owner of the aeroplane, and Roy Darrell, her pilot and navigator, have flown the plane from California. With a wingspan of 36 feet, the plane is unable to completely fit in the 30 foot hanger.

1935 Lord and Lady in Sydney

Lord Baden-Powell, founder of the Boy Scouts, and his wife, Lady Baden-Powell, Chief Guide, and their two daughters are welcomed to Cape Breton. After a morning reception in Sydney with the Scouts, Guides, Brownies, their leaders and others, they have lunch at the Cove, the official residence of DOSCO. A huge rally is held in the badminton court building this afternoon, where, among other celebrations, Miss Katherine McLennan will be invested by Lady Baden-Powell as Divisional Commissioner. (See also February 19, 2005.)

1944 D-Day

While the 7th and 8th Canadian Brigades fight their way ashore at Normandy, the 9th Brigade, which includes the North Nova Scotia Highlanders, commanded by Lt. Colonel Petch, waits to land.

At 11:40 a.m., the Brigade begins landing at Bernieres-sur-Mer. This afternoon, delayed somewhat because of congestion on the beach, the North Novas lead the Brigade advance towards the village of Beny-sur-Mer. The next morning the North Novas lead the advance towards Caen. In the village of Authie, platoons of "C" Company, the vanguard of the 9th Brigade, are overrun by Colonel Kurt Meyer's 25th SS Panzer Grenadiers, officered by battle-hardened veterans of the Russian front and manned by Hitler youth. (See also June 7, 1944.)

A few days later the North Novas retake Authie. Their casualties in the advance from the beaches are considerable; of 242 soldiers, 84 die and 128 are taken prisoner.

1967 Woman of the century

Mrs. Nina Cohen of Sydney, the chairman of the Cape Breton Miners' Museum Foundation of Glace Bay, is awarded the "Woman of the Century 1867-1967" Centennial Award of the National Council of Jewish Women of Canada for the province of Nova Scotia.

1976 Main-a-Dieu fire

The Church of the Immaculate Conception, built in 1885, is destroyed by fire. It was only two weeks ago that Father Dolhanty took part in the annual ceremony of the Blessing of the Fleet in Main-a-Dieu Harbour with a Mass following at the church. Today, with forest fires raging on five fronts, the church is destroyed as well as the Glebe House and seventeen other structures, automobiles and fishing boats. Fires burn in Main-a-Dieu, Big Ridge west of Louisbourg, Beaver Cove and the Georges River area.

1981 Petersfield Park

Petersfield, Senator J. S. McLennan's estate in Westmount, will be made a Provincial Park, it is announced today.

Fig. 6.6 Petersfield.

Petersfield's history goes back to Colonial Cape Breton. It was settled first by Loyalist, David Mathews, former mayor of New York City, who became the first Attorney General and a member of the Executive Council of the new Colony of Cape Breton. Mathews' estate was bought and added to by Thomas Crawley, Surveyor General of Cape Breton and a Superintendent of the coal mines. In Senator McLennan's time, according to a family friend, "when anyone interesting came to the area, they came to Petersfield." The government expropriated the property during World War II. Had Britain fallen, the Royal Navy would have used Sydney Harbour as a base in exile with Petersfield House as a residence for officers. The Mathews-Crawley house was destroyed by fire in 1894, and the McLennan house was destroyed in the early 1960s. (See also Sept. 15, 1939.)

June 7

1801 First resident missionary

Father Gabriel Champion arrives in Cheticamp as the area's first resident missionary. Within the year he establishes a school, the first Catholic school on Cape Breton since the French were in Louisbourg. The school is either a Sunday school or a private school because at this time no Catholic is allowed to be a schoolteacher without taking the oaths against transubstantiation and popery.

1944 Murder

In the Abbaye d'Ardenne, near Caen in Normandy, ninteen Canadian soldiers, captured in the battle following the landing at Normandy, are taken into the garden by men of the SS 12th Panzer Division and murdered. Among the Canadians are twelve from the North Novas. They included Private Charles Doucette and Private George Richard MacNaughton of Sydney, and Corporal Joseph Macintyre of Sydney Mines.

After the war, SS General Kurt Meyer, who was headquartered at the Abbaye, is sentenced to death for the murders. This is commuted to life in prison. Meyer returns to Europe after six years in Dorchester prison and is freed soon afterwards.

2003 Low Strike

Cape Breton ranks 50th out of 57 communities ranked by Maclean's magazine of the best and work places to receive health care in Canada.

June 8

1758 Wolfe lands

Gen. James Wolfe's brigade lands at Kennington Cove enroute to the Fortress of Louisbourg.

2005 Sicker

Cape Bretoners have more health problems than other Nova Scotians. In fact, according to a recent heath information report, we are twice as sick with diseases such as cancer and asthma. We're also more likely than other Canadians to die in hospital shortly after having a heart attack or stroke.

June 9

1793 Isle Madame settlers

Several hundred French settlers arriving in Cape Breton threaten to leave if they can't settle in Isle Madame.

1901 Early ad

Dr. Roger Varian,
Veterinary Surgeon
and Dentist
HORSES
BOUGHT & SOLD
ON COMMISSION
(Castration a Speciality)
All mail and telephone
orders attended to
promptly
Telephone 128
P.O. Box 151, Sydney

June 10

1727 Replaces cabarets

Gov. Saint-Ovide gets permission to have a canteen set up and run by the officers. Stocking wine, spirits and tobacco, by 1739, each company at the Fortress will have its own canteen. This is considered less harmful than the dozens of cabarets around town.

1869 Name changed

Plaister Cove officially changes its name to Port Hastings.

1901 Another death at the steel plant

Archibald Russell from Conception Bay, Newfoundland, is killed in an accident at the steel plant. The accident is due to carelessness on the part of the officials. "A very pathetic incident occurred in connection with this accident. The young man's father had come all the way from Newfoundland to visit his son. Arriving that day at the entrance to the Steel Works he was, in accordance with the rules of the company, refused admission."

1983 Rail centre opens

The Cape Breton Development Corporation's new rail centre at Victoria Junction opens ahead of time and under budget. The rail centre is adjacent to the coal preparation plant and maintains all of Devco's rolling stock. It is located to efficiently route the cargoes from the mines to the preparation plant and on towards their markets.

1988 Ian MacNeil

Ian MacNeil, former executive editor of the *Cape Breton Post*, dies. He started at the *Post* in 1945 as a proofreader. He is remembered for his years as producer of the Rotary spring musicals and for "Between the Lines" (ChitChat) column of *The Post*. Urban legend has his most discussed entry as "There is no truth to the rumor that there is a wife-swapping circle in Coxheath."

June 11

1925 William Davis dies

Miners in New Waterford grow more bitter in their three-month strike. Yesterday, they picketed the nearby power plant at Waterford Lake and expelled maintenance men. Before dawn today, company police pushed through the picket line to take possession of the Plant.

Later this morning, a parade of miners, led by former war veterans, marches in an orderly procession to the Plant. As they draw near, the mounted company police open fire and, in the confusion that follows, thirty-seven-year old William Davis, a miner and father of a large family, is shot dead. Other miners are hurt, and a few police beaten. Fire destroys No. 12 Colliery wash house, No. 12 and 15 company stores and Udovin's store. Things quieten down after the arrival of 500 soldiers from Halifax and other towns.

The anniversary of Davis's death is celebrated every year. Davis Day is a memorial for all miners who have lost their lives in the coal industry.

June 12

1775 Highlanders form
The Royal Highlanders are formed in Scotland and become the first Scottish Regiment posted to Cape Breton and to be specifically garrisoned on the Island.

1918 King of charm
Wallace MacDonald started out as a junior clerk at the Royal Bank in Sydney. He is now a movie actor and has recently been proclaimed the "King of Charm" by the Motion Picture Classic magazine, in the States.

1968 Searching for oil
The seismographic ship *Fred H. Moore* arrives in North Sydney for fuel and supplies. Surveys are being conducted by Mobil of Canada Ltd. to see if there is oil bearing strata off the coast.

1998 Bicycle built for two
Jacques Cote and Micheline Guillot leave their home in Westmount to begin a 106-day, 8,000-kilometre trek across Canada. No ordinary vacation, this trip is done on a 24-speed tandem bicycle. Their route zigzags across Canada and through three states, taking them to places they want to see rather than sticking to the Trans Canada highway. Says Jacques, "It's a great way to travel."

June 13

1883 Coal Mine for sale

> **COAL MINE**
> **FOR SALE**
> New Campbellton Coal Mine.
> Situated at the Bras d'Or Lake,
> with farms, lands, tenements,
> wharves, stores, buildings,
> engines, locomotives, rolling stock,
> tools, and everything in
> connection with the property
> which can be made ready to
> ship coal in a few days.
> C. J. Campbell, Baddeck

1931 Up to Boston
Cape Bretoners going to Boston can travel on any of the three round trips made weekly. One route goes by CN Rail to Halifax and then to the Yarmouth Docks. Another changes at Truro to the Dominion Atlantic Railway, also going to the Yarmouth Docks. The entire fare on the

SS *Yarmouth* from Sydney to Boston is $23.95. "One receives excellent accommodations and fine meals." The boat sails Tuesdays, Thursdays and Saturdays at 6:30 p.m. (AST) and is due in Boston at 8:00 a.m. (Daylight Time) the following morning.

1982 Micmac restaurant opens

This week the Island View Restaurant in Whycocomagh is officially opened. Owned and operated by the Micmacs of the Whycocomagh Reserve, the restaurant features eels and wild blueberries and other traditional Indian foods. The basketwork decorations are handcrafted by the weavers of the Reserve.

June 14

1831 Sprightly judge

Archibald Charles Dodd, former Chief Justice of His Majesty's Supreme Court for Cape Breton Island under its former Government and after annexation, dies at the age of 91 as a consequence of injuries sustained by a fall from his horse.

1931 Runner dies

Billy Taylor, of Sydney Mines, aged 29, dies in Montreal of sunstroke. Billy Taylor won the Nathanson three-mile road race classic, held every May 24th, three times, as well as many other races—short distance and modified marathon events. He also competed satisfactorily in the famous Boston Marathon.

1951 Beer OK

The City of Sydney votes in favour of selling beer in taverns, but it rejects a proposal to sell beer and wine in hotels.

1956 Innovative fisherman

George Bungay of Alder Point installs this month in his 60-foot longliner *Jane Marie* the first Rolls Royce engine to come to Cape Breton. He now uses three gallons of gas an hour instead of the usual ten. Ten years earlier, Mr. Bungay had invented a metal cage to cover and protect the propeller of his lobster boat. He also purchased what is believed to be the first sounder in Cape Breton for finding fish off the coast.

1968 Maiden run for ferry

Captain C. N. Brown takes the new 8,400 ton CN ferry *Ambrose Shea* on her maiden voyage on the North Sydney to Argentia run. The luxury ship will make three return-trips a week.

1980 Boxers honoured

Tonight in New Waterford, ten Cape Bretoners are inducted into the Canadian Boxing Hall of Fame. They include Gussie MacLellan of Glace Bay in the boxer-promoter category, the late Louie Nemis of New Waterford, the late Johnny Corbett of River Ryan, Archie "Bear" Hannigan of New Waterford, Stevie "Kid" MacDonald of Glace Bay, and Buddy "Dobbin" MacKinnon, Les Gillis and Donald "Red" MacPherson all of New Waterford. George Lewis of River Ryan is in the trainer-promoter category, while Lauchie MacEachern in the club builder category recalls that boxing was a family tradition in New Waterford.

1984 Point Edward soccer player leaves

Twenty-two-year-old John Evans of Point Edward, a Riverview High School graduate, is the only representative of Canada's National Soccer Team from east of Niagara Falls, Ontario. John took part in the '82 World Student Games in Mexico City, and he's played against Norwegian teams. Today, the Canadian team leaves for Peking, China, and the Great Wall of China Tournament, June 17-30th.

1984 Cape Bretoners to Boston

Six Cape Bretoners from around the Bras d'Or lakes, following in the Cape Breton tradition, leave this morning for the Boston States. These Cape Bretoners are young bald eaglets, sent by plane to Bedford, MA. as part of the 28 eagles gathered in Canada to be sent to various parts of the United States. Wildlife biologists collected one or two 8-week-old chicks from each nest, leaving at least one for the adult to raise. The 6 eaglets will live in selected sites in large cages on top of 12-metre poles until they can fly. They'll be released and should return to the site to nest.

On the average, about 112 young eagles are raised every year in Nova Scotia, 90 of these on Cape Breton, which has a very healthy eagle population.

2000 Last day

Today is the last day of work for the RCMP here in the Cape Breton Regional Municipality. Amid protests, especially from the more rural areas where the Mounties work, council votes to expand the city police force—instead of keeping with a dual force—that has municipal police in the city and towns and Mounties in the other rural areas.

2004 - Kings Road

The $8.5 million upgrade of Kings Road gets underway and causes traffic bottlenecks, congestion and headaches for motorists, businesses and pedestrians before officials try to alleviate some of the problems by installing traffic lights on Kenwood Drive. The construction is to take six months, with the road opening for general traffic in December.

June 15

1876 Captain Kidd's Treasure

A Sydney man dreams that Captain Kidd discloses where his treasure is buried. Tonight, the man and a friend secretly go to the spot, just west of the Bentinck Street bridge at Wentworth Creek. Capt. Kidd specifies midnight and gives instructions to sprinkle the blood of a rooster in a circle and dig inside it. But other friends have discovered the fortune hunters' plan and one, dressed up in a soldier's uniform with whiskers made of rope, and carrying a broad sword, appears suddenly and scares them. One faints and the other, frightened, races home. The treasure is never found.

1985 Terry MacLellan dies

Terry MacLellan dies. Devco's Director of Corporate Affairs, she is more familiarly remembered as Ann Terry from her days as a radio and TV personality, as hostess of CJCB Radio women's morning program and as a master of ceremonies much in demand. She was a guest panellist numerous times on CBC's *Front Page Challenge*.

She is warmly remembered for her gracious style.

1992 Plant closed
With only two weeks to go, this year's lobster season is almost over. To let emotions cool down, Clearwater Fine Foods Ltd. officials close the doors of its strikeridden lobster plant near Arichat indefinitely.

2004 Not healthy
According to a Stats Canada survey, Cape Bretoners are not healthy. We eat, drink and smoke more than other Canadians; 24.7% of Cape Breton males and 17.7% of Cape Breton females are obese; 23.9% of the population smokes daily compared with the national average of 17.8%; and 28.1% are considered heavy drinkers compared with the national 20.7 %.

June 16

1899 Early disaster
An explosion at Caledonia Mine this morning kills Underground Manager Tom Johnstone and ten miners. This is Cape Breton's first great mine disaster.

1992 Synfuels gets go-ahead
A Senate committee has okayed Scotia Synfuels Inc's using a mixture of coal and imported heavy oil from Mexico and Venezuela and turn it into liquid fuels like naphtha and diesel heating oil. Synfuels plans to use an old Gulf Canada oil refinery at Point Tupper. More than 2,500 jobs are to be created which is good news for an area with a 20 per cent unemployment rate. Two hundred will be at the Synfuels plant, 350 kept or created at the coal mines, and about 2,000 as indirect spin-off jobs.

June 17

1745 Louisbourg falls
After a six-week siege, Louisbourg surrenders to the British under Sir William Pepperell.

1789 On the road
Troops work on road construction. One road leads from Sydney to the Northwest Arm, where several prosperous farms, including Capt. Cox's, are located. At the moment there are only two streets in town, Charlotte Street and the Esplanade, which meet at the south end to form the path leading to Louisbourg and the Mira River, where winter supplies are obtained.

1895 Big day
Passenger service on the S & L Railway is officially inaugurated this morning as the "Big Train," some twenty open cars hauled by the engines *The Pepperell* and *The Whitney*, leaves Sydney about 7 a.m., bound for Louisbourg, picking up passengers along the route.

Conductor Lauchlin McLean (later to become the superintendent of the S & L) helps thousands of passengers board, including Sir Wilfred Laurier and his party. Everyone is on their way to the unveiling at Louisbourg of a monument erected by the American Society of Colonial Wars. Some 2,500 people attend the ceremonies marking the anniversary of the First Siege of Louisbourg. It was 150 years ago that the New Englanders took possession of the Fortress. (The French, using a different calendar at the time—the one we use today—reckoned the date to be June 28th.)

1930 Remember first world war
Residents of Dominion No. 11 want the name of their Post Office changed to "Passchendaele," the name they have given the local branch of the Royal Canadian Legion there.

1966 Long life ends
Mary Sarah MacDonald of Scotch Lake dies at the age of 108.

1984 Doctoral first
Marie Battiste of Chapel Island is the first Micmac to receive her Doctorate. Dr. Battiste studied at the University of Maine, received her Masters in Educational Administration from Harvard, and today she earns her Doctorate from Stanford University in California. Returning to her home at Chapel Island, she is instrumental in getting a bilingual (Micmac-English) program in the local school.

1988 Murmansk run veterans
Thirty-four Cape Bretoners, veterans (and veterans' widows), are decorated for their role in the Murmansk Run during the Second World War by Soviet ambassador Alexey Rodionov at a ceremony at the Coast Guard College.

June 18

1784 Province of Cape Breton
King George III establishes the province of New Brunswick and Cape Breton.

1966 Mitchell Island church
Mitchell Island Union church, near the Rudderham Road, Point Edward, celebrates its 100th anniversary. It is unique as it was established as a church for any denomination. Services are held on a first-come-first-served basis.

1967 Canoes go west
At noon today, Father Paul MacNeil blesses the fleet of three 19-foot canoes which leave on a special Centennial voyage with their four-man crews to Expo '67 in Montreal. There, at the Canadian Indian Pavilion, they will help re-enact the 1894 treaty signing.

1968 New resort
A new ski resort will be built in the Cape Breton Highlands near Ingonish. The first stage will consist of a day lodge, cafeteria, ski shop and a 2200-foot T-bar lift serving a five-mile run trail and slope.

2003 Prestigious award
Sydney native Dr. Arthur McDonald has won $1 million in research funding for his work on clearing up a fundamental question about the basic structure of matter. A professor at Queen's

University, Kingston, Ontario, Dr. McDonald, is named the recipient of the 2003 Gerard Herzberg Canada Gold Medal for Science and Engineering in Ottawa. It is the country's most prestigious science award.

June 19

1905 Animal farm

North Sydney residents have the feeling that the cattle, which are allowed to run around the town, are taking over. Complaints are also being lodged against the piggery on Brook Street. The squealing at night is very disturbing.

1945 Distinguished flyer

John "Wendy" Reid of Sydney, at an investiture at Government House, Ottawa, is decorated with the United States Distinguished Flying Cross, for his patrols over the Normandy beachhead.

"Wendy" Reid received his flying licence when he was only 17 at the Cape Breton Flying Club. He volunteered as soon as war was declared, trained pilots; ferried Hudsons, Liberators and Fortresses to Britain; ran the gauntlet with supplies to Malta; commanded a fighter squadron; and piloted Generals Wave II and Brooke and Prime Minister Churchill on their mission to Moscow and also the Prime Minister and Sir Anthony Eden to Washington to meet with President Roosevelt. Today, he is only 24 years old and he is the youngest person in the British Empire to be appointed a Wing Commander.

June 20

1685 In Praise of Cape Breton

Nicholas Denys sends the King of France a fox from Cape Breton and he writes, praising the Island, "I assure your Majesty, that by Bestewing on this country, only one-quarter of the expence you have bestewed on Quebeck it would produce you more in one year, than Quebeck can do in fourty, it being a country that would produce wine salt and corn in plenty it is full of wood fit for plank and shipping there is also tarr and other things fit for the sea in a very great plenty with very good trade of Cod fish Herring Mackerell and Salmon of which hitherto we have been beholden to England and Holland for a supply; which trade being well established; would bring in a revenue of near two million [a] year to your Majesty and besides would be Nursery of Able Seamen to serve in your Majestyes Fletts." (This is an early translation of his letter.)

1981 Margaree salmon

A concern in the Margaree area over the dwindling salmon stock in a river that was once among the most famous in North America for its fishing, leads to the formation of the Margaree Salmon Association.

1982 New York opening

The Cape Breton Concerto, composed by Daniel Goode premieres tonight at New York's Lincoln Center with the one-hundred-member Guggenheim Wind Ensemble and Cape Breton musicians.

June 21

1920 New lamps for old

Miners threaten to quit unless the company installs electric lamps like the ones now in use in the Springhill mines. The next day, miners are asked to help pay for the installation of electric lamps in the mines. They cost $7.80 each. By the end of December, the old mine lamps will be discarded.

1935 Leading producer

The development of a gypsum mine complex at Little Narrows is proceeding with the first shipment of material scheduled to leave for New York in early September. The loading piers have already been constructed and a road built to the nearby quarry. A warehouse to store the winter output of over 20,000 tons will be erected soon. Canada is the third largest gypsum-producing country in the world, and the bulk of the mineral comes from deposits in Cape Breton.

June 22

1717 Civil courts established

The French King establishes three courts and one Superior Council at Louisbourg, Port Dauphin (St. Ann's) and at Port Toulouse (St. Peter's).

1915 Fly the flag

The Post urges Cape Bretoners to fly the Union Jack. *The Post* has complete flag kits for all patriotic homes.

1944 Scorched earth

Two weeks after the Normandy invasion, believing the tide of war had turned, the Canadian government destroys its plans for the destruction of Sydney, Halifax, Shelburne, Saint John, Quebec City and Gaspe. The British plan for the destruction of St. John's, Newfoundland, then a British dependency, remained in the archives until their recent release. In March 1942, the Canadian War Cabinet, headed by Prime Minister Mackenzie King, approved a "scorched earth policy" for the above cities which planned for their complete destruction. St. John's plan was to deny the enemy the enormous reserves of fuel and ammunition stored there as well as the hospitals and all buildings. Two or three merchant ships filled with rocks were to be sunk to block the entrance to the harbour. At that time the Battle of the Atlantic had yet to be won by the allies, and there were fears that Britain could fall and that the Germans, whose submarines had been active along the coast, would occupy Newfoundland. The frontline in the battles against the Axis powers would then be the eastern seaboard, and their cities were also listed as potential recipients of this scorched earth policy.

1977 *The Rise and Follies*

The Rise and Follies of Cape Breton Island, a satirical musical revue of, for and by Cape Bretoners, opens at the Lyceum in Sydney. This popular revue was conceived by and contributed to by a number of talented Cape Bretoners, including Kenzie MacNeil, Maynard Morrison and

Max MacDonald, who had been part of the College's Dramagroup in 1969, '70 and '71. The show runs for ten days plus another week in August.

A second version with new material is performed in a limited run in 1980 at the Savoy Theatre in Glace Bay and the Rebecca Cohn Auditorium in Halifax. In 1981, the *Follies* is presented in tandem with *Cape Breton's Greatest Hits*. The comedy in this version is more humourous than satirical.

The three versions are recorded on albums, issued by the College of Cape Breton Press.

1984 Dame Isobel

Isobel MacAulay of St. Ann's receives a silver Canadian Tourism Medallion for her contribution to the tourist industry. Mrs. MacAulay established and promoted the Nova Scotia tartan, designed by Bessie Murray, in the early 40s. She established a company to produce the tartan and for ten years it was the sole producer, employing some forty-five people. Mrs. MacAulay, also a weaver, made the first kilt from the new tartan. Her latest work has been decorating and selecting clothing artifacts for the Great Hall of the Clans at St. Ann's.

Mrs. MacAulay was given the title "Dame of Grace of the Order of St. John of Jerusalem" by the Governor General in 1958 for her work with the St. John's Ambulance Corps.

June 23

1597 *Hopewell* reaches Cape Breton

The *Hopewell*, enroute to the New World from England, has been off the Cape Breton coast for a few days. The crew has caught great amounts of codfish. In little more than one hour, they caught 250 fish, using only four hooks. On the 25th, the ship arrives at the two Bird Islands, where they see "great store of Morses" (walruses) asleep on the rocks. As the boats get close to the shore, the animals rushed into the sea and "pursued us with great fury that we were glad to flee from them."

1897 Cape Bretoner at diamond jubilee

William Levis of Portree is a member of the Canadian contingent at the celebration of Queen Victoria's Diamond Jubilee. He later is one of the Canadian volunteers to fight in the South African war.

1914 Illegal immigrants

A considerable number of West Indians are brought illegally to Cape Breton on small schooners and many are making for Sydney. (See also June 30, 1894.)

1979 Rescue teams

A Devco team from No. 26 Colliery, Glace Bay, captained by Willie MacNeil, wins the National Mine Rescue competition, held this year in Whitehorse, the Yukon. This is not Devco's first national victory. In 1977 a team from No. 26 won in Yellowknife, NWT; in 1973 the Lingan team won in Glace Bay; in 1972 a team from No. 26 won in Victoria, BC; and in 1969 a team from No. 20 Colliery in Glace Bay won in Saskatoon, Saskatchewan.

1984 Gardener of the year

Dr. Milford Jackson of North Sydney is chosen the Gardener of the Year at this weekend's convention of the Nova Scotia Association of Garden Clubs. The Green Thumb Award, presented by Freda Robb of the Westmount Club, provincial secretary and herself a one time Gardener of the Year, goes to 100-year-old Frank Jackson of North Sydney.

1992 "Private ownership better for rail line"

The final report of a controversial sale of the CN rail line between Sydney and Truro declares that the line is to be privatized. Devco, Stora Forest Industries and the Sydney Steel Corporation, Cape Breton's major employers, testify that "they depend on the line for their very existence."

June 24

1497 Cabot lands

The day is recognized as the one on which John Cabot lands at Cape North. Sailing out of Bristol, England, Cabot accomplishes many firsts: as the first Royal Commissioner to set foot on American soil, he is able to proclaim sovereignty and take possession in the name of the King; the first raising of the first English flag, a flag quartered with lions and *fleur de lys* (referring to the claims of the Kings of England to be the Kings of France) and a winged lion pennant, a present of Henry VII; the first use of the English language in the New World; and the first European explorer to see and set foot on the mainland of the Western Hemisphere.

There is a story that Cabot's ship was literally stopped by fish. There was such an abundance of fish that baskets lowered overboard filled right up.

1610 Grand Chief Membertou

Micmac Grand Chief Membertou, a great spiritual and political leader and a prophet, is converted to Christianity. Chief Membertou was believed to be over one hundred years old when the French came to Nova Scotia in the early 1600s.

A Reserve in Sydney is named in honour and recognition of the Grand Chief. Their first reservation on the Harbour waterfront is mapped out in 1820 by Cape Breton's Surveyor General Crawley. This is the first time the reservation system is put in place. In the early summer of 1927, Membertou Reservation, at a different location in Sydney, is formally established as an Indian community.

1985 No more

Shutdown of the Glace Bay Heavy Water Plant begins and it will be completely decontaminated by the end of August after which it will no longer require steam from the NSP Seaborne plant.

1997 *Matthew* arrives – in Newfoundland

The replica of John Cabot's ship the *Matthew*, recreating its original voyage across the Atlantic to the New World, is sidetracked into making a landfall at Bonavista Bay, Newfoundland where it is greeted by Queen Elizabeth and hundreds of well-wishers. The first *Matthew* had been searching for a sea route from England to the spice-rich Orient. Instead, it came across the eastern coast of North America.

Both ships were built and sailed from Bristol, England. The tiny ship measures 24 metres from end to end, has a flat bottom and tends to ride the waves like a toy, or, as one crew member describes it, it rolls "like a pig on rough waters." After making various stops along the Newfoundland coast, the *Matthew* is scheduled to finally make its landfall in northern Cape Breton—at Cabot's Landing, below the Cabot Trail. There are many who contend that Cabot discovered Newfoundland first. And that he was the first European to visit our shores.

1992 Arctic char for the Bras d'Or

A Co-Op in St. Peter's the Salmon Propagation Association (SAD) plans to raise arctic char in the Bras d'Or. Using new technology including submersible spherical cages made of aluminium tubes, the co-op hopes to cash in on the high demand and low supply of the char.

1992 Mobile communications are here to stay

Members of the industrial Board of Trade hear latest news about mobile communications. Carl Dexter, Vice President of Sales and Operations for MT&T Mobile Inc, waxes eloquently about the possibilities of wireless technology. Productivity is being increased. Communications will be very convenient.

June 25

1930 Canada First

Mr. H. J. Kelly, General Manager of the British Empire Steel Corporation (BESCO) in a recent radio address commented that the Corporation is large and "with the exception of the great railways, it gives work to more people and pays more money in wages than any other company in Canada."

1957 New furnace

Miss Jody Anson, daughter of the Sydney Steel Plant's general manager, pulls the lever which sends the first heat cascading into the ladle and so opens the new 225-ton tilting open-hearth furnace. This furnace will cause a 25 per cent increase in DOSCO's ingot-producing capacity.

1992 GST is here to stay

"I think it's time now for those who have been fighting to realize that it's here to stay and to get on board with us." Federal Reserve Minister Otto Jelinek reports that the 7 per cent tax on goods and services which came into effect eighteen months ago is legally valid and requires no changes. Says one critic, "Canadians will keep paying the levy on everything from haircuts to funerals—and an estimated $17.5 billion annually will continue to flow into federal coffers."

2004 - BUSTED!

A large stash of cocaine is found hidden in two duffel bags in the rudder area of the ship, the *Sheila Ann*, which is delivering bulk coal at the Emera Inc. coal piers at the bottom of Dominion Street in Whitney Pier. The 83 kilos are discovered during a routine inspection by RCMP and Canadian Border Service Agency officials using an underwater camera. It is believed the drugs come from Venezuela. The bust is the largest of its kind in Cape Breton. (The *Sheila Ann*, owned by the Canada Steamship Lines, is named after Prime Minister Martin's wife.)

June 26

1833 Pickle patronage?

A local man is appointed to be chief inspector of pickled fish for Cape Breton County.

1905 Celebration

Rev. John Cameron, pastor, and the congregation of St. John's Church at New Aberdeen publicly celebrate the Feast of Corpus Christi for the first time in Cape Breton. More than five thousand people watch the procession and the service.

1982 Sydney soprano

Deborah Jeans, soprano, of Sydney, appears in a special program at the Savoy Theatre tonight. She'll be accompanied by Marguerite MacDougall of Glace Bay, who has accompanied many musical performers, including those in Rotary shows. Deborah Jeans sang with the Beinn Breagh Chorale and was a soloist in 1967, when the group performed at Expo. She has pursued her singing career in New York and Toronto.

2004 Priest escapes trial

While waiting trial, Father Hugh Vincent MacDonald, 81, dies in Ontario. He was charged with 27 offences involving sexual molestation of children while he was a parish priest in Sydney, New Waterford and Ingonish.

June 27

1901 Shaft at Dominion No. 2 the largest

Almost two years have passed since the sod was broken in October 1899 for the new shaft of the Dominion Coal Company. Today, the Phalen seam at Dominion No. 2 is tapped at about 850 feet and the shaft, 37 feet x 11 feet, the largest on the continent and ranked among the deepest, is finished.

1930 Kempt Head booze boat

The first liquor seizure of the season is carried out near Kempt Head on the Bras d'Or Lakes when a patrol boat from North Sydney intercepts a motorboat with 102 ten-gallon kegs of rum and 14 cases of whiskey on board and no crew.

It should be noted, however, that carbonated beverages are very popular. The Home Bottling Company of North Sydney, organized by Mr. D. V. Mancini, is doing well with its speciality "Alpine Ginger Ale," while Sydney's newest business, Sandou Beverages, is the exclusive bottler of "Orange Kist."

1976 Nature centre opens

The Scotsville Nature Centre; with wildlife and natural history exhibits, opens to the public.

June 28

1745 Battle over
New Englanders take possession of the town of Louisbourg and the Island Battery. All soldiers and townspeople capable of bearing arms are taken prisoner and will be transported to France.

1901 Russian and Polish Jews
The Intercolonial Railway lays on a special train at North Sydney to take the 450 survivors, mostly Russian and Polish Jews, of a wrecked ship called the *Lusitania* to Montreal.

1923 Police see red
Charges of Bolshevism and Communism in union ranks cause hundreds of provincial police to arrive on railway flatcars armed with machine guns to "cleanse" the Sydney Steel Plant. Workers have left their jobs and many pitched battles occur. BESCO refuses to give steelworkers at the Sydney Plant higher wages or a decrease in working hours or recognition of a union. At present, steelworkers work two shifts—eleven hours by day and thirteen hours by night, seven days a week. It is said that a steelworker coming home in the winter never sees his family until the spring.

1927 No Monte Carlo here
The Diamond Jubilee Number of the *Post* urges Cape Bretoners not to make getting money from the tourist their main objective. Let us not "fall from a position of self-respecting independence to the standards of the gambling places of Europe."

1974 College begins
The College of Cape Breton is founded, continuing a tradition of higher education on Cape Breton started more than one hundred years ago. In 1975, Dr. Donald F. Campbell, president of the College, announces that the Sydney campus will offer Bachelor of Arts degrees. In June, 1982, the College is granted University status. (See also August 10, 1853 and January 16, 1952 and February 25, 2005.)

1980 *Fresh Air*
CBC's radio show, *Fresh Air*, goes on the air. The first of many communities visited is Baddeck. Every week, *Fresh Air* spotlights a different community in Cape Breton, talks to some of the residents and learns about life in that community today and yesterday. (See also photos January)

1982 Musicians go international
Cape Breton musicians, Doug MacPhee and Carl MacKenzie, arrive in Port Townsend, Washington, to give workshops in Cape Breton piano-playing and fiddling at the Festival of American Fiddle Tunes.

June 29

1926 Bridgeport "Kid"

Stevie "Kid" MacDonald of Bridgeport becomes the Maritime Lightweight Champion, beating Roy Chisholm of Halifax. In July, in Sydney, the "Kid" beats Chris Newton of Toronto for the Junior Lightweight Champ of Canada. In 1929 in Indianapolis, Indiana, in a 4th-round knockout over cowboy Eddie Anderson, he wins the Junior Lightweight Championship of the world. On June 4, 1980, he is inducted into the Canadian Boxing Hall of Fame and on September 20, 1980, into the Nova Scotia Sports Hall of Fame.

1985 Prince visits

Prince Andrew arrives as part of a four-day visit to the province. He visits North Sydney; has lunch at UCCB where he is entertained by the Cape Breton Chorale and Sydney School Band; inspects a guard of honour of the 2nd Battalion Nova Scotia Highlanders, and receives a 21-gun salute at the airport on his departure.

June 30

1894 Waves of immigration

J.H. Whitney of Boston is given a long-term lease on Cape Breton coal deposits. Large-scale industrial development continues in 1899 with Whitney's formation of the Dominion Iron and Steel Co. (DISCO). Large numbers of labourers are needed.

One of Cape Breton's MLAs, D. O. MacKenzie, wants to encourage immigration and he feels that Sydney is much like a World's Fair, where people of all nations can live a happy and prosperous life. But opponents of immigration believe "that hordes of degenerate foreigners would swarm into Cape Breton and keep native sons away from employment."

Nonetheless, immigration to Cape Breton is part of a general movement of Europeans to take part in the industrial expansion of North America. A "migration chain" is set up, for example, when a son comes over, finds work and sends for his family and neighbours.

Italians are recruited from Boston to work on the construction of the steel plant. Other Italians and Greeks are brought directly from Europe to work in the mines and the Plant. DISCO entices workers with promises of high wages and inexpensive housing. Some immigrants, though finding conditions different from what is expected, leave for Ontario. Other labourers arrive in Quebec and Halifax and find it cheaper to buy a ticket to Sydney than to continue out West.

By 1904, Poles, Ukrainians and Lebanese have arrived to work at the Plant. Some stay, others move on to other work, or to other areas. Many Chinese come from Western Canada after the completion of the CPR. Syrians also arrive, as do Jews from New York and Eastern Europe.

Blacks, not particularly wanted by the government, arrive from the West Indies, mostly from Barbados. They arrive by schooners already engaged in the coal and molasses trade, landing near Port Hawkesbury where there are no immigration officers and where they can catch a train to the industrial area.

Although trying to encourage British mining officials to immigrate, by 1910, the Nova Scotia government also wants to encourage "intelligent, practical farmers (who) had some money of their own" to come to the rural areas. When this fails, the government brings British children over from the Middlemore Home and Dr. Bernardo's Home to work on Cape Breton farms.

By 1914, there is such an influx of labourers into Cape Breton that several are out of work, and many are working for reduced pay. Premier Murray asks DISCO to stop recruiting. At the same time—and for the first time—the government acknowledges that Newfoundlanders, who have already been migrating for years, are desirable immigrants. They aren't far from home and can always return home if things don't work out.

In the early 1950s, as a result of increasing land pressure in Holland, several Dutch families come here to farm.

In the 1960s Cape Breton sees the arrival of many Americans disaffected by the Vietnam War while the 70s bring Vietnamese "boat people" displaced by that same war. (See also March 17, 1748 and August 3, 1802.)

1898 Newfoundland ferry begins

Late tonight, the SS *Bruce* will leave Port aux Basques for North Sydney, chosen by financier Robert Reid to be the mainland ferry terminus. The new ferry service is to develop into North Sydney's largest industry.

1930 Shipping schedule

The SS *Bras d'Or* begins her regular service from Sydney at 7 a.m.

The SS *Richmond* begins its run on the Bras d'Or Lakes at 7 a.m. The steamer loads freight for Grass Cove, Marble Mountain, West Bay, Irish Cove, Johnston's Harbour, Pulamond and D'Escousse. SS *Aspy* will leave Sydney at 7 a.m.; North Sydney at 8 a.m.; Mondays for St. Ann's; and Tuesdays and Thursdays for Neil's Harbour, Bay St. Lawrence and Ingonish.

1962 Craftsmen

Cape Breton coal miners are hired to learn traditional crafts to use in the reconstruction of the Fortress of Louisbourg.

1966 Second plant

Point Tupper is chosen as the site of Canada's second heavy water plant.

1967 John Allan

Mabou folk singer John Allan Cameron is one of the young Canadians to entertain the Queen in Ottawa and will perform again on Parliament Hill in the Dominion Day celebrations. John Allan has played on Nova Scotia stages, local TV and radio, and entertained audiences in Canada and the States.

1981 Musical home

Michael Murphy of North East Margaree invites guests to use (but not abuse) the musical instruments in his home-cum-museum. More than 60 instruments from all over the world are in the collection started by his father, including a 91/2 foot Alpine horn, a Bolivian flute and an 18-stringed instrument designed and made by his father.

Top left to right ***Fig. 6.7*** *Mrs. John Meloney, c. 1860.* ***Fig. 6.8*** *Whycocmagh pioneers, Jul-34.* ***Fig. 6.9*** *Inverness pioneers, c. 1900.* ***Fig. 6.10*** *Richard Brown, cir. 1866. R. H. Brown.* ***Fig. 6.11*** *Ranna Cossit.* ***Fig. 6.12*** *Rose Schwartz, two of her children and a Mr. Conter, n.d.* ***Fig. 6.13*** *Immigrants landing in Canada, n.d.*

July

Song for the Mira

Out on the Mira on warm afternoons,
Old men go fishin' with black line and spoons,
And if they catch nothing they never complain.
I wish I was with them again.

As boys in their boats call to girls on the shore,
Teasin' the ones that they dearly adore,
And into the evening the courting begins.
I wish I was with them again.

Chorus:

Can you imagine a piece of the universe
More fit for princes and kings?
I'll trade you ten of your cities for Marion Bridge
And the pleasure it brings.

Allister MacGillivray
Cabot Trail Music, C.A.P.A.C.

Top right to left - ***Fig. 7.1*** *Platform, Mira Railway Station, Mira Gut.* ***Fig. 7.2*** *Picnic, c.1916.* ***Fig. 7.3*** *CB Press Club, July 4. 1904.* ***Fig. 7.4*** *With Capt. Phillips on a Mira steamer.*

Summer in Cape Breton

Top left to right **Fig. 7.5** *Swordfish, Dingwall Harbour, c. 1910.* **Fig. 7.6** *Camping party at Indian Brook, c.1897.* **Fig. 7.7** *Fresh fish, n.d.* **Fig. 7.8** *Picnic, c. 1910.* **Fig. 7.9** *Social event, Pt. Edward, 1911.* **Fig. 7.10** *Swimming at Port Hood, c.1930. J. E. Evans.*
Fig. 7.11 *Mi'kmaq camp.*

July 1

1855 New port of entry
Effective today, North Sydney is declared the "Port of Entry and Clearance, and for the Registry of Shipping instead of Sydney" (*The Royal Gazette*)

1884 Keep the Sabbath
The Session of the Presbyterian Church at Grand River hopes there is no truth to the rumours that liquor is being sold at the time of Communion. The Session is also concerned about those people who leave their fishing nets out in the water on the Sabbath Day.

1898 Dominion Day
Nova Scotia finally celebrates Dominion Day—for the first time. The four provinces had accepted Confederation "with mixed feelings, for the benefits were by no means equal. It was said that Ontario was jubilant, Quebec doubtful and expectant, New Brunswick sullen and Nova Scotia rebellious."

1899 "Brawling Bedlam"
More than three thousand residents gather around Muggah's Creek in Sydney to see the first sod turned to mark the start of construction of the steel plant. Within three years, Sydney will change from a community of muddy streets, a marketplace for farmers and fishermen and a place to load coal to "a crowded brawling bedlam" (Sydney "*Post*").

1923 Strike turns ugly
The steelworkers' strike in Sydney turns ugly. Today becomes known as "Bloody Sunday." Provincial police ride on horseback up and down the streets of Whitney Pier and strike out with four-foot hardwood batons at everyone on the sidewalk. This includes a number of women and children coming from church. The Riot Act is read and volleys fired over the crowds, who disperse when a machine gun is set up. In a later Royal Commission Inquiry, it is revealed that the provincial police were to "put on a show" and aggravate the workers. J. B. McLachlan leads the coal miners out on strike in sympathy. John L. Lewis, leader of United Mine Workers International, revokes District 26's Charter when they won't return to work. He comes to Cape Breton to demote McLachlan, remove the radical Executive and get the miners back to work. J. B. McLachlan and secretary/treasurer, Don Livingstone, of the UMW are arrested.

Without the miners' support, the steelworkers' cause is weakened and soon afterwards they return to work. Some are blacklisted while others are given dirty jobs. None of their grievances have been answered.

1929 First airman
The first airmail flown to Cape Breton lands shortly after noon at the aerodrome of the Cape Breton Flying Club at Reserve. A large crowd turns up to greet the plane—and the first passenger from this airport on a mail plane, aviation fan Bruce Jefferson, editor of the *Sydney Record*.

1941 Highlands National Park

The Cape Breton Highlands National Park is officially opened by Federal Minister of Mines and Resources, Hon. T. A. Crerar, and Nova Scotia Premier A. S. MacMillan.

The Cape Breton Highlands Golf Links at Ingonish also open. Designed by Stanley Thompson, world-famous golf links architect, this *Beinne Mare* (mountains and sea) course, complementing the natural setting, is physically demanding, circling cross-country for six to seven miles. (No motorized carts are allowed).

The Cape Breton course, a revolutionary concept in golf course architecture in North America, imitates the traditional links at St. Andrews, Scotland. Each fairway has a name, including the particularly difficult "Heich O'Fash" (Heap of Trouble), "Bonnie Burn" and the 6th, for its sand bunkers shaped like a pair of lips, "Muckle Mouth Meg," a name borrowed from the Scottish poet, Robert Burns.

In 1965, Shell's *Wonderful World of Golf* broadcasts a match between George Knudsen and Al Balding from the course. CBC-TV also televises matches played on the Highland Links between members of the Canadian Professional Golfers Association.

In 2005 the Highlands Golf Links are named the best in Canada.

1973 Medicare

Designed by Cape Breton native, federal Health Minister Allan J. MacEachen, the Medicare plan goes into effect.

1977 Dundee

Dundee golf course opens. In 1983, it expands from 9 to 18 holes and the Devco-run facility includes tennis courts, swimming pool, cabins and a marina.

1986 Sewing baskets to large baby cradles

For more than twenty years, basket-making has been a family affair for the Poulettes of Eskasoni. Recently, son Bill Poulette, a police constable in Eskasoni, took a selection of baskets to Toronto to display at a Native Business Summit. The baskets, made from black ash, "should last more than fifty years," he says.

July 2

1909 Canada's first flying field

Early this month, J. A. D. McCurdy and Casey Baldwin, who formed the Canadian Aerodrome Company in Baddeck, find 300 acres in Big Baddeck Valley. They want to start manufacturing aircraft. This land is Canada's first flying field and is known as an "aerodrome park," the first time this term is used. The *Silver Dart* will be housed here and the *Baddeck I* and *II* built.

1928 Grand picnic

Grand picnic today at Boisdale. Electric cars from Glace Bay can connect, at reduced rates, with the special train which will leave Sydney at about 8:30 a.m. "Come everybody swell the crowd and meet your friends. Entertainment galore. We'll have everything shining except the moon."

1971 *St. Ninian*

The *St. Ninian* sails today for St. Pierre. The first vessel of this size - a renovated 2,224-ton cruise ship accommodating some three hundred passengers—to operate out of a Cape Breton port, she will sail twice weekly from North Sydney to St. Pierre-Miquelon.

1986 "Worst industrial dump site"

Headline: "Tar pond clean-up to begin immediately. The coke ovens will apparently close in July of 1988.The tar pond has been labelled the worst industrial dumpsite in Atlantic Canada. It has also been something of a thorn in the sides of local politicians who have hoped to promote Sydney as a place to invest."

2003 Cape Breton Highlands

The Life Network's Website names the Cape Breton Highlands as the number three rated campsite in Canada. It is noted for "'green mountains and unsurpassed coastal beauty' rivalled by a 'bog-bound eco system along a boardwalk that is home to rare orchids.'"

July 3

1744 Early convoy

Because of war with England, six large merchant ships, loaded with porcelain, spices and silk from the Orient, bound for France, are diverted to Louisbourg Harbour. Two are armed with 28 guns; two with 54 guns. Also in port, along with other merchant ships, are 103 English prisoners of war.

Later in November, the flotilla increases to 53 ships with some 4,000 men on board and sails for France.

1983 Back to Barra

Mary Janet MacDonald of Port Hood teaches Cape Breton stepdancing at the Barra Festival, a children's festival on the Isle of Barra, Scotland. It's the first time Cape Breton stepdancing is taught in Scotland.

July 4

1951 First black KC

F. Alan Hamilton, Sydney lawyer and Canada's first black King's Counsel, dies in Sydney.

1961 Discovery

A skin-diving team from Acadia University discovers the wreckage of three 18th century French ships used to block the channel at Louisbourg Harbour.

1975 MacPuffin

This month the first MacPuffin dollar, portraying the map of Cape Breton, goes on sale. Each year, with a different design on one side, the MacPuffin dollar is legal tender on Cape Breton until December 31st. MacPuffin, related to the hardy puffins who live in Cibou, one of the

Bird Islands off St. Ann's Bay, decked out in bonnet and with a cromack tucked under his wing, is the official tourist symbol of Cape Breton.

1986 New superferry

CN Marine operations manager, Gordon MacLeod, says "the new *Caribou* ferry has had little difficulty meeting traffic demands. The real test will begin the July 18-21 weekend, traditionally the busiest time of the year."

1991 Time capsule

A time capsule is discovered buried within the walls of the old Sydney Academy. The copper box, deposited eighty-one years ago, contains the July 1910 editions of *The Sydney Record* and *The Sydney Daily Post*, along with photographs of municipal politicians, and city and county annual reports.

July 5

1904 Hardwood Hill burns

Forest fires destroy houses and barns in the Hardwood Hill area of Sydney. Within a week, fire will sweep through the Ashby district but the only building destroyed will be the old smallpox building on St. Peters Road.

1913 Where is Cape Breton?

A writer in the *Mining Journal* complains that the federal government doesn't know where Cape Breton is. A short while ago a letter addressed to the "Old Dominion Coal Company, Little Glace Bay, South Cape Breton" was received from a government office. And a central Canadian newspaper referred to Glace Bay as "a little cove on the bay of Fundy." Government advertising ignores Cape Breton as well, never giving a square deal in the matter of immigration and labour supply. Immigrants and workers are being lured to Central Canada.

1913 Manna?

Mrs. Hugh McDonald of Grand Anse, while taking a morning stroll around her house, discovers that rain from a recent shower still hasn't dried, even though the sun has been out for fifteen minutes. The raindrops aren't water. They are sticky, like honey, and they cover stones, pebbles, bushes and trees. The sticky substance will not evaporate until late tomorrow morning.

1927 Archibald D. MacKinnon

Archibald D. MacKinnon, of East Lake Ainslie, is ordained in the newly built St. Andrew's Church in Whycocomagh. He is the first minister of the congregation of Whycocomagh and Little Narrows, recently combined to form one charge as it had been one hundred years earlier. He is to spend over forty years of his ministry in this charge. In 1957 he becomes Moderator of the General Assembly, the highest court in the Presbyterian Church, and later writes *The History of the Presbyterian Church in Cape Breton.*

July 6

1851 Threepenny Post

Under the new Postal Act, as of today, Cape Bretoners and others are not allowed to "forward letters by private opportunities." All letters must now go through the Post Office. A letter will cost three pence to be mailed to any part of Nova Scotia or British North America. Here on Cape Breton, a more efficient postal system is needed because the existing post offices are few and far between.

1906 British Canadian Co-Op

The British Canadian Co-Op Society Ltd. starts in Cape Breton with 180 square feet space in a rented room on Fraser Avenue in Sydney Mines. The Co-op will expand and flourish until a walk-in grocery and department store brings in a new system of customer services. In December 1907, Vincent MacDonald of Sydney Mines will become the first Canadian to be elected to the Board.

1905 SS *Amelia*

The SS *Amelia* leaves North Sydney tonight, and every other Wednesday night, after the arrival of the early express from Halifax, for St. Pierre, Miquelon and Placentia, Newfoundland. Starting Monday night, and every other Monday night, she will sail from Meat Cove, Pleasant Bay, Cheticamp, Margaree, Pictou and Charlottetown.

1905 Sons of Temperance

The Cape Breton District Division of the Sons of Temperance meets at Mira and passes a resolution affirming the strict prohibition of the liquor traffic and the enforcement of the Canada Temperance Act.

1968 Governor General arrives

Gov.-Gen. James and Mrs. Michener arrive in Sydney. Tomorrow will be a busy day for them going first to St. George's, on to Louisbourg and then to the Miners' Museum in Glace Bay where he'll unveil a restored steam locomotive, Number 17, used for many years to haul coal.

1973 Glendale Festival

The first Glendale Festival of Scottish Fiddling takes place this weekend. Performing individually and in groups and with over one hundred en masse in Sunday's finale, Cape Breton fiddlers prove that they are not a vanishing breed, as suggested by a recent CBC film. Major Festivals are to

Fig. 7.12 Glendale Festival, n.d.

be held at Glendale every two years, with the number of massed fiddlers growing to two hundred.

1991 Men of the Deeps

The Men of the Deeps, North America's only coal miners choir, celebrates their 25th anniversary year. "Thirty-Inch Coal" recently opened their first concert of the summer series at the Miners' Museum theatre. It is a musical tribute to their founder, Dr. Nina F. Cohen.

July 7

1784 Governor appointed

Major Frederick Wallet Des Barres is appointed Governor of the new Colony of Cape Breton.

1905 Letter to Louisbourg

A letter to Mr. D. J. Kennelly, KC and secretary of the Louisbourg Memorial:

Oyster Bay

"My Dear Sir,

Mr. Choate (U.S. Ambassador) has forwarded to me your letter with reference to the Louisbourg Memorial. It is hardly necessary for me to say, I trust, how heartily I sympathize with you in your purpose. It is in every way fit and proper that there should be a memorial, for it commemorates an incident that links the history of our continent in a peculiar way with that of the old world. With cordial good wishes for the success of your undertaking.

I am sincerely yours,
Theodore Roosevelt" (See also June 17,1895.)

1967 Highlanders meet

Cape Breton Highlanders meet in their first reunion since the association was reorganized. The famed battalion served in England, Italy and Northwestern Europe as part of the 11th Infantry Brigade of the 5th Canadian Armoured Division.

1991 "We need help right now"

Cape Breton longline fishermen need help. "This is something we can't wait for ... the situation is extremely urgent and we need help right now." About 400 fishermen on 200 boats fall deeper into debt. There are almost no fish to catch.

2001 No smoking

A tough smoking bylaw is enacted. The ban on public smoking in establishments such as restaurants, bars and the Sydney casino, as well as outdoor eating patios, is to be phased in over three years. Mayor John Morgan says, "We're leading the province in that regard. I don't think there is a geographic region in the country that has such a broad-based restriction about smoking in public places."

July 8

1884 Liberal gesture
The Fisheries Committee of the Session of the Presbyterian Church at Grand River decides to permit passive Sabbath fishing. That is, allowing fishermen to leave their nets in the sea on Sunday.

1913 Dry Broughton?
Following yet another liquor seizure, Councillor Neil Ferguson is determined to make the Broughton and Homeville areas completely "dry." A miner recently received some liquor from a dealer who had a cache hidden in the woods near the Homeville station. When the miner snuck back later to let some more, he was driven off by rifle fire.

1975 Early man at Ingonish Island
Dr. Ronald Nash and his archeological crew discover evidence of pre-Micmac man on Ingonish Island, called Geganisg (remarkable site) by the Micmacs. Stone tools were made here by at least two different types of Early Man: one group about 8,000 years ago, the second group occupied the site about 6-7,000 years ago.

1982 Protest
Whycocomagh Indians tear up 2,000 seedlings in protest against the chemical forest spraying of 2,4-0 and 2,4,5- T.

July 9

1866 To repel Fenians
Volunteers at Gabarus and the surrounding districts form the Sixth Regiment, Cape Breton Militia, gathering in the 5ummers (until 1870) to guard against and repel any Fenian Raiders, Irish Nationalists who have been raiding from the United States into Canada.
Forty years later, long after Fenian raids end, a grant of $100 will be authorized to any Fenian Raid Volunteer still living. At that time, there are eighty-nine known survivors of the Sixth Regiment, Cape Breton Militia.

1952 Explosion at No. 20
An explosion at No. 20 Colliery in Glace Bay kills seven miners. Another 250, who had just begun work in the mine, survive the explosion.

July 10

1917 First convoy
With multicoloured designs camouflaging ships' sides and funnels, the first convoy from Canada to leave Sydney Harbour sails today for Europe. Within the next month, ships are segregated according to speed; the faster ones sailing from Halifax. While waiting for the convoy to form, ships carrying explosives are anchored in the Northwest Arm opposite

Fig. 7.13 First convoy.

Upper North Sydney. With the increase in shipping safety, an anti-submarine net defence with guarded gates in the middle, is laid across the Harbour at Centreville.

1981 The Cape Breton fiddler

The Cape Breton Fiddler by songwriter Allister MacGillivary is published by College of Cape Breton Press. Cape Breton has many fiddlers and their music owing much to Scottish roots is unique, for unlike fiddle music in Scotland, it has been less exposed to outside influences. On Cape Breton, for example, the strathespeys, as an accompaniment to stepdancing, retain their syncopated rhythm.

Most Cape Breton fiddlers started playing when they were young. They play at picnics, dances, concerts, "kitchen rackets" and other ceilidhs. During the 1940s and 50s, fiddlers who had an extra impact through the medium of radio programs and early recordings included Winston "Scotty" Fitzgerald, Joe MacLean and Dan Joe MacInnis.

Cape Bretoners appeared on the *Don Messer Show*, the *John Allan Cameron Show* and *Ceilidh.* TV exposure took Cape Breton fiddle music across Canada and through the States and back over to Scotland. Some of these later musicians included Winnie Chafe, Carl MacKenzie, Buddy MacMaster and Jerry Holland. Cape Breton fiddlers play the traditional Scottish music as well as many of their own compositions.

July 11

1839 Port of Arichat

The bustling port of Arichat is declared a free port. With its numerous wharves and warehouses lining the shore, the town is described as being "five miles long and five inches wide." The town's importance gradually diminishes as shipping patterns change. The use of small steamers reduces the coastal trade and with the opening of the St. Peters Canal in 1869, more shipping is diverted from Arichat. Finally, the Great August Gale of 1873 destroys many vessels, which are never replaced.

1883

UNTIL, FURTHER NOTICE
John Morrison of St. Peter's will run a line of covered coaches between Sydney and East Bay connecting with the SS *Neptune* each trip.

1930 Bronx idol really a Bay boy

Glace Bay born boxer, Eddie Provie, is proclaimed, "the Bronx Idol" by New York sports journalists watching him train for the World Lightweight Championship.

1984 Parade of Sail

Twenty-six Tall Ships sail out of Sydney Harbour to start a transatlantic Race to Liverpool, England. The first of the ships arrived at Sydport, Point Edward, last Friday and since then thousands of Cape Bretoners and others have enjoyed visiting with officers and cadets from around the world. The Russian Class A ship *Kruzenshtern* is the overall winner of the handicap race, while the British Class C ketch *Donald Searle* is the first to cross the finish line.

Fig. 7.14 Parade of Sail, 1984. Pamela Newton.

Ian Stott, of Ports Canada, Dr. John Reid, of the Canadian Coast Guard College and Blaine Gillis, of Devco, have been described as modern "dream makers" who masterminded this visit by the Sail Training Association.

July 12

1828 Immigrants arrive

A shipload of Scottish immigrants arrives at Ship Harbour (Port Hawkesbury) with 250 chests, 20 trunks, 50 barrels, 40 bags and 208 people. There are 9 infants, 37 children under ten years of age; 30 people are fifty years and over. The oldest are Rory McIssac, 85, Allan McLean, 89 and Marion McMillan, 88.

1978 Maritime-bred horse

Donmar Shalom, bred by Donald Rankin of the Frenchvale Road, is the first Maritime-bred horse to break the two minute mile in a time of 1.59.4 at Meadowlands, New Jersey.

2003 Checkmate

Early this month 16-year-old Gary Ng becomes the champion in the under-18 division at the Canadian Youth Chess Championship held in Kapuskasing, Ontario. Born in Hong Kong, he moved to Dartmouth at age 2, then on to Port Hawkesbury a few years ago. He won the Nova Scotia Chess Championship against adults in May of this year. Gary works on-line with a Toronto coach every week.

July 13

1907 Dry Sunday

No one can get a drink of liquor in Sydney today. "Dry Sunday" has been proclaimed and guests at hotels, being refused even a beer, are annoyed.

1925 Fire escape

Mr. Verner of Sydney, a member of the 85th Overseas Battalion and the first man in the corps to be wounded at Vimy Ridge, devises a new fire escape especially for hospital patients.

July 14

1905 Enviable time

The special fast mail train from North Sydney to Montreal arrives ten hours earlier than ordinary express. Brought from England on *The Virginian,* 750 sacks and 138 baskets of mail, along with eighteen passengers, were transferred to the cruiser *Canada* and transferred again at North Sydney. The special train left at 10:45 and reached Pt. Tupper in two hours and nine minutes. In some parts of the Cape Breton section, it reached a speed of 60 m.p.h. It took only 18 minutes instead of the usual 35 to transfer the train at the Strait of Canso. And ten and a half minutes after leaving the rails at Pt. Tupper, the train was on them again at Mulgrave. The train took 24 hours and 38 minutes to reach Montreal, where the mails were sorted and put on the western mail train. Even with a slow ocean trip and a double transfer, it is faster using North Sydney as a port to land the mail.

July 15

1924 Good vibrations

Eighty-seven-year-old Hugh Roper of North Sydney has been practically blind for almost eighteen months now. A few nights ago, while listening to a neighbour's radio, he experienced heavy sensations across his forehead. The effect of the electric vibrations became apparent next morning when he found he could see clearly. The visibility lasted for some hours and even now his sight—and his hearing—are better.

July 16

1914 To the far country

A *Post* reporter, offered his first round trip on the *Aspy* on her trip Down North, says he had a strange concept of the area. And he was very surprised not to run into bears, wildcats or icebergs.

1924 Ross Ferry

A new modern ferry is preparing to carry passengers between Big Harbour and Ross Ferry. Seventy feet long and twenty feet wide, she will carry eight cars in one trip. A propeller at each end means that the boat can make the return trip without turning.

Fig. 7.15 Ross Ferry.

1967 Queen Mother here

The Queen Mother on her brief visit to Sydney visits St. George's Church and attends a concert in Wentworth Park. St. George's Church has a Royal Charter and members of the Royal Family attend services here when in Sydney.

1969 St. Pat's

St. Patrick's Church Museum officially opens this afternoon. Three years ago, a small group of students and professors from Xavier College pitched in to help clear out the old plaster and dirt, repair and paint, and convert the deteriorating church into a museum. This real community effort was also the beginning of the Old Sydney Society, formed by citizens with an interest in local history and the preservation of historical buildings.

1983 Jeux Canada Games

It is announced that the Canada Winter Games will be held in Cape Breton in 1987. New facilities at the University College of Cape Breton are to be augmented by those at seventeen other locations around the Island. UCCB's Dr. Carl "Bucky" Buchanan, directing the organization of the Games, says that some three thousand volunteers will be needed. The Games are expected to attract more than 2,900 athletes from all provinces and territories of Canada. (See also January 2, 1987.)

2005 - Lone Coyote

A lone coyote, believed to have traveled on ice floes, is destroying nests and young birds on Hertford Island, one of the Bird Islands off the eastern coast. The Islands are bird sanctuaries for several types of birds including the Great Cormorant and the Puffin. The coyote is now trapped on the Island – and he remains hungry.

July 17

1746 Early beer

During their occupation of Louisbourg, the British drink spruce beer because they think the water may be contaminated. And they continue to drink spruce beer during the second siege. Twice a week, ten soldiers from each Brigade are delegated to gather the spruce boughs and make the beer. The British use a ratio of six quarts of molasses to a barrel of water, similar to the Newfoundlanders' recipe, while the French use a ratio of four quarts of molasses to the barrel. Tender strips of spruce or pine are boiled for three hours, the liquid is strained into a wooden cask, and the molasses added.

1961 "Hinge of History"

At a reception in Louisbourg, Resources Minister Dinsdale calls the restoration of the Fortress the greatest undertaking ever made by his Department. The restoration will show the grandeur of the "hinge of history," when the French gave way to the English.

1967 Devco is born

"The only way to prevent an economic debacle is to lay new foundations," says Mines Minister Jean Luc Pepin. "It's a choice if planning or failing to plan for something that is inevitable."

The new crown corporation, formed following The Donald Report, an inquiry into the coal industry in Cape Breton, will take over the mines and faze down production. It will also seek through industrial development to create new employment in other sectors of the economy. Cape Breton's Allan J. MacEachen, federal health minister, is Devco's chief architect. The new crown corporation will be busy developing new industries for Cape Breton as it closes down the coalmines.

July 18

1745 The pit from the pulpit

Cape Breton has the first and probably the only coal to be advertised from a church pulpit. The incident takes place when Rev. Thomas Prince, while preaching a thanksgiving sermon in Boston in commemoration of the capture of Louisbourg, remarks, "that Cape Breton abounded with the best pit coal in America: easily dug, easy to put into vessels."

1842 Lost, strayed or stolen

Ad in the newspaper, *The Spirit of the Times*: "Lost, strayed, or stolen from the pasture of the Subscriber, a Mare, of the most beautiful vermillion tint, almost rivalling the gorgeous hues of the rainbow. Said mare has a bob-tail, whose hue of jetty blackness strongly reminds the beholder of 'Nights descending robe,' and her mane, dark as Erebus, hangs gracefully adown a neck of the most exquisite symmetry. She has two feet growing upon hind legs, which feet, called by the vulgar 'crooked,' only possess in reality an involute curvature. Whoever will give any information respecting the above truant and erring animal, to her anxious and disconsolate friends, will be rewarded by the consciousness of having done a good action—by the gratitude of her owner—or, if required, in a more substantial manner."
Robert Hill - Northwest Arm

1905 Day's outing

Four special plus the regular tram cars with excursionists from Aberdeen, Glace Bay, Bridgeport and Reserve will meet the special train at Sydney, which will then make connections with the North Sydney special to go to Iona for a picnic. Adult fare from Sydney to Iona and return: 65 cents. Children: 35 cents.

1912 First Montessori class

The first Montessori class in Canada is held at Beinn Breagh, home of the Bells, outside of Baddeck. Mrs. Mable Bell has arranged for Roberta Fletcher to accompany the family from Washington, DC, where she has been teaching two of the Bell grandchildren. The class consists of Graham Fairchild, aged 5, and Barbara Fairchild, aged 3, Alec Grosvenor (Bell grandchildren); Robert and Sadie Rose, Ruth and Mabel Davidson (children of men working on the Estate) and Georgiane Frost, aged 4. Following the principles of Madame Montessori, an Italian physician and educator, the teacher is supervisor and observer, and the children have great freedom of expression.

July 19

1781 Battle of Spanish Harbour

Two French frigates, cruising local waters in support of the Americans in the Revolutionary War, sight a convoy of twenty-one English ships leaving Spanish (Sydney) Harbour. Sixteen of the English ships are unarmed sloops and schooners which have been chartered to collect coal for the garrison at Halifax. They are escorted by five small, armed English ships, including the small 100-ton *Jack,* commanded by R. P. Tonge.

The French ships outgun the English. Commander Evans on the frigate *Charleston* orders the unarmed ships to return to Spanish Harbour and, putting his own vessels in line ahead, sails in to attack the French. The battle is over in an hour. Sixty-three British sailors and forty-three French are dead or wounded. Young Commander Evans is killed. The *Jack* is captured by the French and R. P. Tonge taken prisoner. (See also October 10, 1782)

1842 Not amused

There are complaints about the wholesale desertions of men from the Sydney garrison. Last year, twenty-four men deserted from the 64th Regiment. *The Spirit of the Times* comments that Queen Victoria had not planned on settling the island of Cape Breton with soldiers and she might withdraw the military altogether.

1844 "Set your country free"

Published in *The Spirit of the Times*
"Hear, you Cape Bretonians,
descendents of the brave;
Enrol yourselves together
And freedom you shall have.
Master all your energies, and
Set your country free,
Despised by Nova Scotia,
No longer shall you be."

A rallying cry for the separation of Cape Breton Island from the province of Nova Scotia. Since the annexation of the island in 1820, there have been Cape Bretoners who want separation. (See also October 16, 1820, May 19, 1846, May 19, 1886, December 13, 1974, September 4, 2002.)

1905 LIGHTS ON

Electric lights are used for the first time at the Sydney "Driving Park" racetrack. Four hundred fans watch trotters and pacers and a "gentlemen's road race for a silver cup." The judges find the back stretch a little dark as some of the arc lights have been destroyed and they decide to have a searchlight installed to help them to see the horses all the way around.

1953 MYSTERY FISH

Eighteen-year-old swordfisherman Lester Fleet harpoons a mystery fish in Louisbourg Harbour. The fish was spotted by Lester's mother from her home. Seeing it swimming around in the shallow waters near the shore, she thought at first it was a swordfish. Local fishermen don't think the large, almost one thousand pound toothless fish is a shark (sharks have four sets of gills and this one has five sets). Nor do they think it's the Fourchu Rammer, the large fish that has been terrorizing the coastline for the past two weeks. But they never do find out. Before tiring, the fish pulls out 25 fathoms of rope. It is 11 feet, 3 inches long with a 10-inch dorsal fin and green and blue specks on its belly and back.

1997 ARKANDOR

Fourteen students aged nine to twenty-five, from Russia. Venezuela, Germany, Korea, America and Canada, arrive at Arkandor on Boularderie Island for the Arkandor Foundation's third annual Arkandor-Albert Markov Summer Musical Festival. The students, all recent winners of international competitions, are attending a six-week camp to fine-tune their skills. Faculty members are from the Manhattan School of Music. Angelika Weller, founder and sponsor of the Foundation and Albert Markov, violinist, composer, conductor, and teacher, say the camp "combines professional training and recreation with the beauty available on the island."

July 20

1923 STREET FIGHTING

Some men are clubbed and one steelworker receives a sabre thrust in the shoulder as police and cavalry troops clash with steelworkers in Sydney.

1960 LONE SHIELING

> From the lone shieling of the misty island,
> Mountains divide us, and the waste of seas –
> Yet still the blood is strong, the heart is Highland,
> And we in dreams hold the Hebrides.

Professor Donald S. Macintosh of Pleasant Bay dies. Under the terms of his will, a small cabin is to be built like the lone shieling on the Island of Skye.

July 21

1905 Broughton seam

The discovery of the Broughton seam will add over 100 per cent to the Dominion Coal Company's coal holdings. Measuring from 18 to 29 miles, it is said to extend from Lingan to Mira, to be a land area of 100 square miles, or about 619,520,000 tons of coal.

1997 Encampment

Last weekend the Fortress of Louisbourg Volunteer Militia took part in a militia encampment lined along the shoreline at Englishtown facing towards St Ann's Bay. During the 1600s and 1700s militia troops travelled to Englishtown from the Fortress to stand guard against possible attacks. Before it was Englishtown, the site was a small French fort.

July 22

1785 Soldiers arrive

The 33rd Regiment arrives in Sydney. The troops help clear land, build houses, barracks and roads.

1812 Bishop taken for privateer

Bishop Octave Plessis, one of Quebec's greatest bishops, visits Cheticamp on his trip to Cape Breton. On their journey from Prince Edward Island, the Bishop and his party are worried about potential trouble from American privateers, who have been especially active since last month's declaration of war between Britain and the United States. But it is Cheticamp fishermen offshore who think the Bishop and his party are the privateers. One Irishman on shore takes his family and valuable possessions and hides in the woods.

Landing safely, the Bishop, among his other duties, performs twelve marriages. Although the wedding celebrations are to take place after the Bishop leaves, there is an air of festivity. The brides are decorated with red ribbons in front from head to waist, while the grooms have a bunch of ribbons in their buttonholes and a cockade in their hats. After declaring Saint Peter the appointed patron of Cheticamp, Bishop Plessis travels down the coast to Port Hood where he tends to the Scottish Catholic settlers.

1905 First in Nova Scotia

Off Baddeck, covering a course of about eight miles, *Tam O'Shanter* wins what is probably the first motorboat race in the province.

1919 Donkin Band

A group of local musicians, mostly coal miners, organizes the Donkin Citizens' Brass Band. Brass instruments are chosen over the more expensive silver-plated ones. The Band

Fig. 7.16 Donkin Band in Centennial Parade, 1967. Ray Martheleur.

makes its first public appearance on Christmas Day, 1919, marching out to the Schooner Pond Dam and onto the middle of the ice. Throughout the years, the Band plays at virtually every big event in the Maritimes. (See also August 27, 1958.)

The Band is still in existence. Donkin resident, Verner Murrant, in the Band from 1922 to 1981, is believed to be the member with the longest continual service.

1938 First Mod

The first Gaelic Mod opens today at St. Ann's. Premier Angus L. MacDonald delivers an address in the language of "the Garden of Eden."

1971 All Cape Breton

About three tons of newsprint, manufactured at the new newsprint mill of the NS Pulp and Paper Company at Point Tupper, is used to make up today's special issue of the *Cape Breton Post*. Printed for the first time on all Cape Breton newsprint, it is also the first paper to use this newsprint.

1982 Long service

St. Margaret's Parish in Broad Cove celebrates its 125th anniversary. The parish has given 31 priests and 30 sisters to the Church.

July 23

1749 French return

The French occupy Louisbourg again. Governor Hopson hands over the keys to the town. On July 30, English ships begin to leave the Harbour.

1958 Sydney River spanned

The last span of the new Sydney River bridge is in place. The bridge, the third largest in the province, is scheduled for traffic late this fall.

1978 Micmac poet

Poems of Rita Joe is published by the Abanaki Press. Rita Joe was born in Whycocomagh and moved to Eskasoni about twenty-five years ago. Working for the *Micmac News*, she started writing stories and poems about her Micmac heritage. Written in English, the poems have been translated into Micmac by Bernie Francis. (See also November)

July 24

1784 Robin's Company

Charles Robin, Jersey merchant and entrepreneur, establishes his second Cape Breton fishery at Cheticamp this season. The first had been established twenty years earlier on Isle Madame. Robin's Company store expands and provides employment and provisions throughout the area. The women and girls who work for the company are paid in credits at the store and initially work seven days a week. The men use the Company gear and boats for a charge of 10 per cent of their catch and the balance of the catch is sold to the company. (See also December 15, 1992.)

1924 Not the last time

Mr. Wolvin, president of BESCO, explains why the steel plant must, for the first time in its history, close down for a limited time. Not only is the Canadian steel business in its worst slump, but costs of producing steel in Sydney have increased along with coal mining costs. It's cheaper to buy steel products from France and Belgium. Cape Breton coal miners don't appreciate this implied criticism of their wages, already the lowest in Canada.

July 25

1917 Tragedy strikes New Waterford

At 7:30 this morning, an explosion at No. 12 Colliery in New Waterford kills 65 miners, including three rescuers—two 17-year-old surface workers and another miner who made nine trips into the mine bringing out survivors before he was overcome by gas. Dead are 12 married men, 18 single men, 22 Newfoundlanders (7 from the same small fishing village), and 10 foreigners. Two horses and one miner survive for several days buried in the mine before they are rescued.

The town seal of New Waterford is a copy of the miner on the top of the Miners' Monument on Plummer Avenue, which commemorates the sixty-five miners who lost their lives.

1924 ID necessary

From now on, travellers from Cape Breton, and the rest of Canada, must carry identification with them when travelling to the United States.

1952 New entertainment

The new Midway drive-in movie theatre opens tonight on the Sydney-Glace Bay Highway. Tonight's show, *Tulsa* in "glorious technicolor," plus a Three Stooges comedy, starts at dusk. Cafeteria service is available. There is no charge for the car. Adults: 60 cents; students: (12-15): 25 cents; children under 12: free. "No babysitting or dressing up now necessary."

1981 Cape Breton Farm Market

The Cape Breton Farm Market Association begins an outdoor market in Sydney with produce from local farms. Initially next to City Hall, next year it moves to Charlotte Street and the following year to the Maritime Tel and Tel parking lot, where a permanent structure is built to house the vendors. Since its modest beginning, this Saturday morning market has become the largest of its type in Nova Scotia.

Fig. 7.17 Fresh vegetables.

July 26

1750 Pierre Maillard

Father Pierre Maillard makes his headquarters on Chapel Island, a small island near Port Toulouse (St. Peter's) where he had preached his first sermon eight years earlier. Pierre Maillard was born in France and, following his ordination, he sailed for Louisbourg. There were enough priests there and Father Maillard decided to move out into the countryside among the native Micmacs. He learned Micmac and devised a script from their oral language. Returned to France with other French nationals after the First Siege of Louisbourg, he was back two years later and the British appointed him the "official missionary to the Indians and Acadians of Nova Scotia."

Following the second siege, the chapel on the island, like so many other French outposts, was destroyed. Despite the feelings at the time, Father Maillard visited Halifax in 1760, and was able to celebrate the first Mass ever offered in the capital of Nova Scotia. Two years later, when he died, he was buried in St. Paul's Anglican Cemetery, there by special order of the Governor since there was no Roman Catholic cemetery nearby.

Every summer Micmacs gather at Chapel Island to celebrate the Feast of St. Anne with a special procession and celebrations. (See also August 12, 2003.)

1758 Louisbourg falls again

Louisbourg is captured by General Jeffrey Amherst.

1842 Beware government aid

William Ayre, teacher at the Combined Grammar, Mathematical and Common School in Margaree, receives word from the Board of Education that funds are not available for establishing school libraries. It will be eight years before government funding for libraries and Teachers' Institutes becomes a reality. At that time, Mr. Ayre is pleased, but cautious, recommending "Let us strive to merit Provincial aid, but to trust to it as little as possible; it is a species of begging, and mendication, like other acquired habits, is difficult to leave off; I never knew a beggar quit his trade, till death parted them." (See also September 1, 1870 & 1915.)

1930 Circus

The A. G. Barnes Circus, part of the great Ringling Brothers Circus, arrives in Sydney after being in North Sydney. With thirty railway cars, it is one of the largest circuses now on tour and features "Tusko," the largest elephant in the world. He stands 13 feet tall and weighs 20,845 pounds.

1939 First in North America

The Gaelic College opens at St. Ann's. Established to foster and develop the Gaelic language, the College also encourages preservation through teaching of Celtic arts, crafts, music and dance. A Gaelic Mod highlights the summer school. The College complex expands to include the Giant MacAskill Highland Pioneers Museum and a Great Hall of Clans.

1940 Urge "dry war"
Members of the Cape Breton Presbytery's annual meeting urge the closing of the provincial government Liquor Commission stores for the duration of the war.

2003 Fort Petrie
Today is Fort Petrie History Day. Fort Petrie, New Victoria, one of the seven fortification complexes around Sydney Harbour during the Second World War, is being made into an historic and interpretive site. Work is being done on installing two Second World War gun emplacements. During the war the harbour fortifications helped defend from submarine attacks merchant shipping and the slow convoys forming in the Harbour.

July 27

1749 Lost in evacuation
A little English girl, about three months old, found in Louisbourg when the French returned, is baptized.

1785 Loyalists arriving
According to the records, "A considerable number of His Majesty's loyal subjects who have retired from the United States of America and other settlers are already arrived here (Sydney) and many others are expected hourly."

July 28

1860 Future King at Sydney Mines
The Prince of Wales, later King Edward VII, while en route to Halifax, makes an unscheduled stop at Sydney Mines. Lt.-Col. Brown of the Militia hurriedly orders the Volunteers to muster, but most of them are working in Queen Pit. The Prince lands at noon and is driven up to Indian Beach by horse and buggy to visit the Micmac encampment. The men are away for their annual ceremonies at Chapel Island, but the women greet the royal party. Returning to Sydney Mines, the Prince inspects the Volunteers and tours the town before attending a reception.

Fig. 7.18 Sydney Mines Volunteer Rifles, c. 1860.

1873 Vooght Building
Thomas and James Vooght arrive from England to join their brother John in North Sydney, where they start construction of a store. The original wooden building becomes the largest store on the Island. After a fire destroys it in 1902, a new, more expansive building is built and it becomes the largest department store east of Montreal.

The building is demolished in the early 1980s.

1905 VON

Nurses meet in Sydney to form a local association of the Victorian Order of Nurses. Started in 1897 as the national memorial of Queen Victoria's Diamond Jubilee in Canada, the VON was originally treated with hostility by several medical boards.

1950 Glace Bay celebrates

The "largest town in Canada" celebrates its 50th anniversary. The four collieries operating within the town limits are the four largest producers in Canada. Caledonia Colliery was opened shortly after Confederation and it is believed to be the oldest continuously operated coal mine in America. It was the first mine to use telephones underground.

1951 Mine mechanization

More than 90,000,000 tons of coal have been taken from the mines of Glace Bay since operations began almost a century ago. Today, a multi million dollar mechanization program heralds a new era for the area, rich in mining firsts. No. 1-B Colliery at Bridgeport has a two-way wireless system to maintain contact between drivers of the underground electric locomotives and the dispatcher. The world's largest hoisting engine is at No. 1-B Colliery, and the mines in the Glace Bay area were the first to use the self-contained breathing apparatus for mine rescue work.

1978 Miners' Museum

The Inverness Miners' Museum opens in the old CN station at Inverness.

1991 Broad Cove Concert

The 35th annual Broad Cove Concert, the "grand-daddy of Cape Breton's famed summer concert circuit" takes place today. "What started as a modest fundraiser in support of St. Margaret's Parish has become a regular summer fixture and sparked a string of summer outdoor festivals across the island."

1995 – The Grand Encampment

Close to 1,200 historic re-enactors from across Canada and the United States camp out at the Fortress of Louisbourg National Historic Site and join Fortress animators taking part in a Grand Encampment (July 28-30). All are dressed in mid-18th century costume. Soldiers mingle with civilians, depicting camp life, period military drill and other ceremonies and manoeuvres. Thirteen Tall Ships along with several smaller boats fill the Harbour. This year, Louisbourg celebrates three anniversaries. It's the

Fig. 7.19 Grand Encampment, 1997.

275th anniversary of the declaration of Louisbourg as the capital of Isle Royale, the 250th anniversary of the first siege and the 120th anniversary of the Sydney & Louisbourg Railway. Several thousands of spectators enjoy the activities.

1999 Final Morse Code transmission

Part of the message reads: "With advances in terrestrial and satellite communications we now sign off the Morse code as a primary safety service to mariners. Today, after 100 years, Cape Breton Island will fall silent on 500khz."

Retired radio officer, Art Lockerbie, handcopies out the last Commercial Morse Code Transmission on original Canadian Marconi Company stationery. Retired area operations supervisor, John A. Weir, sends the message from the Coast Guard College's radio station to the Marconi Museum in Glace Bay. The once high tech Morse Code is replaced by more recent technology. (See also Dec 15, 1902)

July 29

1850 Cape Breton *News*

The *News* replaces the *Herald* in Cape Breton. Newspapers appear to have difficulty succeeding on the Island.

1918 Journey to Yarmouth

This summer it takes W. V. Hoyt six days to drive from North Sydney to Yarmouth with the aid of two sets of chains.

1967 New hope

Industrial development in the Strait of Canso area has slowed the exodus of young people from Cape Breton and has enabled many Cape Bretoners, especially Richmond County residents, to stay here on the Island instead of seeking jobs elsewhere in Canada. Development started with the construction of the Nova Scotia Pulp and Paper Company, which opened in 1961. Later, expansion projects provide more employment. About 1,000 people are employed directly with Nova Scotia Forest Industries, while another 1,000 work in the woods.

Further development starts in the late 60s and early 70s with the construction of the Gulf Oil Refinery (mothballed in 1980), the Canadian General Electric Company's Heavy Water Plant (later turned over to Atomic Energy of Canada Limited) and the Nova Scotia Power Corporation's thermo-generating station. In this integrated complex, the refinery produces oil for the thermo-generating station which produces steam for the Heavy Water Plant. The expansion and modernization of the Breton Industrial and Marine Shipyard at Point Tupper provides further employment, as does Georgia Pacific's ocean terminal and its gypsum mine at River Denys.

The large Gulf Oil Refinery dock has two berths. The outside one, built for supertankers, is later taken out of service, but the No. 2 inside berth continues to service coastal tankers.

1981 Royal wedding

Lydia Adams and Stuart Calvert of Glace Bay take part in the Royal Wedding of Prince Charles and Lady Diana by singing in the Bach Choir, under the direction of Sir David Wilcox, at the marriage ceremony in St. Paul's Cathedral, London.

1984 Connie Smythe
Near the end of his life Connie Smythe, the man who got money to build Maple Leaf Gardens and promoter of the Toronto Maple Leafs, visited Baddeck and stayed at the Inverary Inn. He wanted to do something to express his appreciation. He said, "I have found peace and contentment for the first time in twenty years at this lovely spot." After his death his family completes his wish. Today, a small chapel on the Inn's grounds is dedicated.

July 30

1722 Subsistence and protection
Annual gift-giving ceremonies started out as a way in which the French could secure good relations with their new allies, the Indians. Officials fear it has deteriorated and become a means of subsistence for Indians and a form of protection for the French. Guns, shirts and cognac are among the gifts distributed at Port Toulouse (St. Peters) and Port Dauphin (St. Ann's).

1921 Fire at Neil's Harbour
Forest fires blaze around Neil's Harbour. Three homes and two sawmills have been destroyed. Taken aboard the *"Aspy,"* 260 men, women and children were served soup, bread and butter, and tea. Next winter's supplies, which must be stored up in the spring and early summer, are destroyed in the fire.

1952 Fire and ice
In less than a half an hour this evening, four large houses owned by the Allan Ice Company are destroyed by fire. One of the buildings was a landmark on the Northside, having been built in 1896.

July 31

1850 Miracle Medicine
"DR. S. P. TOWNSEND'S COMPOUND EXTRACT OF SARSAPARILLA—The Wonder and Blessing of the Age. The most Extraordinary Medicine in the World—This Extract is put up in Quart Bottles, it is six times cheaper, pleasanter, and warranted superior to any sold. It cures without vomiting, purging, sickening or debilitating the patient. This Extract has cured more of the following diseases than all other advertised medicines have done.

Scrofula or King's Evil: Obstinate Cutaneous Eruptions—Pimples or Pustules on the Face—Blotches, Biles, Chronic Sore Eyes, Ring Worm or Tetter, Scald Head, Enlargement and Pain of the Bones and Joints, Stubborn Ulcers, Syphilitic Disorders, Lumbago, Salt Rheum—and all diseases arising from an injudicious use of Mercury, Ascites or Dropsy, Exposure or Imprudence in Life. It invariably cures Rheumatism, Indigestion or Dyspepsia, Neuralgia, General and Nervous Debility, Palpitations of the Heart, Liver Complaint and Inflammation of the Kidneys.

Ladies of pale complexion and consumptive habits, and such as are debilitated by those obstructions which females are liable to are restored, by the use of a bottle or two, to bloom and vigor.

For sale at the CALEDONIA HOUSE South Sydney - by C. H. Harrington."

1905 Vice-Regal visit

Lord Earl Grey visits Glace Bay for the graduating exercises of the nurses from St. Joseph's Hospital. It was his distinguished predecessor, Lord Minto, who four years ago marked the spot on which the hospital was built.

1905 Educated horses

It's Summer Carnival in Sydney. There are horse races, a mercantile fair in the Rosslyn Rink and, in the Lyceum, Professor Crocker's "25 educated horses." The stage is covered with sawdust, and there are two ropes across the front to prevent accidents. The closing number is a battle scene where the horses fire off the cannon. One horse, holding a Union Jack, mounts a platform and amid a blaze of lights, a very effective patriotic tableau is presented.

1907 Boom town

There is a building boom in Sydney Mines, but the train from North Sydney allows workers to commute to Sydney Mines. It is said that a man can leave the coal mine in the morning and get a job in the steel plant in the afternoon—or vice versa. With a steel plant and five mines in the area, Sydney Mines is a boom town.

1920 To build new world

The Governor General, The Duke of Devonshire, and his wife, visit the industrial area. A special train carries them to Glace Bay and Louisbourg, where the residents are urged to "carry on and build up a new world." After a welcome at Sydney's Wentworth Park, the Duke and Duchess attend a garden party at Senator McLennan's home at Petersfield in Westmount.

1953 "Victory" closes

No. 24 Colliery, "The Victory," officially closes. Last month No. 1-B Colliery, top producer for years, was closed, but it will be mechanized to resume production in the fall.

1967 Miners' Museum

The Miners' Museum at Glace Bay is officially opened. The Museum is a memorial to all coal miners on Cape Breton and the work they have done in the development of the Island.

A fire in August, 1980 destroys the Museum and 80 per cent of the artifacts. Just twenty-two months after the fire, the new museum will be back in operation.

"The Men of the Deeps," a miners' choir, dressed in work clothes complete with helmet and headlamp, perform at the opening of the Miners' Museum. "The Men of the Deeps," all veteran coal miners, are named for the coal mines that run under the floor of the Atlantic and they are believed to be the only miners' choir in North America. They perform at Expo next week.

They travel throughout Canada and the United States and in 1976 become the first amateur Western group to be invited to perform in China. "The Men of the Deeps" entertain at the Olympic Village in Montreal in 1980, on a Christmas TV Special with Anne Murray in 1982 and on *Front Page Challenge* after their China trip. They record three albums.

2004 Congres Mondial Acadien

Nova Scotia is host to the 3rd World Acadian Congress. This year marks the 400th anniversary of French settlement in Nova Scotia and the 125th anniversary of the Cape Breton community of St Joseph du Moine. Events are celebrated all across the province. Here in Cape Breton, over 10,000 Acadians and their friends and families celebrate with 16 days of family reunions, concerts, parades, church services and an abundance of Acadian cooking.

August

The Causeway Crossing

Chorus:

Oh the Canso Causeway's a wonder they say
It's mainland rock and it's mainland clay
And many do come but they don't plan to stay
It was built for going away.

From where the sun rises and where the sun sets
They leave this fair isle for the gold of the west
There is many a young heart that's full of regret
For in seeking to find they find something less.

Albert MacDonald
Music – John Gillis

Fig. 8.1 Road to the Isles, 1955

Fig. 8.2

Summer Work

Fig. 8.3 Scything, Ingonish, c. 1910.

Fig. 8.4 A group effort.

Fig. 8.5 Spinning frolic at Englishtown, n.d.

Fig. 8.6 Cutting hay near Neils Harbour, 1942.

August 1

1892 First observations
The first recorded weather observations, three per day, begin today in Sydney. The first, at 1 a.m., records 54°F. No wind.

1904 First ore
A Norwegian steamer, the first ore steamer for the Nova Scotia Steel and Coal Company, arrives in North Sydney from Wabana, Newfoundland, with 3,500 tons of iron ore.

1907 Comfort of a cigar
An ad in the *Post* suggests that

> *Old Age is Often*
> *Solaced By a*
> *Comforting Smoke*
> The rich, full flavor
> of a
> LORD TENNYSON
> Cigar
> **10 cents**
> is much appreciated
> by old smokers
>
> For 200 bands of any cigar manufactured,
> We will give a painting "Solitude"

1952 Memorial
The Alexander Graham Bell Park is opened by Mrs. Gilbert Grosvenor, daughter of the late Dr. Bell. The recreation centre on Kidston Island is on land owned by Mersey Paper Co., who turned it over to the Lions' Club of Baddeck for a park. The Bell museum opens August 18, 1956, and an expanded complex opens in 1978. The Museum "commemorates the humanitarian and scientific achievements of Alexander Graham Bell (1847 -1922) and his associates, Frederick W. Baldwin, Glen H. Curtis, John A. D. McCurdy and Thomas E. Selfridge."

1995 New CBRM
A new regional government is formed. The Cape Breton Regional Municipality (CBRM) combines eight local municipalities: Sydney, North Sydney, Sydney Mines, Glace Bay, New Waterford, Dominion, Louisbourg and Cape Breton County.

2002 Sydney, Australia?
Two 19-year-olds from London, England arrive at Sydney, Nova Scotia airport instead of their planned destination of Sydney, Australia. They have purchased their tickets over the Internet. They are befriended by Air Canada Jazz representative Angela Batten. Thursday (August 2) they are escorted around various tourist sites by a representative from the *Cape Breton Post*, and later that evening are handed the key to the municipality in a ceremony before a holiday crowd watching "Rock the Dock" on the Sydney waterfront. Emma Nunn

and Raeoul Sebastian find their story is featured in England and Australia. More than a hundred media phone calls are received. They also get free tickets to return next summer.

2003 Thirsty golfers
Because of health risks water coolers are being removed from Cape Breton golf courses.

August 2

1831 Horse haulage
Coal production has increased. Coal was shipped from Sydney Mines in July in 5 brigs, 11 schooners and 14 coasters. Horses are now being used to haul the coal from the Mines to the new wharf at the nearby harbour at North Sydney. The horses pull the coal cars up a grade, then ride down the grade to the wharf in a car at the back. The process is reversed coming back, but the horses always get a ride part way.

1904 Lit up
The first electric lights in Sydney Mines illuminate the streets tonight. Tomorrow night, houses and stores will be lit and, in the near future, an arc light will be placed at Thompson's Corner where the traffic is quite heavy.

1930 Fires
Forest fires in the Margaree area destroy about 300 acres of valuable timberland. What began as a brush fire accidentally started by blueberry pickers, quickly gets out of control. On the other side of the Island, forest fires threaten No. 11 Colliery and homes in the Reserve area.

2003 Donkin firefighters
Donkin Volunteer Fire Department celebrates 100 years of protecting the community. The department was formed when Dominion No. 6 Colliery was opened by the Dominion Coal Company in 1903.

August 3

1802 Early arrivals
The ship *Northern Friends* arrives in Sydney with 299 Highland immigrants from Scotland. They have arrived too late to plant any crops and they have to be given relief by the Executive Council to get them through their first winter.

These Scots arrive in Sydney, but most immigrants simply land anywhere on the Island, some arbitrarily put ashore by ships' captains. They come directly from Scotland or via PEI and Nova Scotia. Without much money and lacking proper supplies, they are confronted by unfamiliar thick forests and suffer extreme hardships. Small numbers of Scots started arriving in the early 1790s to settle along the western shore, spreading as far as Margaree. A few go further inland, like Donald Og MacNeil, who had seen the land he wanted (at Iona) when he travelled through the Bras d'Or as a British soldier fighting in the Second Siege of Louisbourg.

By 1827, larger numbers of immigrants pour into Cape Breton. Many are sick with smallpox, measles and dysentery. Much of the front lands are taken and land acquisition is confused. Immigrants start settling the backlands while squatters roam the Island. In February 1829, Judge Marshall reports to the government in Halifax that 2,300 immigrants have arrived in Sydney during the past year. The Relief Fund is rationed out, but still there is extreme suffering. There is a danger of running out of all supplies before Sydney Harbour is opened to navigation in the spring. Some relief is provided, and Judge Marshall suggests cheaper PEI potatoes be purchased to supply seed potatoes and needed food, as well as oatmeal which the Scots prefer to Indian cornmeal.

The settlers farther from Sydney are unable to get any of this relief. In the spring of 1834, for example, in one settlement in the backlands of Baddeck, there are 40 families, and 130 of the 170 are children. They might get one meal of poor-quality potatoes a day. There is much sickness and diarrhea. Parents try to have the children sleep more so they won't be so hungry.

By 1838 about 10,000 Scottish emigrants have taken the *aiseag mhor*, the (big ferry), ocean crossing to Cape Breton. Repeated crop failures add to the settlers' hardships and, in 1850, Rev. Norman McLeod decides to leave Cape Breton with a shipload of settlers for Australia.

1936 Richmond County sees the light

Electric power starts in St. Peter's this week. Richmond County has been the only county in Nova Scotia without such a service.

1960 Johnstown church

The 100th anniversary of the Johnstown Sacred Heart Church is celebrated. Originally, spiritual needs were ministered by missionaries on occasional visits. But these missionaries didn't speak Gaelic, the only language the settlers spoke. It wasn't until local people trained as priests that Gaelic speaking priests became available.

The church's treasure is a French altar brought from France in 1691 for use at Port Toulouse (St. Peter's). The French hid it in the woods when the English captured Port Toulouse, but the Indians later found it and for many years it was used in Indian churches.

1979 World Snipe Championship

August 3-20, the World Snipe Championship is held in North Sydney.

2003 Novelists honoured guests

At Mabou's Strathspey Place Ceilidh, novelists Beatrice MacNeil and Alistair MacLeod are honoured guests. Beatrice's novel Butterflies Dance in the Dark, now in its second printing, is a Canadian bestseller. In March, Book Television came to Beatrice's home in East Bay and then on to Lower L'Ardoise where she grew up. The novel is chosen for a Atlantic Fiction course at McGill in Montreal and is selected for the summer reading series on CBC's *Cross Country Check-Up*. Alistair remembers the previous year when the audience acknowledged his recent winning of the International IMPAC Dublin Literary Award, "the richest literary award on the globe," for his novel *No Great Mischief*.

August 4

1833 CAPE BRETON

The steam vessel *Cape Breton* arrives at North Sydney with a load of pig iron, machinery and rolled rails of the "fish belly" type to replace the old rails of the tracks for the Sydney Mines train tracks. The *Cape Breton* arrives in Sydney Harbour after leaving Plymouth, England, some 44 days ago. This is 14 days before the *Royal William* departs Pictou on her voyage, which has always been celebrated as being the historic "first across the Atlantic." The *Cape Breton* is the first steamship to cross the Atlantic east to west and the first to or from Canada. It isn't until 1963 that this truth is discovered.

The ship is built by the General Mining Association for services in the company's coal mining operations. Samuel Cunard works for the GMA and is responsible for the management of the company's coal leases in Nova Scotia. Soon the ship will be purchased by the Cunard family and will therefore become the first in their long line of distinguished transatlantic steamships.

1874 "THICKEN WITH FLOUR"

Barrels of flour are released from a sinking ship off Cape Rouge this summer. Many Cheticamp residents rescue three or four barrels, but Martin Deveau finds thirty-eight barrels. During the storm, some of the other barrels break open and the flour spills out into the water, mixing with it and thickening it, so that the stormy seas are calmed.

1904 *INVERNESS NEWS*

Published by A. S. MacAdam, the first issue of the weekly *Inverness News* sells for two cents. It boasts of Inverness's prosperity, and features the Hussey family coal enterprise at Broad Cove.

1916 THE SIXTH ARE FIRST - 732ND DAY OF WAR

About five thousand Cape Bretoners have enlisted in the past two years. Several complete units have enlisted here including the 6th, the only complete unit from the Maritimes to sail with the first contingent from Canada. (See also August 28, 1914.)

1962 SETTLERS FROM BARRA

The First Highland Village Day is held at Hector's Point, Iona, Organizers hope the event will draw attention to the proposed Highland Village Museum, depicting life of the Highland Scots in Cape Breton. The Village will include a carding mill, forge, country store, school, a log cabin and other types of homes built by the residents' Scottish ancestors from Barra.

August 5

1789 ONE POINT OF VIEW

One visitor to Sydney certainly doesn't like the town. "Sydney can never prove of any very essential service to the Empire at large, as its harbour is impenetrably shut up with ice and inaccessible to the whole world for at least seven months of the year. What they dignify with the name of a town consists of about 50 hovels and stands twelve miles from the entrance of

Spanish Bay. [T]here appears here and there a few attempts to form settlements but as far as I can judge they do not seem likely to succeed. [I]n Sydney itself, there is not the smallest trace of industry as the habitants live by selling rum to the soldiers, and were they withdrawn—which God Almighty soon grant—it would be instantly deserted."

2003 Caribbean festival

The Whitney Pier Caribbean festival celebrates its 20th anniversary with the best of West Indian culture, food and music. The festival is a major fundraiser for St. Philip's, the local African Orthodox Church. The 83-year-old church was one of the Steel Corporation's buildings in the 1920s. Rev. Vincent Waterman is retiring as archbishop and his wife Isobel, daughter of the former minister Father Francis, is a key organizer of the event.

August 6

1736 Bet on anything

A baby girl is born in Louisbourg to Marie Catherine Auge, wife of an ex-officer, now a stonecutter. In addition to the baby, she wins a pair of shoes from a wager on the sex of the child made earlier with a navigator on a visiting ship. She, like so many others in Louisbourg, has been caught up in the very real passion for gambling.

1905 Fashion

Fashion news reports that some very smart women are wearing low, dark brown shoes in the forenoon. Parasols, with short wooden or hinged sticks, are also in fashion.

1936 Record swordfish catch

The first broadbill swordfish exceeding 600 lbs (601 lbs) hooked in North American waters is caught by Michael Lerner of New York in a four-hour battle off Louisbourg.

2003 Cows escape

During a severe thunderstorm a stream washes out a fence and seventeen Highland cows escape from their summer pasture in Millville. Their owner, Charles MacDonald of Charrick Celtic farm of Point Edward, family, friends as well as Air Search & Rescue, who use the search as a training exercise, try to capture the cows. Six are recovered quickly, but ten, spooked by the storm, and perhaps by ATVs and coyotes, take to the woods. They remain very hard to herd. One is killed b a transport truck on Highway 105. One breaks its leg and has to put down. The last cow isn't corralled until two months later on a farm in Groves Point, about three miles from the break-out site.

August 7

1843 Kennel coal

Mr. Dodd of Sydney has a beautiful specimen of Kennel coal that he plans to send to England. The smooth, finely grained specimen is about two feet long by six inches wide by four inches deep.

1883 Labourers Wanted

LABOURERS WANTED
Forty Men Wanted Immediately
to work on the Railroad
at the Victoria Mines near Sydney.
Wages to good men
One Dollar and ten cents per day
Alex Beaton Contractor

1932 Family tradition

Peter J. MacKay of Scotsville starts delivering the mail with a horse and wagon and continues a tradition started by his grandfather Hector "The Post" MacKay. Hector was the first man to carry the mail on foot from Whycocomagh to Margaree. That's a distance of more than forty miles. In 1983, Peter J. is still driving that distance over his route. The mail has been delivered by MacKays for sixty-five years.

1957 Centennial

The Centennial of St. Margaret's Church, Broad Cove, is celebrated with the first Broad Cove Concert.

1967 Museum is opened

Dame Flora MacLeod formally opens the 29th Annual Gaelic Mod and unveils a plaque on the front of the new Giant MacAskill Highland Pioneer Museum. Mrs. William Matheson of Glen Tosh, the only surviving niece of Angus MacAskill, cuts the tartan ribbon across the entrance and the museum is opened.

August 8

1750 First observatory

Joseph-Bernard Cabert de Cogolin, a French naval officer and astronomer commissioned to correct the maps of the coasts of Cape Breton, Nova Scotia and Newfoundland, arrives in Louisbourg. He has brought with him eight telescopes, globes of the earth, maps of the stars and an octant. He needs an observatory, and he has an enclosed wooden cabin built on the southern flank of the King's Bastion, so he can work in all weather. This is Canada's first observatory. After he leaves for France in September 1751, the observatory continues to be used and is recognized by the French Royal Academy of Sciences as a centre for astronomy in New France.

1863 Giant MacAskill

Angus MacAskill, the Giant of Cape Breton, dies today and is buried at Englishtown. He was born in 1828 on the Island of Lewis, Scotland, one of thirteen children.

When Angus was a small child, his parents left the Hebrides for Cape Breton. Although his parents and his brothers and sisters were normal size, Angus is reported to have been 7 feet, 9 inches tall when mature and to have weighed 425 pounds, yet he was perfectly proportioned. In addition to his strength and size he was noted for his good humour and generally amiable disposition. Because of hard economic times, Angus left Cape Breton in 1848 (a year when the potato harvest failed on the Island) and toured Canada, the United States, Europe and the West Indies delighting thousands with his feats of strength. He met with Queen Victoria who presented him with two gold rings.

Because of his strength, there were often wagers about his lifting ability and while in New York, one story goes, there were bets that he could not lift a 2,700-lb. anchor. He set the anchor on his shoulders and walked with it, but as he set it down, one of the flukes slashed across his body, resulting in internal injuries which kept him from ever again standing erect. He returned to Englishtown and set up in business with a store and a gristmill.

1918 Victoria Cross - 1,466th day of war

Private John B. Croak of Glace Bay, serving with the 13th Battalion, Royal Highlanders of Canada, is killed in action in the Battle of Amiens. His citation for bravery reads, "Having attacked and captured a machine gun nest single handed, Croak, though badly wounded, later charged another German strongpoint and with the aid of other members of his platoon, silenced three machine guns, bayoneting or capturing their crews. Wounded a second, time he died just after the last resistance was overcome." Private John Croak is posthumously awarded the Victoria Cross

Fig. 8.7 John Bernard Croak, VC, 1918.

1900 Westmount

Public Notice: "The West Side Sydney River will hereafter be known as Westmount—a very appropriate name. The Sydney Ferryboats will call at Westmount three times a day during the remainder of the season."

2003 New park

Louisbourg Royal Canadian Legion members turn an old skating rink, acquired in 2001, into a Veterans Memorial Park.

August 9

1750 Early Acadians

One-hundred-and-thirty-six Acadians settle at La Pointe a la Jeunesse (Grand Narrows). But the settlement doesn't last long. Most of the stock starves to death over the winter, and stones in the soil make tilling difficult. By the next year the Acadians are ready to leave.

1906 New town

The town of Dominion is founded.

1970 Compensation demanded

Noel Doucette of Barra Head, the president of the Union of Nova Scotia Indians, reports that Nova Scotia Indians want compensation for the loss of their lands, or grants of additional land instead.

2002 Sewage
Three levels of government announce multi-million ($8 million) sewage treatment plant to be constructed near Battery Point in Sydney.

2003 Peacekeepers
In a ceremony in front of Sydney's Civic Centre, Cape Breton peacekeepers and their fallen comrades are remembered. More than five hundred Cape Bretoners have served as UN peacekeepers.

August 10

1853 Arichat Academy reopens
Bishop Colin MacKinnon has long encouraged education in his diocese at Arichat, even teaching the advanced pupils himself. Today he reopens Arichat Academy and he has "procured the services of clerical gentlemen—the most eminent scholars in his Dioces— to take charge." Arichat Academy, originally opened in 1833 by Father John Chisholm, has been closed for some years now. One of Bishop MacKinnon's teachers, Malcolm MacLellan, had taught at Cape Breton's first institution of higher learning. "The College," as it was known, was established at East Bay by Rev. William MacLeod in 1825, trained students in the Classics and prepared them for studies in Theology. In 1855, the Church moves the Academy, now St. Francis Xavier University, to Antigonish, where the Bishop's family lives. Cape Bretoners have to wait until January, 1952 for the return of a college to the Island. (See also January 16, 1952 and June 28, 1974.)

1890 Angus L.
Angus L. Macdonald is born in Dunvegan. He becomes Premier of Nova Scotia from 1933 to 1940 and again from 1945 to his death April 13, 1954. During the War, he is Federal Minister of Naval Affairs. A cairn in his memory quotes Justin Daly, "Angus L. has all the characteristics of a Cape Bretoner. Vigor, courage, sincerity, and a splendid personal charm."

1930 Run aground
All passengers and crew on the Newfoundland Railway Company's steamer *Caribou* are transferred ashore. They took to the lifeboats when the steamer ran aground three miles outside Port aux Basques on the regular run from North Sydney.

1955 Record edition
The *Sydney Post Record* today publishes the biggest newspaper in the history of publishing in the Maritimes. This special edition, marking the formal opening of the Canso Causeway on Saturday, weighs almost two pounds and has 120 pages.

August 11

1947 Massive fire
Fire in Pleasant Bay destroys the village. In eleven days, the fire consumes several thousands of acres of woodland. It is 1976 before the scars of the damage are covered.

2003 Long paddle

Sixty-one-year-old Peter Quade of Blacketts Lake paddles a 5-metre kayak through turbulent waters from Bay St Lawrence to Grand Bay Newfoundland in around 20 hours.

2004 Top statistician

Point Edward native, Dr. Michael Newton, is awarded the prestigious Presidents' Award for 2004, given to the world's top statistician under the age of 40. The presidents of the American Statistical Society, the Biometric Society, the Institute of Mathematical Statistics and the Statistical Society of Canada give their Award annually. The award is given in this case for "ingenious and wide-ranging contribution to statistical theory and methodology, including Bayesian inference, the bootstrap, and tree reconstructions for applications of statistical methodology, especially in genetics and genomics and for outstanding training of graduate students." Michael Newton is a graduate of Riverview Rural High School, Dalhousie University and the University of Washington. He is a professor of statistics and of biometrics and medical informatics at the University of Wisconsin.

August 12

1869 Merrier party never witnessed

Fig. 8.8 St. Peter's Canal, 1886.

Many years ago, Bishop Plessis suggested that it would take a regiment about four weeks to dig across the narrow isthmus and clear a canal from the Bras d'Or lakes to St. Peter's Bay. The canal, started in 1854, has taken fifteen years of blasting, drilling and digging to get a 100-foot wide cut through a solid granite hill 60 feet high. With the opening of the Canal today, the trade which has formerly come to Arichat, is diverted through to Sydney Harbour.

Formal ceremonies of the opening take place at noon. A thousand people on the shore cheer as the drawbridge is swung back, and a flag-bedecked schooner with about 200 people on board, towed by a tugboat, passes through from the Bras d'Or to St. Peter's Bay. After an hour, the schooner returns to the Canal and passes through to the Lakes again, where she cruises around the islands. "Refreshments were provided on board, and a merrier party I never witnessed," remarks one guest. After lunch some guests go sailing, driving, rowing or fishing before attending Mr. Purcell's evening party at the St. Peters Hotel, where they dance until daylight.

1978 Les Trois Pignons

Les Trois Pignons (The Three Gables) officially opens in Cheticamp on the Feast of the Assumption of the Virgin Mary, an Acadian holiday. Les Trois Pignons will serve as a focus for Acadian traditions and as a cultural and information centre. It was built by La Societe St. Pierre, formed in 1947 to preserve Acadian culture.

2003 (Chapel Island) Potlotek

Chapel Island, Cape Breton's smallest First Nations' community, is designated a place of national significance. Now known as Potlotek, Chapel Island, contains burial sites dating back hundreds of years and, since the mid-18th century, when the French first erected a Catholic church here, it has been an important centre of the Roman Catholic faith for the Mi'kmaq and the location of an annual historical pilgrimage celebrating the Feast of St. Anne in late July. (See also July 26, 1750; November 28, 1792.)

Fig. 8.9 St. Anne's Mission, Chapel Island, 31-Jul-94. Raytel Photography.

August 13

1955 Causeway opens

At 2:25 this afternoon, Trade Minister C. D. Howe slashes a tartan ribbon with a claymore used at the Battle of Culloden. A salute is fired by the Royal Canadian Navy and Air Force and a lament to the late Angus L. Macdonald, who spearheaded the drive for causeway construction, precedes the historic march across the causeway. Leaving his place at the head of the procession empty, Angus L.'s widow, kilted Lt.-Governor Alistair Fraser and his wife, CNR president Donald Gordon and Trade Minister Howe, carrying crook-shaped *cromaks*, lead the dignitaries, 25 lines of pipers and 40,000 people, the largest crowd to ever congregate here, across the mile-long causeway.

The causeway is the deepest in the world and the result of hundreds of people pooling their talents in a campaign that dates back to 1880. The lock is the largest in Canada. The concrete used would make a solid sidewalk 4 feet wide by 4 inches thick from Sydney to Halifax. The rock that filled the roadway is equal to that of the great Pyramid of Cheops with one of the smaller pyramids added.

August 14

1830 First Steamboat
The *Richard Smith*, believed to be the first steamboat into Sydney Harbour, arrives with miners on board amid cheers and a 13-gun salute.

1914 Sydney Battery to war
The 17th Sydney Field Battery is accepted as part of the 2nd Brigade of Artillery, soon to be sent overseas. Only a few units have been so honoured. Mobilization begins tomorrow. War service drill follows with the soldiers leaving next week for Quebec.

On August 2, 1914, two days before Britain declared war on Germany. Canada offered troops to Britain. Her offer was accepted on August 6th.

1940 First convoy
There are 92 ships in Sydney Harbour. SCl, the first of the Sydney-Clyde convoys, with forty ships, sails into the Atlantic for England.

August 15

1903 Filles de Jesus
A group of Filles de Jesus (Daughters of Jesus) arrives in Cheticamp. Their new convent, constructed by Father Fiset, is almost ready.

1922 Miners against besco
Cape Breton miners go on strike against the British Empire Steel and Coal Company (BESCO). Late in 1920, a yearly contract was signed that provided for wage increases. But this January, BESCO tried to reduce wages by 35 per cent.

Against arguments of "returned soldiers" who believe that the presence of troops aggravates matters, Federal troops are brought to Glace Bay to quell any disturbances. A wage settlement is reached August 26th. With provincial police and federal troops aligned with BESCO, the miners return to work. (See also June 28, 1923 and June 11, 1925.)

1931 Finest Rails
I. C. Mackie, chief of DOSCO's metallurgical department, has improved the process of producing rails, creating rails free of "shatter cracks." He believes the steel plant is now manufacturing the "finest rails" in North America.

1939 Arichat celebrates
Arichat celebrates the Golden Jubilee of Rev. A. E. Mombourquette and the 100th anniversary of Our Lady of Assumption. In 1844, the decision was made to divide the diocese of Halifax, and Arichat was chosen as the centre of the new See. During the next forty years it was used as a cathedral by three bishops. In 1886, the seat of the diocese was changed to Antigonish.

1983 Elizabeth LeFort

The Elizabeth LeFort Gallery officially opens in Cheticamp as an extension of Les Trois Pignons. Elizabeth LeFort has transformed the craft of rug hooking into an art. Some of her tapestries hang in Buckingham Palace, the White House, the National Museum of Man in Ottawa and in the Vatican. She begins by drawing a design on burlap, and then she dyes the wool, using as many as 20 shades in a face. Elizabeth LeFort can hook 55 stitches a minute, making 3,300 an hour.

In 1961 La Societe St. Pierre obtained a gallery to display her tapestries, but her collection has expanded to over three hundred and these, plus other hooked rugs of Cheticamp artists, are now in the new extension.

1997 Bras d'Or Stewardship Society

The Bras d'Or Stewardship Society is incorporated as a public non-profit corporation. Its main objectives are to "Protect, Conserve and Restore the Bras d'Or Lakes." Operating costs are not dependent on government funding, but on individual membership and other private sources. They get legislation in place to make the dumping of raw sewage into the Lakes illegal and are instrumental in getting a new sewage system in place for the village of Baddeck.

2003 Facelift

A program to enhance the storefronts of downtown businesses in CBRM has begun.

New Waterford has its own slant on the renovations. It hopes the murals on its building fronts will make it the largest mural community in Atlantic Canada. So far, sixteen murals are in place with a further five expected to be finished soon. Subjects include the history of the community, a Canadian naval vessel HMS *New Waterford*, classic cars, the Men of the Deeps. The "crown jewel in the downtown area" is the Rose Schwartz Memorial Park. The family is turning the land where her store once stood over to the community to be used as a park, in honour of the family matriarch, one of the community's most well-known citizens. A pond area will have an artificial ice surface for skating in the winter. A bandshell pavilion is also planned.

August 16

1858 Burning up the wires

Queen Victoria and American president Buchanan exchange greetings by transatlantic cable, via Cape Breton.

The telegraph fleet met mid-ocean on July 28 but the splice parted, and it wasn't until today that the first greeting crossed. The message didn't exactly burn up the wires. The Queen's message started at 10:50 a.m. August 16 and is completed 17 hours and 40 minutes later at 4:30 a.m. August 17. The message is 99 words with 509 letters, averaging two minutes for each letter and ten minutes for each word.

In 1935 the permalloy duplex cables allow 1,400 letters a minute each way, or 3,000 letters a minute combined.

1905 Howling mob

The Westward "Harvest Train" leaves Sydney. About six hundred men going west for work are on the train by the time it departs New Glasgow. The car with ladies in it, is cleaner and quieter than the others which are "filled with a howling, swearing, singing mob. Drunken fiddlers squeaked for dear life with drunken tunes on drunken fiddles, while drunken dancers danced to the drunken music. The air was foul in the extreme and filled with the odour of stale tobacco smoke."

Changing to the special "Harvest Train" at Saint John, an average of sixty-five people are crammed like cattle into each of the eleven cars. There is one lavatory in each car and one small tank of ice water and one with water for washing and cooking. The cars, with the exception of one with the other passengers, is cleaned out once on the five-to-seven-day trip to the wheatfields. Cape Bretoners, "wild men from the Far East," are known for their brawling, although they are blamed for a lot of damage they probably don't do.

Strong, hardworking Cape Bretoners flock to the west to help with the harvest from the 1890's until the Depression and drought out west bring an end to the annual harvest excursions.

August 17

1873 Enthusiastic tourist

American author Charles Dudley Warner becomes a most enthusiastic visitor to Cape Breton. His book *Baddeck, and That Sort of Thing*, originally published in monthly magazine instalments, is instrumental in encouraging other summer visitors.

"We stopped at the door of a very unhotel-like appearing hotel. It had in front a flower garden; it was blazing with welcome lights; it opened hospitable doors, and we were received by a family who expected us. The house was a large one, for two guests; and we enjoyed the luxury of spacious rooms, an abundant supper, and a friendly welcome; and, in short, found ourselves at home....

(Outside) The scene was enchanting. And we respected then the heretofore seemingly insane impulse that had driven us to Baddeck."

1927 Harbour swim

Thousands of spectators gather on shore, in boats and aboard the *Aspy* and the *Lakeview*, to watch the annual Sydney Harbour swim for the Dave Epstein trophy. They cheer as sixteen-year old Warren Anderson comes in the only finisher of the five-mile swim. A 20-mile-an-hour Northwest wind blows in the swimmers' faces and causes twnety-nine of the original starters to quit after the first mile. Of the seven girls who enter, two last until they reach Point Edward.

August 18

1928 Doctor C. L.

Dr. C. Lamont MacMillan begins work in Baddeck as the medical practitioner for an area that extends from Smokey to Iona—and frequently beyond. Born in 1903 in Guysborough County, he had graduated in May 1928 from Dalhousie University and for a short while practiced in Lunenburg County. Dr. C. L. decides to move to Baddeck following the death there of Dr. Dan MacAulay. He becomes widely known and respected throughout the region. Travelling at all hours, in extremes of weather and frequently under primitive conditions, he delivers babies, helps the injured and the sick for forty years. He becomes a member of the legislative Assembly in 1942 and continues as an MLA until 1967. In 1972s he is elected to the Order of Canada and in 1975 will publish his life story *Memoirs of a Cape Breton Doctor*.

1935 Record high

Weatherman Rollie Richards, taking observations at his home on St. Peters Road, Sydney, records a high for any year: 36.7 C or about 98.5° F.

1937 Grand Chief honoured

Grand Chief Gabriel Sylliboy, elected chief of the Micmacs of all Nova Scotia, is congratulated by the Director of Indian Affairs on receiving the King's Coronation Medal. (See also Oct. 7, 1947.)

1982 4-H'ers Celebrate

4-H'ers in Cape Breton celebrate their 60th anniversary at their 4-H Day at the Cape Breton Farmers' Exhibition at North Sydney. Clubs in Cape Breton started in Cape Breton County and Inverness in the early part of 1924, in Victoria County in 1929 and in Richmond County in the early 30s.

August 19

1824 Early Baptism

Reverend John MacLennan, the first Presbyterian minister to visit Baddeck, baptizes eight children in the first of four visits to Cape Breton.

1918 Liberated women - 1,477th day of war

The War has opened up many new industries to women. Here on Cape Breton, fourteen young women are employed by Dr. Bell at his boat-building plant at Baddeck. The best of food is provided for them at their well-furnished camp. They wear khaki uniforms, riding breeches and coat, with puttees and brown shoes.

Fig. 8.10 Female boat builders, Beinn Bhraighe, 1917-18.

1927 British PM visits

British Prime Minister Stanley Baldwin briefly visits North Sydney, concluding his cross-Canada tour during our Diamond Jubilee Celebrations. He boards the CPR liner SS *Empress of Scotland,* the largest ship ever to enter Sydney Harbour, brought here from Quebec by Capt. Everett Cann of North Sydney.

1991 Champs again
The Glace Bay Kentucky Fried Chicken Colonels win a championship game in Victoria, BC, and are the National Little League Champions for the third time. They won in 1987 and in 1988.

August 20

1971 First legal police strike
The first legal police strike in Canada takes place in Sydney and there is some disorder when police leave the streets. Thirteen years later, in September 1984, the police strike again. This time there are no noticeable disorders—the Mounties are on the streets immediately following the police walkout.

1981 Cream shipped again
A farmer with ten cows in River Denys is shipping cream to the mainland. It's been more than seven years since the last cream was shipped, then from Margaree, to be processed at Eastern Dairyfoods. In 1960, Nova Scotia had some 8,000 farms producing cream. The number went down to 300, with none from Cape Breton.

August 21

1856 The wrestling doctor
Dr. Hugh (Hoodie) MacDonald is born at Lake Ainslie. At twenty-two years, he will win every event at the Highland Games at Princeville. In Truro, he will later win the light hammer throw, come second in the heavy hammer throw, comesecond in the running high jump and win first prize in Gaelic singing.

In Halifax as a medical student, he issues a challenge (August 16, 1881) to Thomas F. Lynch, the Irish Champion athlete, who comes up from Boston to wrestle. Winning two of the three events, Hugh MacDonald becomes the wrestling champ of North America. Dr. MacDonald serves as surgeon during the construction of the Point Tupper-Grand Narrows section of the Intercolonial Railway, which begins in the fall of 1887 and practises in Whycocomagh for forty-eight years until his death in 1940.

August 22

1966 Exhibition
Today marks a new early opening date for the 50th annual Cape Breton County Exhibition. Admission is adults: 75 cents; children: 35 cents. Entertainment features include the Bill Lynch Shows, Rockin' Saints and the Go-Go girls, the MacDougall Girls' Pipe Band, Trainor Donovan and his Radio Ranch Boys, and Bernie and Ruth MacLean. All this and agricultural displays.

2003 Olympic try

Twenty-five-year-old yachtsman Mark Coakly of Baddeck and his teammate Eric Holden of Vancouver have arrived in Athens, Greece, to take part in today's pre-Olympic regatta sailing challenge. It's the test event for the Olympic Games. All 20 boats entered from around the world had to qualify to compete. The top 16 countries to qualify will be in the Olympics.

August 23

1705 Boularderie born

Antoine Le Poupet de la Boularderie is born in Port Royal. He will be a page in the household of the Duchess of Orleans until he is 19 years old. Antoine arrives at his father's concession at Ile Verderonne (Boularderie Island) in July, 1737, and a year later, after his father dies, Antoine discovers the property rights are not clear and there are a great number of debts.

Within a few years, he is growing wheat and has a large garden and orchard. He also has a dairy, a stable, a dovecote, a windmill, and a watermill to grind his corn. He is officially given command of his father's concession as well as those at Niganiche (Ingonish).

In 1745, New Englanders attack Louisbourg. Antoine is wounded and taken prisoner, eventually being sent to Boston. A model prisoner, he is put in charge of taking other French prisoners back to France. His property on Cape Breton is destroyed by the British. After the war, he is destitute, but he still tries to get funds to rebuild. The farming enterprise of the Boularderies doesn't come up to their expectations. It is never large enough to supply Louisbourg. (See also February 15, 1719.)

1914 Church parade

Catholic soldiers attended church services this morning. This afternoon, others in the 17th Battery take part in a parade to the old garrison church of St. George's. The last time such a church parade was held, was sixty years ago in 1854, when a regiment of soldiers stationed in Sydney paraded before they left for the Crimean War. After the service, the men parade back to the field where, after the singing of "God Save the Prince of Wales" and the National Anthem, they read the Army law, under which every unit in active service is governed.

1930 Big raid

Three booze joints are raided in the first seizure of liquor to be made at North Sydney since the New Act came into effect. All the police can find at the Queen Hotel is an empty pitcher that smells of liquor.

1934 MacLeans of Washabuck

A tablet is unveiled at Lower Washabuck commemorating Lachlan MacLean, the progenitor of the clan and the first of his line to settle in Cape Breton, by his oldest surviving granddaughter, 84 year old Mrs. George MacNeil of Baddeck.

August 24

1745 "Darling of the nation"

Comments of Lord Chesterfield, the future Secretary of State for Britain, on Cape Breton: "One almost insurmountable difficulty I forsee in any negotiation with France, is our new acquisition of Cape Breton, which is become the darling object of the whole nation, it is ten times more so than even Gibralter was, and the people are laying in their claims, and protesting against the restitution of it upon any account. But, on the other hand, I forsee the impossibility of keeping it."

1821 Rankinville Road

Fifty-three residents of Mabou and Port Hood gather to sign a petition requesting that Rev. William Miller be appointed as their minister. In 1981, in the Pioneer Cemetery on the Rankinville Road, the Mabou and Port Hood Presbyterian (now United) Church celebrates its 160th anniversary.

1873 August gale

A Sunday; the day of the "Great Gale." A savage two-day storm hits Cape Breton, other counties of Eastem Nova Scotia, Prince Edward Island and northern New Brunswick. Many people are killed, an uncounted number of houses and barns are smashed, livestock drowned and fishing boats flung ashore. Many vessels at Cow Bay are blown ashore and among those drowned is Capt. Leonard of Main-a-Dieu. Bodies are washed ashore for days afterwards. All hands are lost on the schooner *Eureka*, sunk off Boularderie Light. The steamer *Saltwell,* 1,160 tons out of Liverpool, England is smashed on the shoals of Scaterie, and many of the crew drowned.

The schooner *Commissioner*, 399 tons, just started on her maiden voyage from Pictou to Bermuda, is never heard from again. The Arichat schooner *Good Intent*, one of the many that are lost, will be found bottom-up off Port Hood several days later. This storm is believed to have been the greatest natural disaster to hit Cape Breton. It is said that over 1,000 seamen never returned home and on Isle Madame alone, the heads of 68 families drown.

August 25

1752 Loud day

Louisbourg residents celebrate the annual Fete de Saint Louis, the day set aside to honour King Louis IX, who died on this day in 1270 from the plague. A strong, fair ruler, he was canonized in 1297. Five separate sets of salutes are fired throughout the day from the Batterie de la Piece de la Grave on the waterfront. Twenty guns announce the feast day at dawn. Later other salutes are fired: 21 guns for the health of Louis XV, 19 guns for the health of the Queen and 17 guns for the health of the entire royal family. During the Te Deum service, a final 21-gun salute is fired. It's a day of relaxation, ending with a special evening bonfire.

1900 Letter to the editor

"Sir – I want to call the attention of the Board of Health to the unsanitary condition which exists at the corner of Great George and Wentworth Streets. Coming from a neighbouring yard and oozing across the sidewalk is a stream of sewerage water unutterably filthy, greenish and slimy. It is disgusting to the eye and a menace to the public health. A sense of decency and cleanliness at least should move residents themselves to prevent this sort of thing."

1931 Road builders

One thousand men find relief from unemployment, and over $500,000 is expended on the reconstruction of 39 miles of provincial highways in Cape Breton and Richmond counties. The Trans Canada Highway will be constructed through St. Peter's to Glace Bay, even though residents of the central route advocate the highway leave the Strait and follow the Victoria Trail through Whycocomagh and Grand Narrows to Sydney.

1969 Arichat musician wins

Cornelia Boucher of Arichat wins both the Canadian and North American College Music titles over more than 10,000 finalists from 1,000 colleges and universities, at the CNE in Toronto. Accompanying herself on guitar, she sings the popular song, "The Beat Goes On," as well as two of her own French songs.

August 26

1725 *Le Chameau* sinks

Early this morning, *Le Chameau* (The Camel), carrying 216 passengers and said to be the fastest ship in the French Navy, sinks off Louisbourg, after striking a reef last night. *Le Chameau* is on her way to Louisbourg to land the newly appointed Governor, Mesuier de Loges, son of the Governor of Montreal. Also on board are senior military and civil commanders, distinguished clergy and 82,000 livres of gold and silver from the Royal Treasury to pay the troops at Quebec. (See also September 19, 1965 and April 4, 1966.)

1793 Surf and turf

Gov. Macarmick reports that the shipbuilding industry in Cape Breton ranks behind fishing and the coal mines but is growing. More than 160 Cape Breton-built boats are now at sea. Baddeck has built five vessels, Port Hood twenty. The Sydney, Cheticamp and Margaree areas are also boat building. The Isle Madame area alone has accounted for 110 boats.

Agriculture is also expanding: 1,766 black cattle, 565 sheep and 95 horses are around the Island, mainly at Isle Madame, Cheticamp, Port Hood and Louisbourg. The Sydney region has 288 black cattle. Small numbers of sheep and oxen are being exported to Newfoundland.

August 27

1621 Codfish = goldfish

Faced with up to 145 meatless days a year, Catholics eat a lot of fish. Codfish are "gold" fish and many European fleets flock to the Grand Banks every summer. Spanish Bay (Sydney Harbour) is especially busy. Each week the so-called "Admiral" of the port retires and at every changeover, the official gives a party. Wine flows, and castanets and guitars accompany singing, dancing and piping. Water sports frequently end the season. These weekly fishermen's parties precede Champlain's Order of Good Cheer.

1798 Eight-year-old banned from taverns

Michael Todd of Sydney, eight years, eleven months old, is formally apprenticed for twelve years to John Muggah, a carpenter and joiner in Sydney. During this period, Michael agrees (John Meloney, Richard Dobbin and Registrar D. McKinnon witnessing) to obey his Master's commands lawfully, not waste his Master's food, not absent himself nor haunt alehouses, taverns or playhouses. He shall not play at cards, dice or any unlawful game. Nor shall he contract matrimony nor commit fornication. In exchange, the Master, John Muggah, will feed, house and clothe Michael and teach him in the trade and mystery of his profession.

1958 Brass band

The Donkin Citizens' Brass Band travels to Toronto to play for the Old Veterans' Club at Warriors' Day at the CNE Queen Elizabeth is in the audience. September first, the Band plays up Bay Street to the Toronto City Hall, and on September 2, the Band wins second place at the competition at the CNE.

Fig. 8.11 Seeing them off.

August 28

1914 Off to war

The 150 volunteers of the 17th Battery of Field Artillery are given a tremendous farewell as they leave for Valcartier, Quebec, before heading overseas. About 2,000 people from the Northside have come over by ferry, while thousands more have travelled by special tram service from Glace Bay. By 3 p.m. all the stores are closed, and more than ten thousand people line the streets. Flags are everywhere and the

Fig. 8.12 Soldiers off to training.

bands of Sydney, Sydney Mines and the 94th Regiment play "Auld Lang Syne," "Our Old Canadian Home" and "God Be With You Till We Meet Again" as the troop train, decorated with bunting, leaves.

1952 On the beach

The rocky beach at Rigby's Cove, New Waterford, is literally covered with huge bodies of squealing and blowing porpoises, left stranded after coming in on the afternoon tide.

1978 Hall of fame

Roddie MacDonald of New Waterford, light heavyweight champion of Canada, and the College of Cape Breton Capers Canadian College Athletic Association National Champs in hockey in 1978 are inducted into the Nova Scotia Sports Hall of Fame.

2001 Call centre

Stream International Call Centre employing nine hundred people recently opened in Glace Bay.

August 29

1899 Bright future

Henry B. Whitney, addressing citizens of Sydney in the old Temperance Hall, proclaims that "next summer those immediate structures which are to produce wealth and prosperity in your land will begin to rise rapidly before your eyes."

1901 Helen Keller visits Dr. Bell

Helen Keller and Alexander Graham Bell fly kites at Beinn Breagh in Baddeck. Dr. Bell has been experimenting with kites to learn about the techniques of flight. Helen Keller, when she was younger, was one of Bell's pupils.

1940 Guest children

The first British "guest children" arrive in Cape Breton. George and Doug Thompson and Robert Turnball remain in Sydney for the duration of the war.

1980 Injunction

Mr. Justice C. Denne Burchell of the Nova Scotia Supreme Court grants an interim injunction against the spraying of the herbicide 2,4-D in the Glengarry Valley area of Big Pond. An out-of-court settlement was reached March 13, 1981.

1932 Hasty landing

Capt. James A. (Jimmy) Mollison, a Scottish flyer, in his single engine Puss Moth *The Heart's Content* unexpectedly lands this afternoon on Cape Breton on his return flight to Ireland from New York. Running into a heavy electrical storm off the coast, he manages in the dense fog to land safely at the John Stewart farm in Coxheath. The plane is dismantled and taken to the Cape Breton Flying Field at Reserve. A month later Captain Mollison breaks all speed records for the eastward flight from New York to England via Harbour Grace, Newfoundland, in 19 hours, 59 minutes.

Mollison's bride is the former Amy Johnson, the famous aviatrix. Soon after, there are reports of Mollison family coolness and the cause is another flyer, the blonde Beryl Markham (see September 5, 1936), who also makes a hasty landing on Cape Breton. She is wearing Jimmy's wrist watch when she crash lands at Baleine. Mollison telegraphs his congratulations on her successful flight, concluding with "Thank God you saved my watch."

August 30

1813 First militia

A holiday atmosphere surrounds settlers and Indians as they gather to watch the first parade of the Cape Breton Militia in Sydney this month. This year has seen a reorganization of the Militia. With few exceptions, all males between the ages of 16 and 60, residing in and belonging to the Island must enlist. Each man will be supplied with a musket, and any officer on active duty found drunk or behaving contemptuously will be court-martialled and cashiered. Fines will be imposed on non-commissioned officers or privates who wilfully interrupt a company at drill, or who exchange or conceal militia arms and ammunitions.

1971 Honorary Chief

Micmac Grand Chief Donald Marshal of Sydney confers the honour of an honorary Micmac chief on Gov.-Gen. Roland Michener at celebrations at Port Royal Habitation.

August 31

1905 Good advertising

The founders ride in their Prowse and Crowell's Department Store entry in Sydney's summer parade. The department store, at 319 Charlotte Street, will last to become the oldest business establishment in downtown Sydney. The original type of department store, it not only features clothing, but also offers groceries and a wide range of the daily necessities for home and family.

Fig. 8.13 Good advertising, early 1900's. C. W. Kelly, Sydney.

First known as Prowse Brothers and Crowell, it opened in 1891 in the same block on Charlotte Street, but not at the same location. Following the Great Fire of 1901, which wiped out a large selection of the downtown commercial area, the present Crowell's Building is constructed. A grocery department is part of the store until the late 1940s. The old-fashioned pneumatic money change tube system was used right up until the store's closure in 1999. The historical building gets a second life with renovations and new businesses in November 2004.

1922 STRIKE ENDS
Twelve thousand Cape Breton miners end the strike that began August 14.

1971 NORTH SYDNEY GARBAGE
The first public collection of garbage from North Sydney begins today.

September

The Beautiful Lakes of Bras d'Or

How I love the sweet rhythm of water
Lapping gently the side of my hull,
While my spirit is lifted immensely
By the circling and grace of the gull,
Look westward at yon glowing sunset
And the many wee islands so green,
They somehow remind me of Scotland
Where many a day we have been.

Please fetch me a dram, oh my fair one
And make it a whisky not wine,
And I'll sing you a wee song in Gaelic
As I breathe deep the smell of the brine,
Come closer and take of my loving
And soothe me with loving galore,
There's no place for loving my darling
Like the beautiful lakes of Bras d'Or.

Stanley Collins

Fig. 9.1 At anchor, n.d.

September 1

1846 Church at Black Cove

Rev. Norman McLeod builds a second church close to the first one at Black Cove at the head of St. Ann's Bay.

The original church was too small and, in summer services, had been held outside. The new church seats about a thousand, but even this size will soon prove to be too small. Rev. McLeod commands a large and scattered congregation. Parishioners from as far away as Whycocomagh come by boat, wagon, sleigh and by foot. Some even leave home on Friday and Saturday to get to church. Norman McLeod is his own authority. He is their school teacher and business advisor as well as their spiritual leader (dictator, some say). In his church he gives neither baptism nor communion.

1870 "TO TEACHERS"

Fig. 9.2 Early Cape Breton school, 1917.

1 – Each day teachers will fill lamps, clean chimneys, and trim wicks.
2 – Each teacher will bring a bucket of water and a scuttle of coal for the day session.
3 – Make pens carefully. You may whittle nibs to the individual taste of the pupil.
4 – Men teachers may take one night each week for courting purposes, or two evenings a week if they go to church regularly.
5 – After school the teacher must spend the time until supper reading the Bible and other good books.
6 – Women teachers who marry or engage in unseemly conduct will be discharged.
7 – Every teacher should lay aside from each month's pay a goodly sum for his benefit during his declining years so that he will not become a burden to society.
8 – Any teacher who smokes, uses liquor in any form, frequents pool halls or public halls, or gets shaved in a barber shop, shall give good reason to suspect his worth, integrity and honesty.
9 – The teacher who performs his duties regularly and faithfully and without fault for five years, will be given an increase of 25 cents a week in pay, providing the Board of Education approves.

1915 RULES FOR SCHOOLTEACHERS

- You will not marry during the term of your contract.
- You are not to keep company with men.
- You must be home between the hours of 8 p.m. & 6 a.m. unless attending a school function.
- You may not loiter downtown in any of the ice cream stores.

- You may not travel beyond the city limits unless you have the permission of the chairman of the board.
- You may not ride in a carriage or automobile with any man unless he is your father or brother.
- You may not smoke cigarettes.
- You may not dress in bright colors.
- You may under no circumstances dye your hair.
- You must wear at least two petticoats.
- Your dresses must not be any shorter than two inches above the ankle.
- To keep the classroom neat and clean, you must: sweep the floor at least once daily, scrub the floor at least once a week with hot, soapy water; clean the blackboards at least once a day; and start the fire at 7 A.M. so the room will be warm by 8 a.m.

1904 Sydney Mines steel

The first run of pig iron in Sydney Mines is made this morning. Senator McGregor and other officials witness the historic event. The pig is said to be of superior quality.

1905 Emery Seam

The Dominion Coal Company starts sinking a new shaft at Donkin to tap the Emery seam, which underlies the Phalen seam. Earlier this summer the old disused shaft was pumped out and a few days ago the first coal in years was taken from this seam.

1908 "Premier Yacht Club"

In the September issue of *Rod and Gun and Motor Sports in Canada*, the Royal Cape Breton Yacht Club is praised as being "the premier yacht club of Canada." The club wins a number of competitions, including those won by the clipper *Cibou* in 1901, which brought to Cape Breton the illustrious Prince of Wales and Wenonah trophies.

1914 Multi-Nippled Sheep

John Davidson, the shepherd of the Beinn Breagh flock, purchases a number of the multi-nippled sheep for his farm at Stewiacke. The sheep represent a unique type of sheep, selected and developed over the past 25 years by Alexander Graham Bell. Twin-bearing ewes with 6-8 nipples, instead of the usual 2, have an increased supply of milk. Ewe Iambs with 6 nipples are going for $10 a head, while those with 8 nipples are $20.

1936 Mauling

A New Waterford boy has his lower eyelid torn as a result of a mauling by a Carnival show bear.

1971 Tom Kent

Tom Kent, formerly Deputy Minister of Regional Economic Expansion, is appointed President of the Cape Breton Development Corporation (Devco). Early in his career he had been a journalist and had worked as editor of the *Winnipeg Free Press* and before that as an editor of the London *Economist* and editorial writer for the *Manchester Guardian*. He later became an assistant to Prime Minister Lester Pearson.

Kent makes major changes within Devco. Policies are formulated which recognize the resources of Cape Breton both in the primary field—particularly in aquaculture and agriculture—and with secondary industry and tourism. A program of capital improvements in the mining industry is begun.

Tom Kent resigns the presidency of Devco in January 1977 to become president of the Sydney Steel Corporation. In 1980, he heads the Kent Royal Commission on Newspapers and later becomes the Dean of Administrative Studies at Dalhousie University.

1997 Pay to park

Starting this month, students and the general public will have to pay for parking at CBU.

September 2

1713 Engineers choose fortress site

A group of French military officers and engineers land on Cape Breton and take possession in the name of Louis XIV. They have been instructed to locate a site suitable for a fortress. Having recently signed the Treaty of Utrecht, France wants to strengthen her hold on Cape Breton, strategically important as the "key to the St. Lawrence." The engineers choose English Harbour (Louisbourg) as a site for the Fortress. During the course of their explorations, they report that Isle Royale (Cape Breton) has a population of one Frenchman and thirty Indian families.

1860 Gaelic scholar

Jonathan G. MacKinnon is born in Dunakin, near Whycocomagh. An outstanding Gaelic scholar, he becomes internationally known for his editing and publishing of the Gaelic newspaper *MacTalla* (see also May 28, 1892). He will translate many English classics into Gaelic. His *Old Sydney Sketches* of the town and the people in days gone by, is printed by his brother, Donald and goes on sale in 1918. Jonathan G. MacKinnon dies on January 13, 1944 and is buried at Stewartdale Church near Whycocomagh.

September 3

1905 Steel demand good

The demand for steel rails is good and the steel plant, exceptionally busy last month, may soon put on a double shift in all departments. The daily tonnage of rods and rails is up to 640 tons and pig iron has reached an output of 900 tons a day.

2002 Ad

Two River Wildlife Park "adopt-a-friend" sponsorship program. Judy the Rabbit, age 3. $25 to adopt.

September 4

1829 Joins Halifax Diocese

Originally under the jurisdiction of Quebec, Cape Breton now leaves that of Charlottetown to become part of the diocese of Halifax. In 1844, the diocese has its eastern seat at Arichat and in 1886 it moves to Antigonish.

1901 Eskimoes on Northside

Residents of North Sydney see two families of Labrador Eskimos, their gear, dress, sleds and nine husky dogs as the families make a brief stop via the SS *Bruce* to Buffalo, New York, where they'll take part in the Pan American Exposition.

1912 Bus run

Using kerosene for fuel and equipped with solid rubber tires, a bus, believed to be the first bus in Canada, makes its maiden run today in Sydney from Charlotte Street to the Cape Breton County Exhibition grounds on Kings Road (where St. Rita Hospital used to be). The bus, constructed by local carriage builders of the firm of J. A. McCallum, is a novelty, drawing large crowds. A policeman is stationed at each end of the bus to keep order, letting the first passengers get seated before others are allowed to enter. Lee Ripley, the conductor, collects 5 cents a ride from the 2,500 passengers today.

Fig. 9.3 First bus, c.1930.

1911 Coxheath celebrates

Coxheath celebrates its Centennial. Festivities centre around a large tent at the Edmund Andrews' farm. Dinners are put on by the Church, and girls from nearby farms help carry pies, bread and cooked hams across fields to the tent.

Old farming techniques are demonstrated, including the use of fanners to fan the chaff from the oats. This makes a mess, covering everyone nearby with dust. A big platform has been erected for dances. There are many musicians in the area and tonight, Coxheath holds a celebration dance.

Fig. 9.4 Coxheath centennial party, Robertson farm, 1911.

1936 CB County Exhibition

September 5-9; competitions for horses, cattle, sheep & swine, poultry including turkeys, ducks, geese and eggs; grains and seed, vegetables, flowers and several categories of fruits, 32 varieties of apples, 28 of plums, 11 of pears. Other competitions are Class 76 for Indian Work and other classes which include everything from Class 84, Canning & Preserving for girls under 6 years, to Class 57, Old Ladies' Work.

2002 Nunavut, the Yukon, Northwest Territories & Cape Breton?

John Whalley, economic development officer for CBRM suggests investigating the feasibility of Cape Breton becoming the country's fourth territorial government if the province doesn't alter its approach to economic development.

September 5

1883 Death in the Arctic

Fears are expressed for the safety of the Greely Polar Expedition and, in particular, for one of its members, George Rice of Little Bras d'Or, well known as a painter on the Northside. George Rice is the official photographer for the Greely Expedition, which left in 1881 on one of the expeditions planned by the International Geographical Conference in Leipzig. The expedition of 25 men has established a camp called Fort Conger, on the northeast shore of Discovery Harbour, Grinnell Land.

After two years of scientific observation, the expected relief ship fails to arrive from Newfoundland, the camp has to be abandoned and the whole party moved southward in small boats to Bedford Pyn Island. After considerable difficulty and many deaths, seven survivors are eventually rescued. George Rice is not one of the survivors.

1936 First woman to fly Atlantic

A light blue monoplane, *The Messenger*, came in low over the water, dived towards William Burke's house, lifted again and crashed into the nearby marsh. Beryl Markham, the first woman to fly single-handedly across the Atlantic, on her way to New York, running low on fuel and into strong winds and fog, tries to find a clear spot to land. She crash lands at Baleine, near Louisbourg. Miss Markham left England at dusk yesterday. She carried no radio and only a minimum of food: some hot coffee, raisins, and a jar of lemon curd.

Once news gets out that she is in Cape Breton, newsmen and photographers arrive. Air ace Eddie Rickenbacker arrives at the Cape Breton Flying Field in Reserve, and CBC announcer J. Frank Willis broadcasts an interview with the aviatrix. "I'm feeling fine, you know," she says. "After all, it's nice to have landed right side up on my first visit to America." (See also August 29, 1932.)

1981 Nursery opens

Strathlorne Forest Nursery, producing seedlings for large-scale reforestation of Cape Breton, officially opens today. Buildings include a 46,000 square-foot greenhouse, production house, cold storage and the office. Approximately 200 of the 425 acres have been cleared for nursery use.

2002 Marathon

The Lake Ainslie Marathon, Cape Breton's only full marathon, is to be run this weekend. No one won last year because of the heat. The course starts out easily over rolling hills, then onto steeper hills.

September 6

1788 King with a memory
Prince William Henry, later King William IV of England, is the first member of the Royal family to visit Cape Breton. He will spend several days in Sydney and attend many functions, including a dance. Largely due to the size of the ladies' hoop skirts, invitations have to be scaled to the size of the room.

The Prince visits Attorney General David Matthews and his family at their home across the harbour at Point Amelia (Petersfield). He becomes fond of one of the girls and promises her that when she grows up and when he becomes King, he will grant her anything she wishes. Years later in 1820, the girl, now Mrs. John Clark, a widow with a large family, writes the King, reminding him of his promise. The King remembers and replies, enclosing a commission for her son, Charles, as commissary. Prince Street in Sydney is named after the future King.

1886 Condemned and sold
Charles Muggah Lorway of Sydney, Master of the sailing schooner *L 'Houlett* makes the first modern arrest of a foreign ship in Canadian waters. The early Coast guard work is carried out this morning as he apprehends the *Highland Light*, out of Provincetown, MA, and her crew, fishing within the three mile limit off Souris, PEI. At a trial in Charlottetown on December 2, the *Highland Light*, her bait mill and the rest of her gear, along with her cargo will be "condemned and forfeited to her majesty, the queen, and sold."

1980 Odessey '77
Ken Langley of Coxheath and Gary Sowerby of Moncton start on their "Odessey '77" to circumnavigate the Earth. 27,000 miles and 74 days, 0 hours and 11 minutes later they arrive in record-breaking time back at their Toronto starting place. Seven years later, "Odessey '84—the Africa to Arctic Challenge"—takes the adventure twenty-eight days to get from Cape Agulhas up to Nordkapp, Norway, with various detours en route due to hostile local situations in parts of Africa.

2002 Unamaki Institute
"Tradition and science meet in Eskasoni." Today marks the grand opening of the Unamaki Institute of Natural Resources. The Institute will help manage the Bras d'Or and be a guardian of the Lakes.

September 7

1850 First French Consul
John Bourinot of Sydney is appointed French Consul, becoming the first in British North America. He is also later to represent Cape Breton in the House of Assembly in Halifax. When the French North Atlantic fleet spends the summers at Sydney Harbour, he entertains the officers at his home on the Esplanade in Sydney.

1870 Father Jimmy

James J. Tompkins is born at Margaree. He teaches school in Cheticamp to finance his own education. Shortly after being ordained he is appointed Vice-President of St. Francis Xavier University in Antigonish. He quickly achieves a reputation for his ability to raise money for university improvements. When the Carnegie Corporation offers large sums of money for a large federated Maritime University, the concept is supported by Father Jimmy Tompkins; but there is considerable opposition, and the bishop has Father Tompkins sent to the remote parish of Canso. It is from here that he succeeds in launching his ideas of adult education among farmers, fishermen and industrial workers in eastern Nova Scotia. Tompkinsville, the first cooperative housing plan in Canada, near Reserve Mines, is named after Father Tompkins, who is instrumental in establishing the cooperative movement. (See also November 27, 1938.)

1988 Horror!

Twenty-three year old New Waterford actor Barry J. Gillis stars in *Things*, the first video horror movie made in Canada. It will be released soon.

2002 Old trousseau

The Highland Village Museum presents the Hundred-Year-Old Trousseau, an exhibit featuring works by the Lake Ainslie Weavers Guild and friends. They have collected and created replicas of handcrafted items that would have made up a trousseau of a bride in 1901. They have created Rachel Campbell, the persona of a young woman of the area. The exhibit is to run to October 20th.

September 8

1629 All's fair?

Captain Charles Daniel, on his way out from France to join Champlain in Quebec is forced to seek shelter in what is now St. Ann's Bay. Captain Daniel knows that war between France and England has ended, but the Scot, Sir James Stewart, at his settlement at Baleine, had left England before the treaty was signed, so Daniels attacks Stewart's fort and Cape Breton's first colony is destroyed. Prisoners are forced to help build a second colony, the first French fort, Fort Daniel, later renamed Fort Ste. Anne.

Father Batholomew Vipont, a Jesuit priest, is on board Capt. Daniel's ship. Later this week a second French ship flounders off the other side of the Island and two Jesuit Fathers on board come to stay with Daniels' group. They start a mission to the Indians with Father Vipont. A chapel is built, named Ste. Anne. Over a period of several years, seven priests, including the brother of Capt. Daniel, share this first Jesuit mission in Cape Breton.

1900 Moxham Castle

Arthur J. Moxham buys the estate "Rockaway" from Jemina L. McKay, widow of Newton J. McKay, barrister and one-time Federal MP. Mr. Moxham, a pioneer in the production of steel in the States, came to Sydney in 1899 as the first General Manager and Vice-President of the new steel plant, now under construction.

The Moxhams' stay in Sydney is brief and tragic as their son is killed while at work on the steel plant. The Castle is used during the First World War as a military hospital, and later as the setting for two films. For many years it is the home of W. N. MacDonald, after which time it is left vacant and becomes the target for vandalism. It is eventually destroyed by fire on April 25, 1966, ending Sydney's claim to one of Canada's two castles.

1908 New Waterford

Rev. Willoughby-Goddard-Frank holds the first Anglican service in New Waterford in a hotel room, used by men engaged in opening up No. 12 mine. On this same day in 1913, New Waterford becomes incorporated as a town.

1969 Governor's apartments

The opening of the Governor's apartments of the rebuilt Chateau St. Louis by the Hon. Jean Chretien, Minister of Indian Affairs and Northern Development, marks the completion of the first phase of the reconstruction of Fortress Louisbourg.

The reconstructed ten-room wing contains the largest collection of authentic mid 18th-century antiques and French period furnishings in North America. The selection of antiques was based on a bankruptcy list for Gov. Duquesnel who died in 1744 and whose possessions were sold to clear his debts.

1988 No more party lines

Ninety-five L'Ardoise telephone customers in the 587 exchange will receive single-line service. Those now paying additional mileage charges may have them removed or reduced. The program is part of MT&T's commitment to a universal single party service province wide by 1996.

September 9

1850 Early bus

W. Snow's new Omnibus starts operating between Sydney Mines and the Bar (North Sydney), leaving "the Mines" in time for the mail steamer.

1909 Snow travel

A letter arrives in Sydney from Dr. (later Sir) Wilfred Grenfell, founder of the Grenfell Mission to Seamen. On his way north, Dr. Grenfell had visited Alexander Graham Bell's home at Baddeck. Dr. Bell had told Dr.Grenfell that airplane engines could be used with sledges in Grenfell's work in Labrador, and Dr. Bell thought that once they were being pushed over fifteen miles an hour, the sledge should lift and, although not leaving the surface altogether, should scarcely touch it, exactly like a hydro-plane.

1919 Plane that can't fly

The HD4, Alexander Graham Bell's 4th hydrofoil (hydrodrome) reaches a speed record of 70.68 mph over a mile course at Baddeck. This record holds until 1929. In 1917, when the United States entered the war, Dr. Bell decided to pursue the use of hydrofoils as submarine chasers and he built the HD4. But it was difficult getting an engine powerful enough to push the 60-foot craft. Two Renault engines couldn't reach the speeds needed. After the war, Dr. Bell acquired two Liberty engines. Both the American and the British Navy had looked at the possibility of the hydrofoil. But naval traditions die hard. To them, the hydrofoil was only an airplane that couldn't fly. Its potential has never been realized here in Canada, although hydrofoils are used in Russia, Hong Kong and Australia. The first International Hydrofoil Conference is held in Baddeck in July, 1982.

1978 Cradle of Boxing

At a special induction dinner at St. Anne's Hall tonight, Tony Unitas, Canadian Boxing Hall of Fame chairman, speaks of Cape Breton as "the cradle of Canadian boxing." Boxers Ronnie MacNeil, Joe Smith, Joey Burchell, Maurice MacDonald, Dit MacLellan and J. B. "Kid" Adshade help prove his point. Boxing builders-trainers, Rudy Plachie, Sid Rideout of Glace Bay and John Cechetto of Sydney are also inducted into the Hall of Fame. Their names will also be placed in the Hall of Fame Directory in Washington, DC.

1988 PCBs to burn

A spokesman for Atomic Energy of Canada states that PCB's "are perfectly safe where they are—we don't have a place to put them, so what do you do with them? We've been storing them for two years, but I have no concern." The bulk of PCBs in Cape Breton are at Atomic Energy of Canada Ltd., Glace Bay (54 45-gallon drums—8,405 litres), and Stora Forest Industries in Port Hawkesbury (111 45-gallon drums—13,710 litres). They are safely stored according to a list released by Environment Minister Tom McMillan. Other PCB sites—Novex Mining & Exploration (East Bay), 9 litres; Nova Scotia Power Corp, Lingan Generating Station (Lingan), 149 litres; National Sea Products (Louisbourg), 3 litres; Marine Atlantic (North Sydney), concentration unknown; Transport Canada, CN Marine (North Sydney), 500 litres; Richmond Fisheries (Petit de Grat), 27 litres; NS Power Corp. (Point Tupper), 87 litres; Ultramar Canada Inc. (Port Hawkesbury), 975 litres; DEVCO (Prince Colliery), 2 sites, 75 and 80 litres; Cape Breton Hospital (Sydney), 150 litres; SYSCO (Sydney), 610 litres; National Defence, CFS Sydney, concentration unknown; Canadian Broadcasting System (Sydney), concentration unknown; Transport Canada Sydney Airport, concentration unknown."

The PCBS are to be burned here in mobile incinerators.

September 10

1864 Say "cheese"

John Robert Fraser arrives in North Sydney to set up a business where he can "attend to customers who might need a faithful and well-executed ambrotype," an early form of a photographic image.

1932 SS *Watford* tragedy

During the night the wind reaches close to 100 mph. The little collier, the SS *Watford*, on its run from Montreal struggles on to Sydney, but to turn into the Harbour there would put her broadside to the waves.

She seeks shelter from the storm between Scaterie Island and the shore. But the seas drive her hard onto a rocky ledge at Cape Percy, near Port Morien. The crew's frantic signals for help are heard in Glace Bay and three carloads of men set out, walking the last three miles through scrub and brush into the teeth of the gale, while two more men work their way round the cliff top from Port Morien.

The Cape Bretoners manage to secure a line from the ship, and one by one the crew is pulled to land. Two die: a stoker of a heart attack and the First Officer, who fell and was sucked into the sea by a receding wave. The last man to be hauled onto Cape Breton is Bosun Murray from Stornaway in the Outer Hebrides.

1939 War
Canada declares war on Germany.

1980 Oil refinery to close
Gulf Canada Oil Refinery at Point Tupper announces that it is closing. There will be no layoffs until March.

September 11

1784 Separate colony
Royal instruction to Gov. Parr makes Cape Breton a separate Colony.

1922 *Sea Riders*
The Canadian Maritime Motion Picture Company will premiere *The Sea Riders*, the first Nova Scotian film, at the Strand. One big fight scene occurs on a schooner off the coast of Ingonish. Most of the exterior scenes were shot at Main-a-Dieu and Ingonish. The company's 1921 film *Big Timber*, also shot on Cape Breton, has not been released yet.

Fig. 9.5 On the movie set of Sea Riders, *1923.*

1929 New Sydney hospital
At the Lyceum last night, graduation exercises of the nurses of the Order of the Sisters of Saint Martha precede the opening ceremonies of the new St. Rita Hospital in Sydney today.

1980 Road to the Isles a busy one
Tokens replace tickets at the Canso Causeway. About 23.5 million vehicles have crossed the causeway since opening on August 13, 1955.

1980 Boat People reunite
More than 60 Vietnamese people gathered recently for a picnic at Whycocomagh Park. The new immigrants now live in many different communities in Richmond, Inverness and Victoria Counties, and they got together for the first time since their arrival.

2001 9/11 - Terrorists attack
This morning two airplanes are hijacked and deliberately crashed into the World Trade Centre in New York City. Minutes later both towers collapse. More than 2,000 people are killed. At the same time, a third plane is hijacked and crashed into the Pentagon in Washington, DC, while a fourth plane crashes into a Pennsylvania field before it reaches its target.

All air traffic into the States is halted. Planes in the air are diverted to Canada with most landing in Vancouver, Halifax and St. John's, Newfoundland. Because of its smaller runway, only one plane lands at Sydney Airport.

Canadians do what they can to help the stranded passengers. Cups of tea, a shower, even clean underwear, are welcomed. Those stranded are left with feelings of fear and uncertainty, and it is days before air traffic begins to move again. Airport security is greatly expanded.

September 12

1874 First embalmer

John Dooley, a carpenter in North Sydney who makes caskets, decides to develop a business. He buys the first hearse in Cape Breton. Custom-made in Sydney with steel tires, it is pulled at funerals by a pair of black horses, covered with fringed black cloth. (Caskets for young people in Sydney are pulled by a pair of white horses with white coverings.) The family expands the business. William Dooley takes a course in embalming in Saint John, NB, and becomes the first embalmer in Cape Breton in 1902, when embalming begins in the Maritimes.

1940 Rural electrification

Thirty miles of pole line are being installed under the Rural Electrification Act. Electricity will light up Homeville, Mira, Catalone and other communities between the Seaboard Power Plant at Glace Bay and Louisbourg. It's the first project of its kind to be carried out in Cape Breton County by the Nova Scotia Power Commission.

1969 First choppers

The first flight of the Okanagan Helicopters out of Sydney is logged today. The fleet has the largest carrying capacity of any chopper company in Canada. Daily trips to the drilling rigs, Sednith I and Serco H are planned. In the next year the company is to fly more than 1,000 hours and burn up to 10,000 gallons of jet turbine fuel.

1975 Bras d'Or Institute

Dr. Donald Arseneau of the College of Cape Breton is appointed director of the Bras d'Or Institute. The organization, begun in 1972, is sponsored by the College to promote research and development of ideas beneficial to Cape Breton. It arranges symposia, sponsors or carries out research and development programs, and maintains a library. It has been involved in agriculture and aquaculture, coal and steel resources, environmental studies and social programs.

1988 New camp

A new Girl Guide camp opens at Big Pond. It is situated on a hill overlooking the Bras d'Or, and there is a sandy beach just across the highway. There are two wilderness camping areas, a small chapel set deep in the woods, several hiking trails, and a small stream and wading pools—ideal for all levels of the guiding program.

September 13

1906 Too few men

The promise of less demanding work in Western Canada has lured men away from Cape Breton. Good fishing this Ssummer has kept Newfoundlanders, who used to come to work in Cape Breton, at home, and Cape Breton industries are suffering from a lack of sufficient manpower. Coal facilities have been improved, and coal contracts have been made. Agents of the Dominion and Nova Scotia Coal Companies have searched the island, but they cannot find enough men to do the work.

1918 Sphagnum moss for the wounded - 1,502nd day of war

Canadian moss is in demand, and Cape Breton moss is being harvested to help the wounded. Moss gatherers, including volunteers from Toronto and Halifax, have taken only 300 bags from the False Bay bog near Grand Anse, and they could easily gather a thousand more. But there aren't enough pickers.

Sphagnum moss, from near the seacoast, is used for dressing and pads by the medical services overseas. The healing properties of sphagnum moss were discovered accidentally about 60 years ago, when a workman on a peat bog crudely dressed his lacerated arm with peat. Sphagnum dressings were first used in the Russo-Japanese War. They've been in use in the British Army since 1914. In 1916, the War Office recognized the dressings as official and the output has progressively increased.

1969 New union

The Union of Nova Scotia Indians is formed in Sydney. It will promote educational, political and economic development.

1988 Frozen clams

The world's first factory freezer clam vessel, the *Atlantic Vigour* out of North Sydney, recently landed its first catch at the Alder Point fish plant.

2002 Horseshoes anyone?

New Waterford brothers, Hughie and Duncan McKenzie, become the new Maritime Horseshoe Champions for "A" division at a recent meet in Sussex, NB. Now pensioned-off coal miners, they learned to play when they were kids and are members of the Horseshoe club in their community. Over the years they have won doubles and singles.

September 14

1716 Licentious officers

The French ship *L'Atalante* arrives at Louisbourg with reinforcements, supplies and pay. The sudden influx of money means that the soldiers and officers can indulge excessively in their favourite pastimes: gambling, drinking and women. Gov. Pasteur de Costebelle has already been ordered by his superiors in France to control and eliminate their licentious ways.

1850 Poisoned rye

Farmers are warned not to use rye grain from certain fields in Sydney or to mix it with other grains. Bread made from it tastes the same, but the blackened ears of rye are diseased, causing high fever and gangrene in the legs and other parts of the body.

1917 Huge increase necessary - 1,137th day of war

An increase in the monthly output is keeping the shell department of Sydney's Steel Plant busy. Ottawa has requested that at least 140,000 blanks be produced every month, as opposed to the present 17,000 average output.

2002 Search & Rescue

Eric Langley of Sydney, a founding member of the Cape Breton Search and Rescue team, receives a certificate of achievement in Halifax from the National Search and Rescue Secretariat.

September 15

1851 Fish fight

Believing their fishing rights threatened by the arrival of foreign fishing boats, 219 Cape Breton fishermen battle with the crews of 93 American and 75 British mackerel fishing vessels anchored in Souris Road.

1930 Impoverished schools

Dominion No. 6 schools have been closed for lack of money. Ratepayers are told that poll taxes may have to be increased so that the schools can be reopened.

1939 Senator John Stewart McLennan dies

Senator John Stewart McLennan, owner of Petersfield, Westmount, dies in Ottawa. Born in Montreal, he came to Cape Breton in 1882 and became the manager of the International Mine at Old Bridgeport. Later, he was Managing Director of the International Coal Company until the formation of the Dominion Coal Company in 1883, which consolidated ownership of the Cape Breton mines.

Senator McLennan became the first Treasurer of the new Dominion Iron and Steel Company when the first steel was produced. He retired a year later and decided to build an estate, "Petersfield", on property on the Westmount side of Sydney Harbour. In 1904, he bought the *Sydney Post*, which he owned and edited for twenty-nine years until it merged with its competitors, the *Sydney Record* to form the *Sydney Post-Record*.

His interest in Louisbourg started when he was asked to write an article for the magazine *Canadian Scenery*. He began collecting material on the rich history of the Fortress, which led to his book *Louisbourg From Its Founding to Its Fall*, and this in turn inspired others and led to the excavation and restoration of the Fortress. (See also June 6, 1981.)

1965 Canadian Coast Guard College

Regular classes start at the new Canadian Coast Guard College at the Point Edward Naval Base. Cadets are able to study engineering or navigation. In 1981, a new College complex opens nearby, adjacent to Petersfield.

1988 Bears beware!

A special two-week bear season is proclaimed, during which hunters may shoot over bait sets. A special licence is required, and the bait being used must be registered with the Department of Lands and Forests.

1996 Daring rescue

Hurricane Hortense slams into Cape Breton. In the pitch dark, in strong wind and rain, a volunteer fireman, 35-year old Tony Fitzgerald from Ingonish Beach, guides a small aluminium boat across flood waters that have swept Linette Hudson's car off the Cabot Trail, to where she is stranded on a fallen tree. In the spring of 1997, he is awarded the Canadian Medal of Bravery.

September 16

1952 The beginning

The first blast at Porcupine Mountain starts construction of the Canso Causeway. A giant truck carries the first load of 18-ton chunks of rock and dumps them on the edge of the first fill. (See also August 13, 1955.)

1977 Allan J.

Allan J. MacEachen, MP for Cape Breton Highlands-Canso, is appointed Deputy Prime Minister of Canada. Born in Inverness in 1921 and educated at schools in Inverness, St. Francis Xavier University, and the University of Toronto, he entered Parliament in 1953 and, from 1958 to 1962, was special assistant to Lester B. Pearson.

Following the election of a Liberal government in 1963, Mr. MacEachen was appointed Minister of Labour. He later held the office of Minister of National Health and Welfare, Government House Leader, Minister of Manpower and Immigration, President of the Privy Council, Leader of the Government in the House of Commons and Secretary of State for External Affairs. He resigns in June 1984, after Prime Minister Trudeau resigns, and he is appointed to the Senate.

1998 "911"

Cape Breton comes on line and now "Nova Scotia is the first jurisdiction in Canada to have a province-wide ground to air medical dispatch service. All ambulance calls are directed—via 911 emergency line—to a central line in Bedford, which sends the closest available vehicle and personnel to where they are needed."

September 17

1745 Mutiny averted?

Gov. Shirley of Massachusetts promises the British troops at Louisbourg an increase in pay. The troops have been dissatisfied and have been threatening to lay down their arms.

1925 Under and over

Mayor MacConnell of Sydney reports that Mr. McLurg, the vice-president of BESCO, will not allow the city to fill in the ravine beneath the Charlotte Street bridge. BESCO may want to use the railroad again he said, even though they haven't used the property since 1906. At the same council meeting, a petition is received for the paving of Kings Road from the city line to Perry Lewis's store at Sydney River.

September 18

1836 Break quarantine

A short while ago, a ship arrived with passengers from Scotland who had smallpox. They were put under quarantine, but escaped and fled to the shore. Health officials are taking precautions, but there have been other cases reported.

1900 – "Where do they get the rum?"

Letter to the editor of the *Daily Record*

"Sir; Any person walking down around the Ferry wharf on a Sunday morning will see two to six young men drinking from a flask, and just as soon as the flask is emptied one of them goes and gets it refilled. Now, this is a Scott Act town. Where do they get the rum? Some one ought to step in and put a stop to this practice. What looks worse than to see men drinking when church bells are ringing? People are being confronted by the fact that the Scott Act is merely a farce. Not only on the wharf, but on the waterfront and park is this practice carried out. Have our police no power to stop this? If not, they ought to have.... It is an awful thing that in a city such as Sydney so much open air drinking should take place."

1959 "Junior" Hanna

Sydney native John "Junior" Hanna signs a contract with the New York Rangers for the 1959-60 season. On September 20, 1980, he is inducted into the Nova Scotia Sports Hall of Fame.

September 19

1833 Murder!

Mrs. Charlotte Flahaven and two sailors, William Johnston and Reuben Easman, are publicly hanged today in Victoria Park in Sydney for the murder of Mrs. Flahaven's husband. John Flahaven, a tavern-keeper in North Sydney, sometimes gave food and lodging to travellers. In the summer of 1833, Flahaven was lured into the woods by two sailors, one of whom had fallen for Mrs. Flahaven, the other for one of the daughters.

Earlier, at Little Bras d'Or, Flahaven bought an ox to fatten for the winter. The sailors let the ox go and then told Flahaven the ox was headed back to Bras d'Or. He set out in pursuit and in the woods he was set upon by the two sailors, who beat him to death with a club and an axe. One of the daughters, becoming suspicious, climbed out a window and ran to tell her uncle in Sydney Mines. Neighbours and the local Justice of the Peace arrested the sailors.

The sailors and Charlotte Flahaven were tried in the Supreme Court of Nova Scotia at Sydney, August 27-30. Difficulty in finding a hangman last night was resolved when a sailor from a recently arrived ship accepted the offer of 5 pounds to do the work.

1954 Mabou wharf
The Mabou Bridge wharf is busy again after fifty-six years of inactivity. Until now, the last cargo of coal to be loaded was back in 1898. The MV *Arichat*, owned and operated by W. N. MacDonald of Sydney, is being loaded with coal at the wharf. An extra 157,000 tons of coal a year will be mined at the MacDonald mine at Inverness and Harbourview Mine at Port Hood.

1965 Treasure
Divers discover the rotting hull of the wrecked French pay ship *Le Chameau* (see also August 26, 1725 and April 4, 1966). Another group that had agreed earlier to find the treasure with one of the divers, sued the finders, and that tied up the treasure for months. In December 1971, the treasure, including silver coins and a rare Cross is sold at public auction at Parke-Burnet in New York City. (The Nova Scotia Supreme Court rules that one-half of the treasure goes to the first group.)

2002 CB Centre for Craft & Design
The Cape Breton Centre for Craft and Design, formerly the School of Crafts, celebrates its 30th anniversary.

September 20

1901 For Canso crossing
The SS *Scotia* is completed, passing sea-tests in England where she was built. The steamer is designed to ferry railway cars across the Strait of Canso to and from Mulgrave and Port Hastings. There are rudders at each end, and she can be handled in either direction. There are also ice-breaking propellers at each end. The *Scotia* can carry nine Pullman cars, 84 feet 6 inches long, or a corresponding number of boxcars. She has been strengthened to take an express locomotive and tender.

Fig. 9.6 First transfer of rail cars on Canso ferry Scotia, *1892.*

1923 "Kid" Adshade

J. B. "Kid" Adshade is born in Glace Bav. The Maritime welterweight king fights between 1946-54 against some of the best light and welterweights of Canada. "Kid" is a courageous fighter and a hard puncher. He scores the fastest knockout in Maritime rings at 41 seconds over New York's Earl Trader at the Glace Bay Forum. He is inducted into the Nova Scotia Sports Hall of Fame, September 9, 1978.

1986 Highlands of Scotland links with Highlands of Cape Breton

Companies in the Highlands of Scotland trade mission follow up on last year's successful trip to Cape Breton. The exhibit, at Mayflower Mall today and the Holiday Inn on Monday, is part of the twinning link between our two regions.

September 21

1812 Tragedy off Cheticamp

Twelve people, including seven heads of families, drown as three ships sink in a great gale off the Cheticamp coast.

1901"Shiver my Timbers," or words to that effect

This morning about 7 o'clock, Capt. Fougere of Cheticamp was sailing past the mouth of Morien Bay when he saw a sea serpent. The creature remained motionless, his body extending for over a hundred feet along the surface, head raised with "red and evil eyes." An old muzzle loader was discharged, there was blood left on the water as the creature disappeared. "Shiver my timbers," the Captain is reported to say, "if I would pass through the same experience. No, not for all the schooners in Cheticamp."

1909 Peary returns

Commander Robert E. Peary returns to Sydney Harbour on the homeward leg of his successful expedition to the North Pole. Peary has made many visits to Cape Breton and bought most of his supplies at North Sydney. Peary was here in 1905 aboard the SS *Roosevelt* and again in 1908.

Fig. 9.7 Admiral Perry returns.

On April 6, 1909, with Matt Henson, a Nova Scotian, Peary reached the North Pole and on this day is met at the entrance to Sydney Harbour by a great flotilla of boats welcoming his return. Two days later, he writes, "There is a very tender place in my heart for Sydney: eleven different summers have I gone north from here, returning with various measures of success until at last I have won that to which I have devoted the best years of my life. Here, I have repeatedly said 'goodbye' to those who are near and dear to me, and here they have greeted me upon my return. The generous ovation given seems a fitting climax to a series of memories which I shall always carry with me."

September 22

1811 First Cheticamp Baptism

Philippe Lelievre is the first child baptized in Cheticamp and entered in the parish registry begun by Rev. Lejamtel.

1844 Bishop of Arichat

Pope Gregor XVI ratifies a decision to divide Nova Scotia into two dioceses. Monsignor Fraser chooses Arichat as his headquarters because it is the most centrally situated parish in the new diocese of Antigonish. He becomes the Bishop of Arichat.

1922 Dancing in the dark

City council spends time discussing the "moonlight waltz" and the corruption of the morals of the young men and women of the city. Alderman M. N. McKenzie is very upset about what he saw one evening last week. About 10 p.m. he was walking down Charlotte Street and was attracted to a large gathering of young people on the sidewalk looking up at a building across the street. Looking up himself, he saw behind window blinds couples dancing to jazz music in the dark. "A man does not need to be much of a moral crank to see the evil which is engendered by an assemblage such as I have spoken of," he comments, and he wants to know if there's a city law to prevent this. Another alderman admits he is a champion of moral reform and thinks that dancing in the dark is going too far. Other aldermen present believe that the dancing is all right as long as there are lights. But the city has no power over dance halls. That will have to be left to the churches to influence.

1939 Progress

Women working in cities in Nova Scotia now have a new minimum wage: 22 cents an hour.

September 23

1967 Early Cape Breton inhabitant

A discovery made in 1959 by Dr. Donald Baird of Princeton and W. E. Rake, then on the staff of the Nova Scotia Museum, has not been reported until now. A fossilized skeleton of the reptile Romeriscus Periallus, which lived around 280,000,000 years ago, the most primitive reptile known so far, has been found on the west coast of Cape Breton.

1988 Jesus at Tim Hortons

The image of Jesus appears on the outside wall of the Tim Hortons at Bras d'Or. Several hundreds, faithful and curious, flock to see the image.

September 24

1909 RECORD?

Local contractor F. L. Dixon may hold the record for fast house construction. It took a staff of fifteen men exactly two days to build a 22' x 16' one-and-a-half storey house on the Mira Road.

1944 STRATEGIC PASSAGE

In a brief on the St. Peter's Canal presented before the Commission of Post-war Development and Rehabilitation, Rev. Leo Keats reminds them of the importance of the Canal. He would like to see two new wharves built and the Canal widened and deepened. In four months in 1943, he argues, more than 250,000 tons of coal passed through the Canal. With ships taking this route, it freed the Navy vessels of escort duty and allowed them to devote their time to chasing submarines in the Atlantic.

2004 *QUEEN* ARRIVES

The *Queen Mary 2* arrives in Sydney Harbour on her first voyage to Canada. The ship, originally scheduled to land here on Monday, was diverted because of Hurricane Ivan's winds and rough seas. The *Queen Mary 2* is twice as big as her sister ship, *Queen Elizabeth 2,* another visitor to our Harbour. The *Queen Mary 2* is almost as long as four football fields and clearly dwarfs the smaller boats that go out to see her at close hand. Residents go to South Bar or Point Edward to look at the ship, the flagship of the Cunard Line and the world's largest cruise ship.

Fig. 9.8 Queen Mary II *visits, 2004.* Cape Breton Post.

September 25

1904 EXPLOSION

An explosion at Dominion No. 2 in Glace Bay kills one miner.

1905 RAID?

The police on the Northside are after a pair of "fakers" who have been operating around the industrial area. The con men have been selling a simple insect exterminator. Instructions say to take a small amount of the powder and blow it into the air where the insects are the heaviest. The next day there will only be dead bugs around. Unfortunately, the mixture costs money and it doesn't work. As a matter of fact, insects seem to thrive on the powder, which is mostly Cow Brand baking soda.

1980 WHYCOCOMAGH SCHOOL
The new Federal school at Whycocomagh is opened, serving the Indians of the Whycocomagh Reserve.

2003 "NATURAL GAS IN LIQUID FORM IS SAFE"
"Natural gas in liquid form is safe." That's encouraging news as plans for an LNG terminal are unveiled at the Strait. The $500-800 million plant will import liquid natural gas for delivery into the Maritimes and Northeast Pipeline.

September 26

1905 WET CITY
There are about 80 places in Sydney where intoxicating liquor can be bought, including 16 hotels and 8 restaurants. The rest are mostly private homes, where liquor is sold in small quantities and to certain people.

1969 POINT TUPPER PLANT OPENS
Premier G. I. Smith officially opens the Nova Scotia Power Commission's multi-million dollar thermal generating plant at Point Tupper. This will supply the steam and electric requirements for the Canadian General Electric Heavy Water Plant.

1983 COAL TO KOREA
The first ship to ship transfer of export coal is completed by the Canada Steamship Line's *Nanticoke* in the Strait of Canso. Nearly 30,000 tons of Cape Breton coal are loaded into a French coal carrier bound for South Korea. This contract, to sell 150,000 tons of Cape Breton coal to South Korea, represents the Cape Breton Development Corporation's first penetration into the Pacific Rim market.

September 27

1790 "LES 14 VIEUX"
The fourteen founders of Cheticamp, "Les 14 Vieux," receive grants from the government at Sydney of 7,000 *arpents* of land. "Les 14 Vieux" are not really old; their names are the first on the land grant list for Cheticamp. There are now twenty-six families in the area.

1961 SYDNEY SHOPPING CENTRE
Today marks the grand opening of the Sydney Shopping Centre.

1980 *THIRD WALKER* OPENS
The Third Walker, filmed in Cape Breton and starring William Shatner (of Captain Kirk fame) premieres tonight at the Savoy Theatre in Glace Bay.

2003 BUSINESS HALL OF FAME
Five local business people are the first to be inducted in the new Cape Breton Business Hall of Fame, created by the Sydney and Area Chamber of Commerce and UCCB. Michael and

Christine Dezagiacomo of Glace Bay (successful Tasty Treat outlets and a rental real estate company); John Eyking of Millville, (came from Holland in 1953 to farm), Jack Yazer of Sydney (arrived from Poland at age 14, peddled clothes from a backpack, then by horse and wagon and finally opened his own store); and the late Joan Harriss of Sydney (insurance, travel and shipping).

September 28

1984 The Bay

The Bay Boy, a semi-autobiographical film by Glace Bay native and film writer/ director/ producer Daniel Petrie premieres at the Savoy Theatre in Glace Bay. The film portrays a sixteen-year old boy's life in Glace Bay in the 1930s. Glace Bay resident Jane MacKinnon is one of several Cape Bretoners acting in the movie filmed here last year.

Daniel Petrie has worked on the New York stage and in Hollywood as a director. He has worked with such actors and actresses as Richard Burton, Darren McGavin, Jane Fonda (*The Doll Maker*), Jane Alexander, Ed Asner and Paul Newman *(Fort Apache - The Bronx*). Daniel Petrie has won Emmies for his productions, including the TV movie *Eleanor and Franklin*. *The Bay Boy* wins Best Canadian film at the Genie Awards in March 1985, in addition to the awards for Best Actress in a supporting role and Best Achievement in overall sound.

1992 "He shoots. He scores!"

Hockey fans flock to Centre 200 to watch an exhibition game between the Edmonton Oilers and the Boston Bruins. This is the first time that two National Hockey League teams have played together in Cape Breton.

September 29

1671 Deny's book to printers

Nicholas Denys' two volume book, *Geographical Description of the Coasts of North America, from New England to the River Saint Lawrence* goes to the printers in Paris. Denys mentions the coal in Cape Breton: "There are mines of coal within the limits of my concession and upon the border of the sea; this is found to be as good as that of Scotland, according to the tests I have had made of it, sundry times, upon the spot and as well in France, where I have had samples taken."

Denys also mentions the walruses, "beasts of the big tooth—two huge teeth, thick and long as half the arm, while the other teeth are four fingers' breadth long ... no ivory is more beautiful." Praising the seal oil used by the Indians, he notices that it's "good to eat fresh, and for frying fish. It is also good to burn. It has neither odour nor smoke.... If one were to bring it to Paris, it would sell there very well." (See also January 30, 1654.)

1918 Spanish flu

Spanish flu has reached epidemic proportions on Cape Breton, and in some homes everyone is sick, some dangerously so. There is no place to go, as hospitals are full. Public gatherings are banned. Schools, theatres and dance halls have been closed and churches may be closed. By the middle of October, Public Health officials recommend that houses with influenza should be placarded. The Spanish Influenza kills more people around the world than the First World War.

1922 Profitable sideline

Large quantities of moonshine liquor are distilled all around Cape Breton. Stills are usually hidden in isolated and practically inaccessible spots. There is a ready market in the towns and much is sold to wholesalers who in turn sell to the bootleggers. One young man in the Margaree area is said to have cleared $2,000 on moonshine rum this summer, and the operation of his still didn't interfere with his farming.

1962 Blair Richardson

Blair Richardson of South Bar wins the Canadian boxing title in Glace Bay when he comes up against Wilfie Greaves of Edmonton. In March, 1966, he dethrones Gomeo Brennan of Bimini, Bahamas to win the Canadian and British Commonwealth Middleweight Championship. In 1963, Richardson is named Boxer of the Year for his win over Greaves. Their fight also rates as the Best of the Year. Blair dies of a brain tumour on March 5, 1971, at the age of 30 and is inducted posthumously into the Nova Scotia Sports Hall of Fame on September 20, 1980.

September 30

1913 Come to the fair

This week's Exhibition on the grounds on Kings Road, Sydney, is expected to attract 50,000 people. The aeroplane exhibitors and the amusement concessions have arrived. Three carloads of cattle are also here and other animals have been coming over by boat and are walked along roads. About 350 head of cattle, 135 horses, 150 sheep, 120 swine and 1,000 poultry are here along with a large display of agricultural, dairy and women's work.

To help the visitors and exhibitors from St. Peter's and western Bras d'Or Lake points, the Intercolonial puts on a special train to connect with the SS *Richmond* at Grand Narrows. The *Marion* brought Cape Bretoners from Whycocomagh and points on that side of the Bras d'Or. Hotel rooms in the area are all booked.

1952 Homeward bound

Eastern Command Headquarters in Halifax have released a list of soldiers from Cape Breton who will shortly be returning home on rotation leave from Korea.

1978 Major sale

Amid hoopla, the first sale of the 1975 importation of North Country Cheviot sheep takes place at noon today in the Athletic Centre, Mabou. Deputy Prime Minister, Allan J. MacEachen, auctions off the first ram. One of the purebred rams sells for over $1,000, believed to be the highest price for a North Country Cheviot ram ever paid in Canada. Concurrent with the sale is a major exhibition by the Cape Breton School of Crafts featuring and demwonstrating wool and other related crafts.

The following year, a second major sheep sale will take place, when Madame Jehanne Benoit, noted Canadian cook, (whose husband is a sheep farmer) auctions off the first sheep. This sale is reported to be the largest of its kind ever held in Canada.

1978 SPCA

The SPCA animal shelter officially opens in Sydney. In 1983, the shelter handles 5,510 dogs, cats, rabbits, hamsters, chickens and one fox, which is turned over to the Department of Lands and Forests. There are far too many unwanted animals around. For example, the people at the shelter say, that if he can find enough female cats in heat, one tomcat alone in one year could father 100,000 kittens.

1984 STAGED BICYCLE RACES

The Cape Breton Pepsi Fall Cycling Classic, a bicycle race in eleven stages, starts at Sydney. Top teams from the United States and Canada, including one from Cape Breton, take part in the race which will take them on courses around the Island.

1997 THIRD OFFICIAL LANGUAGE

Mi'kmaq is to be the official language of the day-to-day municipal affairs in Chapel Island (Potloteck).

October

Cape Breton Coal Miners

We are the miners from Cape Breton isle.
We don't make much money but manage to smile.
Workin' hard for our living a mining the coal.
The dust and the sweat seep into our souls.

Chorus:

So come all you miners and listen to me.
Be proud of our country and good old C.B.
When we get to heaven and God reads the scroll,
He'll say step right in boys for you've loaded coal.

Ray Holland of The Men of the Deeps

Fig. 10.1 c.1945. National Film Board

Fig. 10.2 Owen Fitzgerald.

October 1

1849 Head For Arichat

The Times and the *Cape Breton Spectator* will soon be published at Arichat instead of Sydney because of a lack of support for these papers in Sydney and the encouragement from Arichat.

1900 A penny a ton

$708.04 was paid in tolls by vessels using the St. Peters Canal last year, according to a report issued today. That's a penny for each ton of freight, which included everything from barley and bricks to cattle and telegraph poles.

1917 The Home Front - 1,165th day of war

More than 300 Cape Breton girls are in the Annapolis Valley harvesting apples as their contribution to the war effort.

1970 First Heavy Water

Canadian General Electric Co. Ltd. starts producing the first heavy water in Canada at their plant at Point Tupper.

1977 Learn to fiddle

The only group program in North America for teaching Scottish fiddle music starts at the University College of Cape Breton under the direction of Cape Breton fiddler, Winnie Chafe.

Winnie Chafe, who was the first woman to win the International Old Time Fiddle Contest in Pembroke, Ontario, was born and raised in Glace Bay in a family that had long established roots in Beaver Cove. She took lessons from the age of nine and three years later appeared as a guest violinist at the Gaelic College. She has studied the classical violin but is particularly moved by the slow airs of Scotland. She was fiddle music arranger on CBC-TV's *Ceilidh* and has played at concerts in Scotland. Today she teaches aspiring students of the violin as well as performing herself.

1982 Run around the trail

Cadets from the Canadian Coast Guard College hold a Cabot Trail Run today and tomorrow. Time for the Run is 23 hours, 8 minutes and 50 seconds—a new record.

1986 First song

"Your memory is still holding on" by Peter MacDonald becomes the first song by a Cape Bretoner to hit No. 1 on the CKPE country music chart.

October 2

Fig. 10.3 H. M. Whitney.

1900 Whitney who?

"In the distant future—very distant, it is hoped—when the last vestiges of the steel works will have vanished, Whitney Ave may help to remind future Sydneyites of the man who, if not the founder, was at least the finder of Sydney."

1903 Diversify

The Dominion Tar and Chemical Company distills its first product. The company has been set up to utilize the by-products of DISCO and change them into such products as creosote, pitch sulphate and ammonia.

1905 Farming at Sydney Forks

The Sydney *Post* reports an increased interest in market gardening, especially in the Westmount and Sydney Forks area. Farmers here have a ready market in the industrial area, and residents get a good buy from them because the produce is fresh and less expensive. One of the most successful farmers in the area is I. N. Shurman at Sydney Forks. He has been operating his property for three summers now. He has 40 acres under cultivation and produces potatoes, turnips, cabbages, cauliflower, beets, carrots and strawberries. He also raises wheat and buckwheat to feed some 780 chickens: light Brahmans, Rhode Island Reds, Buff Orpingtons and Plymouth Rocks. Cracked corn and sunflower seeds are grown to feed ducks and geese and his prize pigs. One Yorkshire sow this year had a record litter of 21 piglets. Mr. Shurman also has a creamery on the farm.

1994 Inventory

An extensive inventory of resources along the coastline from Forchu to Mira Bay begins this month. Information will be gathered on everything from bogs and shipwrecks to cemeteries and local historic sites, as well as bald eagle nesting sites and good areas for lobsters.

1998 Unsung heroes

CBC's Wayne Rostad interviews a local "unsung hero" for his TV show *On the Road Again*. He talks with Charlie Seward, a young man known around Sydney for going with his shopping cart and, unpaid, helping to clean the city's sidewalks. Rostad also interviews Piper John MacLean about his helping people rediscover the old authentic way of playing the pipes. There's also a follow-up on the late Joe Delaney's scarecrow family in Grand Etang.

1998 Wrench-turning ceremony

In Point Tupper, the president and general manager of Sable Offshore Energy Inc., John Brannan, turns a wrench (instead of digging a traditional spadeful of dirt) to start construction of a processing facility of natural gas liquids from Sable.

October 3

1838 Young town

About one half of the 203 people at Englishtown are school children. Twenty-three heads of household are farmers who fish as well. There are two carpenters, two merchants, a weaver, a fisherman, a blacksmith and a sailor. Englishtown is a Scottish community with names like MacDonald, MacAulay, McIver, Fraser, Campbell and MacAskill.

The Scottish settlers named the community Bhal na Ghul or the town of the English, because the original English settlers couldn't speak Gaelic. The area's history goes back to the time it was a French outpost. (See also Sept. 8, 1629.) Later Simon Denys, brother of Nicholas Denys operated a trading post and a farm here.

1900 No homework

The Ladies Home Journal recommends as a step toward a reform of the abuses inflicted on children "that every parent who has a child at school will send a note to the teacher that, under no circumstances whatever, will the father and mother permit any homestudy by the child."

1972 Reaching for roots

Six Inverness schools become the first in Nova Scotia to have Gaelic on the curriculum.

October 4

1851 Sydney and Pictou linked

The last of the telegraph poles between Sydney and Pictou is planted in Sydney. It has taken workers fifteen days to put the 106 miles of poles up between Plaister Cove (Port Hastings) and Sydney.

2000 Trans Canada Trail

Phase one of the local leg of the Trans Canada Trail is underway. Workers are clearing the trail, grading and filling in potholes, limbing trees, burning brush, picking up garbage and cataloguing the flora and fauna as well as the present users of the trail. This first 3-kilometre part begins at the old Branch Road off Johnston Road in North Sydney and continues on to Scotch Lake Road. Trail manager, Jim Redden, says "soon our focus will be on teaching trail etiquette. This is a multi-purpose trail and we can't have someone on an all-terrain vehicle causing a problem for the individual riding a horse or someone hiking. We can't have people on dirt bikes and ATV's speeding along the trail."

October 5

1910 First licence

J. A. D. McCurdy of Baddeck and *Silver Dart* fame gets his pilot's licence—the first Canadian to receive one.

1940 Convoy devastated

The Sydney-Clyde convoy, SC 7, leaves today. It becomes the first convoy to be attacked by a German submarine wolf pack. Twenty of the convoy's thirty-four ships will be sunk.

1951 Library on wheels

The Cape Breton Regional Library's new bookmobile, designed by librarian, James F. MacEachern, is completed and has been delivered to the headquarters at the Courthouse in Sydney. This library on wheels makes its maiden voyage to Louisbourg to deliver books for their new branch, opening soon.

1975 Flying sheep

A Pacific Western Airlines Boeing 707 lands at Sydney Airport with a cargo of some 500 North Country Cheviot sheep, imported from Scotland by Devco, a notable event. It is the first flight of the biggest importation of sheep in British-Canadian history. It is the first occasion that livestock left the U.K. double-decked in an aircraft, and the largest single consignment of air freight ever to land at Sydney airport.

Fig. 10.4 Flying sheep.

This is the first of three flights this year bringing 1500 sheep, including 52 registered rams, to upgrade the Island sheep and stimulate the Island's sheep industry. Next year (1976) 1100 sheep are brought over on two flights. They spend two weeks quarantined at the Point Edward Naval Base before moving on to farms throughout Cape Breton for a three-year quarantine period. The sheep importation was engineered by Devco's Primary Production head, David Newton. Premier Gerald Regan and Devco's president, Tom Kent, are among the thousands who gather at the airport to welcome the sheep. (See also September 30, 1978.)

2002 Dutch medal

Veterans and spouses of veterans who participated in the Liberation of the Netherlands in 1944-45 are recognized with a Dutch Medal of Remembrance. Today's ceremony is at the Armstrong memorial Royal Canadian Legion Branch No. 19, but other legions have recently held ceremonies.

2002 Big pumpkin

The 10th annual Octoberfest gets underway in Millville. One of the main events is the showdown of pumpkin competitors. In 1999, Ken Rose of Lingan breaks the record for a giant Cape Breton pumpkin. At 362 kilograms (just under 800 pounds), it is the 7th-largest pumpkin in the world.

October 6

1977 Spruce budworm
Cape Breton has the most concentrated spruce budworm infestation in North America and there is little hope for improvement next year. Although the province has had a spray program in effect since 1952, there is no such program in Cape Breton. A group of landowners is unsuccessful in its fight to stop Nova Scotia Forest Industries, when the latter does decide on an extensive spray program.

1997 New owners
Ownership of the Sydney Airport is officially handed over from the federal government to the newly organized Sydney Airport Authority (SAA). Chairman Vince MacLean officiates.

October 7

1763 Annexed
Cape Breton and Prince Edward Island are annexed to Nova Scotia.

1896 Wreck off Neil's Harbour
Heavy seas prevent the men of Neil's Harbour from reaching the stricken Norwegian ship *Ariadne* which is wrecked nearby. Altogether five bodies are recovered. On the day of the burial, the school will be closed and the blinds lowered in the homes as a token of respect for the dead seamen. Residents of New Haven and Neil's Harbour attend the funeral. A wooden cross with a picture of a full-rigged ship in the centre marks the graves. A few months later, the minister receives a communion chalice with the thanks of the Norwegian government for burying the dead seamen.

1947 Centralization
Micmac Indians are being centralized into two areas: Shubenacadie on the mainland and Eskasoni on Cape Breton. Many of the Indians from Whycocomagh, Wagmatcook, Barra Head, Membertou and Malagawatch have moved into Eskasoni, an area where the Micmacs have always lived. Centralization causes a great deal of anguish for many Micmacs. This is a time of change and hardships. As an incentive to centralize, they are promised all kinds of things from new houses and jobs to insulation, clothing, furniture and medical attention. For many, these promises don't live up to their expectations. Before, many Indians had been subsisting on small farms, but their farms didn't move with them, and a number are forced to be dependent on welfare.

Because of the issues of centralization, Gabriel Sylliboy, Grand Chief of the Micmacs on Cape Breton for 25 years, resigned as chief in 1943.

1909 The first and the last
This fall, Dolly MacLeod, her family and several of her friends gather and watch Casey Baldwin flying in the *Silver Dart* at the new aerodrome park at Baddeck Bridge.

When Casey Baldwin lands, he asks if any of the women want a ride in the *Silver Dart*. Dolly MacLeod accepts. The flight isn't very long. She remembers, "We circled around within a radius of about three miles, and I was back on the ground before many of them realized that I had gone." In taking this impromptu flight, Dolly MacLeod becomes the first woman in Canada, first in North America and in the British Empire and probably the first woman in the world to fly in an airplane. The flight was also her last.

1998 Irish President visits

Irish president Mary McAleese, her husband and entourage of about twenty-five arrive in Sydney. They visit the Fortress Louisbourg and UCCB where they see a special Irish Archival display, various exhibits in the Art Gallery, and are guests at a Cape Breton Ceilidh. This year is the 200th anniversary of the first Irish settlers to these shores. They came from County Wexford after the unsuccessful uprising of 1798.

October 8

1973 Should this be a surprise?

Two young women, the first to train at the Canadian Coast Guard College in Point Edward, show they can keep up with the men. Cathy Walker of Bathhurst, NB, and Oksana Peczeniuk of Sudbury, ON, have just returned from a weeklong training session at sea. John Forest, the College's Director of Studies says, "They know their way around the bridge and engine-room just like any of their male counterparts."

1987 Too much?

A recent survey shows that in the Sydney-Glace Bay area over half the households with a TV also have a VCR. This is higher than the national average, making the area the "VCR capital of Canada."

1991 Special Rosary

Noel Doucette, Band councilor in Chapel Island, is making a cassette tape of the Rosary in the Micmac language.

October 9

1910 New prayer house

Father Pacific blesses the new prayer house, the Chapel of the Holy Family at Eskasoni. Micmac and English copies of historic documents are encased in the cornerstone.

1955 Fleet found

John Sweeney of Halifax, assisted by divers from Halifax and a group from the Sydney Skin Diving club has discovered remains of a French fleet, sunk to barricade the harbour at Louisbourg during the Siege in 1758. In addition to the ships, they find seven cannons, a few stubby mortars, pig iron ballast and fourteen cannon balls. It is quite an adventure for divers Bob MacDonald, Dr. Gyorfi of Glace Bay, Gordon Naish and Ed Bolinger, the photographer.

1997 *"The Jewish People of Glace Bay"*

Minyan on the Mira: The Jewish people of Glace Bay airs on CBC-TV's *Man Alive* series. Elliot Marshall, president of the Congregation Sons of Israel synagogue in Glace Bay, says, "We've been here since 1901, since Glace Bay has been a town, that's when we began our congregation," believed to be jusy the first or second Orthodox community in Atlantic Canada. The show airs between Rosh Hashanah (Oct 2) and Yom Kippur (Oct 11).

October 10

1782 Battle at Petit de Grat

Commander R. P. Tonge, who had been captured by French warships off Spanish (Sydney) Harbour fourteen months ago, has been released from prison and returned to Halifax where he is given command of another vessel, a cutter which he names the *Little Jack*.

Arriving at the Gut of Canso today, he runs into two heavily armed American privateers, and he makes his escape to Petit de Grat. He knows the coastline well from the days before his capture, and at the entrance to Petit de Grat, he turns his vessel broadside and prepares to meet the bigger and heavier gunned Americans. His crew manhandles a nineteen-pound cannon into a rowboat and takes it ashore. With superhuman effort, the gun is dragged up the 140-foot rise of land that overlooks the entrance to the harbour. As the Americans come into view, they are hammered from both the shore and from the small guns aboard the *Little Jack* and after hours of pounding, the Americans, damaged though still afloat, take flight. (For Commander Tonge's earlier CB exploit, see July 19, 1781.)

1906 Lake Ainslie exploration

The Cape Breton Prospecting, Mining and Developing Co. Ltd. has acquired 100,000 acres in North Lake Ainslie. There are said to be large deposits of natural gas, oil and salt. Land has been selected in Inverness where wharves and piers will be constructed. (See also March 29, 1911.)

1997 Celtic Colours International Festival (Oct 9-18)

"Fosgail An Fheis" (Open the Festival!) a Celtic extravaganza at Centre 200 is one of the highlights of this ten-day event highlighting Celtic music and culture. The world renowned Chieftains are performing tonight. Cape Breton performers Ashley MacIsaac, Natalie MacMaster and Gaelic singer Mary Jane Lamond have all recently toured with the Chieftains as well, and Natalie MacMaster and Tracey Dares will be part of their next album. Other performers include the Mabou Scotch Four and the Mabou Square Set dancers. The festival is said to showcase "the finest Celtic music and culture ever to be held this side of the Atlantic" and to spotlight the connection between Ireland, Scotland and Cape Breton.

Concerts are held at venues of varying sizes around the island. The festival coincides with nature's festival of fall colours. In 2001, the event is a top bus tour destination. At the February 2005 ECMA, the festival is presented with a special award for Event of the Year.

October 11

1727 First school

Cape Breton's first school is started in Louisbourg by Marguerite Roy (Soeur de la Conception) of the Congregation of Notre Dame and her two assistants. By mid-December there are twenty-two students.

October 12

1853 Religious experience
A major Pentecostal experience occurs at Whycocomagh during a service held by the Reverend Peter Maclean.

This service is part of a "long Communion." People have come from all over the Island and stay with relatives or set up camp for the week-long ceremonies. Five thousand people attend this particular long Communion, which is so powerful an experience that it changes people's lives. People see flames, speak in tongues, and truly believe that the Holy Spirit is descending.

These long Communions continue into the 1950s, although usually only for three days. One lady in the Black Rock-The Points-West Bay area remembers being driven home to milk the cows and helping feed seventy-nine people staying at the house for the Sacraments.

1910 Finer than Halifax
The 2nd Annual Cape Breton Farmers' Association Agricultural Fair is held in temporary buildings at Victoria Park in Sydney with some 1,421 exhibits. The first fair was held in North Sydney with 991 exhibits. At the formal opening, D. O. MacKenzie, KC, MP, comments that "the display would do credit to any country...."

Dr. Kendall remarks that our present agricultural progress is due to the great industrial development that has taken place here. Fifteen years ago, a farmer was lucky to sell his butter at ten cents a pound, and many times he would return to the farm with his mutton, being unable to sell it for even four or five cents a pound.

October 13

1909 First exhibition
The first Cape Breton County Exhibition is formally opened at North Sydney. A large crowd is attracted in spite of the rain. At the end of the Exhibition, many of the vegetables and fruit displays are given to the new Hamilton Memorial Hospital. A ten-pound tub of butter is important. It wins its maker a gold watch, and it brings pleasure to the largest family in town, Mr. and Mrs. Archie MacDougall and the fourteen of their eighteen children living at home, to whom it is donated. Next year the farmers' Associations of the other counties take part in the Exhibition. Moving over to the Sydney side of the Harbour for many years, it returns to North Sydney in its 21st year, where it remains to this day.

1962 NDP convenes
Today's founding convention of the Nova Scotia New Democratic Party formulates a constitution. To date, the CCF, forerunner of the NDP, has one member in the 43-seat Legislature, Mike MacDonald of Reserve.

1967 Black Friday
Ian MacNeil, editor of the *Cape Breton Post* comments that this day will go down in the Island's history as Black Friday. "Shock waves thundered throughout industrial Cape Breton today in the wake of an announcement by Hawker-Siddley and DOSCO that the big Sydney Steel Mill, economic backbone of this city, will be closed completely by April 30, 1968.

"The cruel, callous and totally unexpected development caught government leaders at all levels completely by surprise and triggered a reaction in the community unmatched since the plant was erected in 1900." (See also November 19, 1967)

1974 Glimpse of the past

Old 42 and the *Repton,* giant steam engines, belching black smoke, bring a glimpse of the past to people waving along the route as they pull some 400 passengers in seven railway cars for an historic run to Grand Narrows and back. Everyone returns to Sydney in good spirits, although the "Highland Cheer," the bar car, runs out of liquor part way home.

1988 "Pass Go. Collect $200"

Nine-year-old Cara Buffet of North Sydney leaves for England, where she'll take part in the eighth World Monopoly Championship at the Park Lane Hotel London on Oct 17. The youngest player ever to participate in the Canadian Championship earlier this year, she is also the youngest international player, and Parker Brothers is flying her parents over with her. She's taking Cuddles, her lucky bear. She wants the horse peg because horses are her favorite animals. She'll also be a special guest on the longest running Canadian TV show *Front Page Challenge* recently taped in Campellton, to be aired later this fall. "I don't play to win. I think I stand a pretty good chance but really I play for fun and so far I've been lucky."

While in England she'll attend the unveiling of a million-dollar bejeweled edition of the game made by a man from San Francisco. The participants will also meet the former Prime Minister, Edward Heath, have High Tea at Windsor Castle, take a boat tour down the Thames River. She's staying at a hotel next to Buckingham Palace and she's excited about seeing the Queen's horses. (The championship is ultimately won by a Japanese International Trade Executive.)

October 14

1931 Pier tram service ends

At midnight, tram car service to Whitney Pier will end after more than 30 years of operation. Ford buses have replaced the tram cars, which will continue to operate on the Sydney-Glace Bay run for a while. A depot will be established later at the Townsend Street car-barns.

1942 Passenger ferry sunk by sub

Between 3 and 3:30 this morning, the German sub *The Laughing Cow* torpedoed the SS *Caribou* on her regular run from North Sydney to Port aux Basques. The ferry sank rapidly, taking to the bottom 137 men, women and children, including Captain Ben Traverner. There are 101 survivors.

"The war isn't so far away. It's right here on our doorstep." This terrible disaster was made more so because those killed were mainly civilians. Angus L. Macdonald says, "If there were any Canadians who did not realize they were up against a ruthless and remorseless enemy, there can be no such Canadians now." The German submarine escapes the depth charges fired by the *Caribou's* escort, but it is believed to have been subsequently destroyed by Allied action.

October 15

1785 Wynyard ghost

Late this afternoon at the Sydney barracks after dinner, during which they had not drunk any wine, Capt. John Cope Sherbroke and Lt. George Wynyard of the 33rd Regiment, sit having coffee in the latter's apartment. The room has two doors—one into the hallway and the other into the bedroom.

Sherbroke notices the stranger first, an emaciated young man about twenty years old, who stands in the hall doorway. Surprised at the presence of anyone dressed in such light clothing, when it is necessary to wear something heavier, he calls Wynyard's attention to the visitor. Wynyard becomes very agitated and is struck speechless. They watch the figure move slowly across the room looking at Wynyard before he passes into the bedroom. When Wynyard recovers, he exclaims that the visitor is his favourite younger brother, John, who is at the time serving in the 3rd Regiment of Foot-Guards in India.

They go into the bedroom, but find no trace of the young man. The window, the only means of escape, is still securely puttied down for the winter. The figure has disappeared as silently and as quickly as he had appeared. Wynyard feels sure that the figure is the spirit of his brother, John, and he fears that something terrible has happened to him. The others in the Regiment become involved in waiting for news from England. The first ships in the spring have no news for him. Finally, on June 6th, word is received that his brother had died at that very hour on that very day in India.

The story is fully documented and researched. Both Sherbroke and Wynyard are noted for their good sense and their honesty. Several years later, in 1811, Sir John Sherbroke becomes Lt.-Gov. of Nova Scotia.

1825 First Baptist church

The first Baptist Church on Cape Breton is started with nine chapter members, who meet in the Union Meeting House until a larger church building is dedicated in 1864 at Upper North Sydney.

1932 Cabot Trail

Premier Gordon S. Harrington sets off the charge that blasts away the final rock barrier and the Cape North to Pleasant Bay section of the Cabot Trail is officially opened. Rev. R. L. MacDonald is the first to cross the Trail. He leaves Inverness shortly before noon on Saturday and arrives on the scene just before the opening ceremonies.

The Cabot Trail has opened up an area of outstanding scenic beauty. It has also "provided a year-round link between the communities of northern Cape Breton and the rest of the world." Many Cape Bretoners make an annual pilgrimage around the Trail, particularly in the Fall. The trip in 1984 takes about eight hours. In the 30s, however, an average driving time just from Cheticamp to Dingwall is eleven hours.

Fig. 10.5 The widest passage, 20-Jul-22.

Many drivers are helped by the first park warden, Johnny Roach, who is known to rescue drivers "frozen" at the wheel. Johnny drives their cars safely down the mountain for them. The driver of one car takes no chances. He is guided by a woman running ahead to spot the curves, while two men run behind the car carrying big rocks to block it, in case it stalls.

Fig. 10.6

Fig. 10.7 Rest stop, c.1933.

Fig. 10.8 National Archives of Canada.

Fig. 10.9 National Archives of Canada.

October 16

1820 Cape Breton annexed

Cape Breton is re-annexed to Nova Scotia "by a dash of a Colonial minister's pen" as the Honourable Mr. Uniacke complains in an address to the House years later. "Sir James Kempt, by proclamation, and without any appeal to the people or the Parliament, attached the Island to a country debt-ridden, and its laws and constitution, in the making of which they had no voice, were forced upon the people."

The re-annexation is officially proclaimed in Sydney on October 19. Government officials here and other Cape Bretoners have known about this political move for over a year. One of the few people happy about re-annexation is Lord Ainslie, who never liked living here. Others are angry that Cape Breton's income will have to pay Nova Scotia's debts. Cape Bretoners try for years to regain their separate status. (See also Dec. 13,1974.)

1833 NO WAY

A negative reply is received from England to the petition for the restoration of the ancient constitution of Cape Breton. On December 11th a petition is prepared for the dissolution of the Union of Nova Scotia and Cape Breton.

2004 "NO"

Nova Scotians say "No" to Sunday shopping.

October 17

1907 FIRST RADIO MESSAGE

Leonard Rosser Johnstone, of Roanoke, VA, a Canadian Pacific telegraph operator, "ticks off" the first radio transatlantic message from Port Morien. Johnstone had been transferred to Montreal at the time the Marconi Company was recruiting operators. In 1904 he transferred to Fame Point in the Gulf of St. Lawrence, the first regular Canadian Marine wireless station. Today, at the official opening, Johnstone handles most of the official dispatches and news stories to dignitaries and newspapers in Europe. A holiday is declared by the coal and steel company.

By the outbreak of the war, service at Glace Bay reaches 1,000 to 1,200 foreign messages in a 24-hour period. The initial letters "G.B." are the radio call for years.

1973 BAND LEAVES FOR CHAMPIONSHIP

The Port Hawkesbury Youth Band leaves to compete in the United States National Championship Marching Band contest to be held in Philadelphia, PA, on Saturday the 20th. It is the only Canadian band invited to participate.

October 18

1890 FIRST TRAIN THROUGH

The first train from the Strait of Canso arrives in Sydney. The five-coach train, Gov.-Gen. Lord Stanley's private train, left Halifax at midnight and arrived at Mulgrave early this morning. Transported across the Strait to Point Tupper on scows, it was placed on the new Cape Breton rails and pulled by Intercolonial locomotive No. 166 to Grand Narrows.

Fig. 10.10 First Train across Grand Narrows.

At the Grand Narrows bridge, Lord Stanley formally declares the new railroad opened. Lord Stanley himself drives the locomotive over the new bridge to the crowd gathered on the other side. Along the route, residents turn out in welcome. Volleys are fired from firearms. At the Shipyard crossing in Sydney, all the houses are lit up. Then "the train plunged through the darkness of the swamp behind the town" before arriving at the new station at 7:10. As the official party disembarked, the guns of the Sydney Field Battery roar a 19-gun salute from the cricket field overlooking the station, church bells peal, and the Sydney Comet Band plays. A parade winds through town, under decorated arches, to the courthouse for more ceremonies. Music and merrymaking continue into the night.

1936 Flying-boats

Despite rain and a southeasterly gale, the German flying-boat *Zephir* is catapulted from the deck of her mother ship, the *Swabenland*, in Sydney Harbour off Low Point. Many people have seen its sister ship, the flying boat *Aeolus*, which rocketed off the *Swabenland* last Friday and went on to beat the record by arriving at Horta, in the Azores, a distance of 1,700 miles, in the time of twelve hours.

When the *Swabenland* arrived in Sydney, there was a reception on board and one of the Canadian guests is Harold "Gus" Edwards, from New Aberdeen, who became Air Marshal of the RCAF (see also May 12, 1937), who would add to his distinguished career fighting the countrymen of those who entertained him that day on the *Swabenland* in Sydney Harbour.

October 19

1741 Indian allies

Gov. DeQuesnel helps cement relationships with the Indians by awarding commissions and medals to the chiefs. The Indians are especially useful in harassing the English both on land and at sea.

1793 Baddeck's founding father

Capt. Jonathan Jones, Baddeck's "Founding Father," receives his land grants. England had been discouraging settlement of Cape Breton because she didn't want the coal mines to be developed and compete with English mines. But now that Cape Breton is opened up for settlement, Captain Jones, an "Associated Loyalist" and a retired naval officer, becomes one of the first settlers. With provisions, three vessels and 140 passengers, Captain Jones settles at Baddeck River. He builds the first sawmill in Victoria County on his land at Upper Washabuckt, and later a second mill at the mouth of the Baddeck River. He exports farm produce to Newfoundland. Three years after arriving in Cape Breton, he is appointed magistrate for the district of Louisbourg, which includes Sydney and Baddeck.

1836 Juste au Corps

A Bill, passed last year, has been assented to and it divides Cape Breton into Cape Breton county, Richmond and Juste au Corps, with no increase in representation. Juste au Corps is renamed Inverness in 1837 on the suggestion of its first representative, Sir William Young, a native of Inverness, Scotland. The new counties are mentioned in the 1836 Almanacs: Belcher's Farmer's Almanack and The Nova Scotia Temperance Almanac.

1901 Great Fire of Sydney

Early this afternoon, in the Gordon and Keith's building on Charlotte Street, glue was being melted on an oil stove in a back room, when the stove overturned and the Great Fire of Sydney began. There is no water immediately available as it has been shut off so that pipes can be repaired. The wind is high and puffy—just right to fan a fire. Within minutes, the buildings on either side are in flames. And by the time the fire engine arrives, the fire is out of control. The North Sydney Brigade arrives shortly before the fifty firemen from Glace Bay. In just over an hour, the fire sweeps the entire west side of the street from Wentworth to Prince, and it progresses on the other side of the street. The wind shifts, driving the fire north—Prowse and Crowell's, restaurants, businesses, homes, Ball's Meat Market—all are destroyed. Only Mrs. C. L. Ingraham's home is left in a two-block area bounded by Wentworth, Charlotte, Pitt and Bentinck. Half of the block between Charlotte, Wentworth and Prince is gone, as is half the block bounded by Wentworth, Bentinck and Prince.

At 6:30 this evening, the fire reaches Moore's Corner, some two blocks away from where it started. Finally, it rains and the fire is extinguished.

Fig. 10.11 1901.

Fig. 10.12 1901.

1991 Ugly deer

Hunters concerned about the safety of the meat from deer with large lesions on their bodies need not worry. According to the Department of Natural Resources most of the lesions are just deer warts and "the meat is fine."

October 20

1826 To relieve some debts

Although the rights to all minerals are reserved to the Crown, in 1825 King George IV gave his brother, Frederick, Duke of York, all the unworked mines and minerals in Nova Scotia for sixty years. But the Duke has had some heavy debts, and he transfers his concession to the court goldsmiths, Rundell, Bridge and Rundell for them to operate on a royalty basis. For this purpose, the General Mining Association has been incorporated.

Originally looking for gold, silver and copper, they discover that coal, the black gold, is more abundant. Royalties from coal mines, paid to Nova Scotia, are to be the province's largest source of income for many years. (See also April 1, 1890.)

1961 Seal Island Bridge

Harry MacKenzie drives his car over the bridge at Seal Island to mark the first official crossing of a passenger vehicle. Mr. MacKenzie is the construction superintendent for the O. J. McCulloch Company, which designed the new $6,000,000 bridge at Big Bras d'Or. The official opening is on November 8 and is attended by Premier Robert Stanfield and about two thousand Cape Bretoners.

2004 Happy anniversary

This week (October 18-24) UCCB celebrates the 30th anniversary of the amalgamation of St. Francis Xavier University Sydney and the Nova Scotia Eastern Institute of Technology, becoming the College of Cape Breton. Various events are held, including receptions, an informal dance, art gallery gala/auction and dance, and a barbeque. Today, a literary tea launches *Perseverance,* Dr. Robert Morgan's history of the University.

October 21

1954 Polio

A polio scare, described as a mild epidemic, has hit Neil's Harbour. There are six confirmed cases and unconfirmed symptoms in others. Baddeck Rural High School has been closed as a precautionary measure after one of the students was taken to the polio clinic in Sydney.

1987 Rally round, boys

There's something for everyone at the upcoming Circuit Cape Breton Motor Sports Weekend. Professional rally drivers from across North America will drive over the 539 kilometre Rally Bras d'Or circuit, much of which borders the lakes. Amateur drivers can compete in the Keltic Cup Navigational Rally and vintage cars will join in a fun-run. Spectators can visit an auto show at Sydney's Centre 200 or look at the vintage cars as they stop along the way at the Miners' Museum parking lot.

October 22

1933 Smell at Glace Bay Post Office

Customs officer McGillvary, assisted by a few Mounties, dumps some $4,000 worth of assorted liquor down the drain in the government building in Glace Bay. The liquor had been seized recently in New Waterford. Four autos and a big truck-full were caught just as they were being loaded. The liquor includes Hennessy's 3-Star Brandy, Buchanan's Black and White, and other choice whiskies, wines and liqueurs, and a number of kegs of rum. This explains the very strong smell of liquor around the Post Office today.

2000 Marijuana raids

The Cape Breton Regional Police recently destroyed twenty-nine mature marijuana plants hidden in a secluded spot in woods back of Sydney River. The plants have a potential street value about $40,000. Two weeks ago in a joint operation with the RCMP they raided some $250,000 worth of marijuana from Howie Centre. Investigations are progressing on at least ten local operations. In some cases the plants are removed just before the law enforcers arrive. According to Sgt. Paul Jobe of the force's street crime and drug section, "Cape Breton is an ideal growing area because of its widespread forested areas, along with plenty of unexplored or infrequently travelled back areas."

October 23

1950 Civil defense

Under the proposed civil defense program for Nova Scotia, Halifax and Sydney have been designated "target areas." The rest of the province will be organized to assist and receive casualties or displaced persons in the event of an enemy attack.

1976 Cape Bretoners in Edinburgh

Cape Breton musicians perform in Edinburgh Castle, Scotland. Linden MacIntyre co-hosts the concert, which includes fiddlers Buddy MacMaster and Winnie Chafe, with Joey Beaton and Doug MacPhee on piano. Other performers are the stepdancing MacPherson sisters from Antigonish, and Gaelic singers Father Alan MacMillan, Tom MacDonald and Malcolm MacLeod.

October 24

1756 High cost of imprisonment

La Grive Des Assises, the regular quartermaster, has finally arrived at Louisbourg from Halifax as part of a prisoner exchange. In June he had been aboard the *Arc-en-Ciel* from France with his own wine, bed, candles and servant, when the ship ran into a British blockade. Inflation is very high in Louisbourg and Des Assises ends up paying double, in some cases quadruple, the cost for replacing his belongings.

1837 Bourinot born

John Bourinot is born in Sydney of a French Hugenot father and a Loyalist mother. He begins his career as a journalist, but in 1880 becomes Chief Clerk of the House of Commons. A prolific writer, he is most remembered for his *Practice and Procedure of Parliament*, published in 1884 and still an authoritative reference. Four years before his death on October 13, 1902, he is knighted.

1950 Hot freight

An important experiment in the Maritime steel industry has been successfully completed. A 30,000-pound hot alloy ingot from the DOSCO plant at Sydney is shipped via CN Rail to Trenton Steel Works in Trenton. The hot ingot was allowed to solidify, then it was stripped and put in a cast iron box insulated with vermiculite. Shipping the ingot hot reduces the process by some two months. Otherwise, the ingot needs six weeks to cool, be shipped and then be reheated, increasing the danger of cracks and increasing costs.

On reaching Trenton, the hot ingot still retains 1,575° F of the more than 1,700° F it started with. This experiment is believed to be the first of its kind.

1955 "Jaws" at Balls Creek

A 300-pound shark, nearly nine feet long, somehow gets past two wire fences across the waters of Balls Creek and beaches itself on the shore of the creek about a mile and a half above Ball's Creek Bridge on the Sydney-North Sydney Highway.

October 25

1917 Two islands join

"The largest and most modern bridge in Nova Scotia," is advertised. The Lennox Passage Bridge, built by the Maritime Bridge Company of New Glasgow, is a steel bridge connecting Isle Madame to Cape Breton Island.

2000 Fast ferry

The Marine Atlantic Gulf ferry service had a good season. The new high-speed catamaran ferry, the *Max Mols,* made the 145-km crossing between North Sydney and Port aux Basques in only two-and-a-half hours. This encouraged many west coast Newfoundlanders to come over to Cape Breton to shop. The Marine Atlantic Gulf ferry service had a good season. Board chairman Capt. Syd Hynes describes "the popular *Mols* is sexy and a novelty for people who wanted to try it on." There were some passengers, however, who didn't care for the movement of the high speed and nicknamed the ferry the *Vomit Comet.*

October 26

1765 Cartographer arrives

Capt. Samuel Holland, having surveyed part of the southwest and southeast coasts, concludes that his survey of the Island will probably take much longer than he thought because of the numerous inlets and lakes.

In the next month, Holland will ask the Indians to provide guides for his party as well as snowshoes and dog sleds. The Indians will help if they are given any hope they may have the spiritual guidance of a priest. Last summer, a formal delegation of Indians went to Louisbourg and promised allegiance to King George as well as asking for the services of a priest.

1786 Governor leaves

Joseph Frederick Wallet Des Barres, first governor of the Colony of Cape Breton, leaves the island and sails for England after nearly two years of antagonistic relations with other leading figures. He is on his way to see the Colonial Secretary, Thomas Townsend, Lord Sydney, so that he can vindicate his name. This he will eventually succeed in doing, and he will later become Lt.-Gov. of Prince Edward Island.

Des Barres, who fathered 13 children by his wife and his mistress, who danced on the table to celebrate his 100th birthday and who died in 1824, 103 years old, was a great believer in the potential of Cape Breton. He wrote "...the value of property in this Island must in a very little time far exceed that of any other in America." He later attributes many of Cape Breton's problems to the attitude of Halifax and believes that merchants in that city ensure high prices for goods to Cape Breton and impede the island's development whenever possible—even by trying to prevent settlers coming to the Island. It is said of him that he was an old fighter who outlived all his enemies.

1850 Sydney residents walk the planks

A Sydney resident comments that the laying down of gravel and planks, allowing pedestrians to walk "without hazarding their persons" on the streets of Sydney is a big improvement, showing "taste and care."

1929 Caledonia rugby

The place is Fredericton, NB, and the action is between the University of New Brunswick and the Caledonia Rugby team from Glace Bay. In their first semifinal match for the McTier Cup, each team scores and they battle for one hour and fifty minutes of actual playing time before the game is called because of darkness. The teams are deadlocked 3-3, and a new overtime record is set. Back home in Cape Breton, some five hundred rugby fans call the *Post* and many gather around outside its Glace Bay office to hear the scores. On November 4, the team returns with the McTier Cup.

Later, the Caledonia team beats UNB again—this time for the McCurdy Cup and the Rugby Championship of the Maritime Provinces. The Caledonia team is never defeated for the cup and is inducted into the Nova Scotia Sports Hall of Fame.

1971 No Micmac or Gaelic

The *Cape Breton Post* reports that Indian children are being encouraged not to speak Micmac in school. This is much like the Cape Breton children a generation ago who were not permitted to speak Gaelic in the schools.

In the 1970s, there is a resurgence of interest in preserving Scottish heritage, and the study of the Gaelic language is introduced into the curriculum in Inverness County schools. Micmac is also being taught to the younger children in some of the Reserve schools. In September, 1984, the school at Chapel Island starts an integrated program of teaching the language to the younger children and reading and writing of Micmac to grades 4, 5 and 6.

October 27

1852 Fishermen detained

One hundred fishing vessels are detained at Port Hood. There is suspicion that an elaborate system of fraud has been organized to carry on fishing in violation of the law.

1963 Tyrone wins

Tyrone Gardiner, Maritime lightweight champion, wins the Canadian lightweight title with a knockout over Marcel Gendron at the Glace Bay Forum. Tyrone Gardiner of Sydney River is managed by Johnny Cechetto of the Venetian Gardens Club, who develops three Canadian title holders: Tyrone, Rocky MacDougall and Ronnie Sampson. Tyrone won the Maritime title in May 1961 and the Eastern Canadian crown in September 1961. He retires undefeated in 1966. He is inducted into the Nova Scotia and Canadian Halls of Fame and, on September 12, 2003, he is inducted into the World Boxing Hall of Fame.

October 28

1784 Loyalists arrive

Abraham Cuyler, ex-mayor of Albany, New York, arrives on Cape Breton with 140 Loyalists. Some of them stay at St. Peter's while the others disembark at Louisbourg to spend the winter there. Only about four houses are left and the area has been stripped of trees, so there are no building supplies.

In 1776, Abraham Cuyler proclaimed his loyalty to the King of England. He was banished and had his property confiscated. He became Inspector of Refugee Loyalists in Quebec and also took charge of American prisoners of war. He went to England to petition for funds and land for himself and other "distressed associates" and also wants a position for himself in the new settlement. In July of next year, Cuyler is forced to take his forty Loyalists to Sydney where the main settlement is. He becomes the secretary and registrar of deeds for the new colony.

1851 Sets sail

Rev. Norman McLeod and nearly 140 followers, including 40 children, leave St. Ann's on board the *Margaret* for a new life in Australia.

In the fall of 1848, with the timber business in a slump and a famine threatening, Rev. Norman had kept his people from being helped by the merchant, John Munro, who was accused of smuggling rum into the settlement. A letter from Rev. Norman's son, Donald, arrived from Australia praising the climate and other advantages of settling there. Feeling even more responsibility for his people, Reverend Norman starts thinking about emigrating.

There are family arguments and people wonder whether their security lies in the settlement they know or with Rev. Norman himself. In June 1849, the keel of a ship is laid below the church at Black Cove. Rev. Norman sells his property to a Loyalist and cedes his church to the Free Presbyterian Church of Nova Scotia.

He preaches his last sermon on the hillside above his church.

This year, St. Ann's becomes part of the new county of Victoria, and John Munro, Reverend Norman's adversary, is elected to the Legislature. (See also March 18, 1848 and April 10, 1852.)

October 29

1979 World record

The world's largest bluefin tuna, weighing 1,496 pounds, is caught on Pomquet Bank north of the Canso Causeway by angler Ken Fraser of PEI, formerly of Port Hawkesbury. It takes forty-five minutes to land. The fish is sold in Auld's Cove and from there it goes to Halifax, New York and on to Japan.

Previous records for large fish: a 1,065 pound bluefin tuna caught by Glen Gibson at River Bourgeois mid-November 1970, and a 680-pound tuna with a three-foot wide tail caught off St. Ann's Bay July 8, 1906.

1982 "Sure was an old bridge"

Two cases of dynamite (500 pounds) are used to demolish the supports of the old Marion Bridge. As one resident puts it, "That sure was an old bridge." The hundred-year old bridge collapsed last March 3 under the weight of a snowplow.

October 30

1987 Who knew?

Cape Bretoners are surprised to hear of a new study, funded by the Federal Research Council and Halifax's Clearwater Fine Foods, to discover why lobster tastes so good.

1991 Keep together

The Cape Breton Regional Hospital is considering changing the way newborn babies are cared for. A practical solution in smaller hospitals, the concept of keeping mother and newborn together in the same room instead of separating the babies into a nursery is becoming mainstream.

October 31

1936 Swordfish centre

Boston is the best market for the more than one million pounds of swordfish harpooned off Cape Breton this year. Some nights there are over 200 boats sheltering in Glace Bay Harbour, and you can cross the harbour by walking on the decks. An even larger fleet is based at Louisbourg. Price per pound delivered ranges from 7 cents to 30 cents.

The swordfish catch in 1984 is about 66,000 pounds, taken by harpoon mostly off Ingonish with small numbers from off Alder Point and Glace Bay. These swordfish are caught as a bonus as the fishermen are already out on other fishing business.

Fig. 10.13 Glace Bay harbour, 1930s.

1945 HALLOWEEN

Wearing big work gloves and big rubber boots, with a wig of frayed rope, and burnt cork or stocking masks to cover their faces, Cape Breton kids dress up to go out from house to house. At each house they'll sit around the kitchen eating cookies or candy while the adults try to guess whom they are. Outside, some of the bigger "kids" put wagons in inaccessible places and tip over outhouses. But times and customs change, and "trick or treating" becomes more sophisticated. And you can't tip over an outhouse that isn't there.

2000 CHILL FEST

Cape Breton's Chill Fest at the Hangar of Horror at Sydney Airport ends today. This fundraiser of artsCapeBreton involves several volunteers from the National School of Learning as well as drama club members from three local high schools and UCCB as the spooky staff. Event producer, Douglas Brown, says the event is "meant to be scary."

November

Fig. 11.1 Rita Joe and her Order of Canada, 1990.

Klusuaqann mu nuku nuta nuk!
Tetpaqi-nsitasin.
Mimkwatasik koqoey wettaqane wasik
Lnueyey-iktuk ta'n keska q

Mu a'tuwaqan eytnuk klusuwaqaney
Panaknutk pewatmikewey
Ta'n teli-kjijituekip seyeimik

Espe'k Lnu'qamiksuti,
Kelo 'tmuinamitt ajipjitasuti,
Apoqonmui kqilm nsituowey
Ewikasik ntinink,
Apoqonmui kqama'lanej app;
Espipukua 'lanej aqq mlkiknewa'lanej.

Mi'kmaw na ni'n;
Mukk skmatmu piluey koqoey wja'tuin.

Translation: Bernie Francis

Words no longer need
Clear meanings.
Hidden things proceed from a lost legacy.
No tale in words bares our desire, hunger,
The freedom we have known.

A heritage of honour
Sustains our hopes.
Help me search the meaning
Written in my life,
Help me stand again
Tall and mighty.

Mi'kmaw I am;
Expect nothing else from me.

Rita Joe

Fig. 11.2 Sawing frolic Cape North, 1947.

Fig. 11.3 Cutting firewood, 2003.

Getting Ready for Winter

Fig. 11.4 Horse delivery oil, North Sydney, 1922.

November 1

1918 Great War veterans

The Cape Breton Branch of the Great War Veterans Association is formed at a meeting of returned soldiers. The actual number of returned soldiers in Cape Breton County is quite small, but the men of the two local Military Convalescent Homes, the Ross and Moxham Military Hospitals, come from a large area. Others have returned and are now working on munitions' inspection work at the steel plant. Close to 150 soldiers gather tonight at the Cape Breton County Council Chambers to form the Cape Breton branch. Another branch has been organized at Sydney Mines to accommodate the men on the Northside.

November 2

1932 Rats as big as deer

It is brought to the attention of council in Glace Bay that there are huge rodents, "some as big as a buck deer," living in the covered drains at No. 11, and these are a danger to children. Council replies that the coal company is responsible for the maintenance of the drains.

Council condemns the relief lists, that is, lists of articles people on relief are allowed to buy in the stores.

1933 Potatoes to Labrador

Sir Wilfred Grenfell writes and thanks Cape Breton farmers for their generosity in sending potatoes to his mission.

One hundred and ten bags of potatoes were sent aboard the *Caribou* to St. Mary's, Labrador, where they helped the people who were in desperate straits, "people who would be very grateful to have a potato to eat with their herring."

November 3

1821 Three districts

The northern district of Cape Breton is divided into three parts: Sydney, St. Andrew's and St. Patrick's.

1914 Red Cross

Some sixty to seventy ladies assemble at the *Post* building in Sydney to form a local Red Cross Society. Their immediate plan is to furnish garments for the soldiers serving at the Front.

1959 Overcoming the odds

Johnny Devison, born with a disease causing separation of the hip joint and the thigh, was told fourteen years ago that he would never walk again. Tonight, he wins the Canadian Bantamweight title. In one of his fights, he concealed tiny weights in the inner band of his trunks so he would qualify for a bout against a heavier opponent. He is inducted into the Nova Scotia Sports Hall of Fame in September 1980.

November 4

1800 Miner bear

Miner Bear, an Indian, leaves everything he owns to "his good friend, John Gruntmier" (Grantmyre), a Hessian soldier who was granted land at Northwest Arm. Miner Bear has land six chains wide next to Grantmyre's land. Miner Bear dies in April 1801 in Grantmyre's home. His will is recorded today on page one of Book A and is one of the first wills probated in Cape Breton. The first will on December 31, 1782, was that of Thomas Moxley of Plymouth, England, a boatswain on board His Majesty's ship *Bombay Castle*.

November 5

1913 Wentworth Park

The city of Sydney is to purchase land around Wentworth Creek to create a park. Once considered "country" by people in Sydney, the Park becomes a bit of country in the city. Ducks on the creek stop traffic on Kings Road. In winter, by this spot at Atlantic Spring, horses and sleighs are able to get out onto the ice to go across the Harbour to Westmount. In later years, in summer, the boys bring their sweethearts in canoes to the Park to listen to the concerts in the old band shell.

1972 Youngest mayor

Earl Tubrett becomes Sydney's youngest mayor.

November 6

1879 Thanksgiving

Cape Bretoners join other Canadians in celebrating the first annual Thanksgiving. Earlier, on March 1, 1871, the first Thanksgiving has been proclaimed "for the restoration of the health of the Prince of Wales." After today, as a harvest festival, Thanksgiving will be proclaimed annually and celebrated on different days. From 1921 to 1931, Thanksgiving and Armistice Day are celebrated together. When Armistice Day becomes Remembrance Day, Canadians want it as a separate holiday. In 1957 Thanksgiving is established on the second Monday in October.

November 7

1925 Time to store cars

It's time to remove the batteries from your cars and set the cars on blocks in the garage for the winter. It is not until World War II that the Department of Highways begins snowplowing the public roads.

2001 Anthrax scare

CBRM police investigate a breach of security in an incident at the Department of Citizenship and Immigration on Dorchester Street, Sydney. It is feared that three suspicious packages contain anthrax. The police are not immediately informed. When they are, they evacuate the entire building. This incident follows a rash of post office anthrax scares in the United States. The anthrax powder turns out to be pieces of crumbled bagel. It is unnervingly coincidental that 62-year old security chief Ross Naylor, who opened the packages, dies unexpectedly the following night but an autopsy confirms that he dies of natural causes.

November 8

1760 "Foul Weather" Jack

"Foul Weather" Jack Byron—so called because he is always running into storms—helps complete the job of destroying the Fortress of Louisbourg today, his 37th birthday. He is aided by 100 soldiers. He returns to England to continue an adventurous and exciting career, fighting the French, sailing the world, and becoming Governor of Newfoundland. He dies a Vice Admiral on April 10, 1786. Two years later, his son, "Mad Jack" Byron, becomes the father of George Gordon Byron who one day achieves distinction as a poet. Among his lines are: "Shrine of the mighty! Can it be that this is all that remains of thee." Perhaps Byron was thinking of his grandfather's work at Louisbourg. (See also Feb 9, 1760.)

1973 Oyster farm

The Crane Cove Oyster Farm Ltd., incorporated in 1971 and owned and operated by the Indians at Eskasoni, harvests its first crop. Although the first crop was suspended from cables, the company has developed a suspension method of cultivating oysters by hanging smooth surfaced scallop shells from rafts in the bays and coves of the Bras d'Or Lake.

1979 Judique Dan

A tribute is paid to the internationally famous wrestler, "Judique Dan" MacDonald, who had 945 wrestling matches and who, in 1910 and 1911, toured North America, defeating every middleweight wrestler he met.

1961 Last ferry

The Ross ferry crosses for the last time. Now motorists will use the new Seal Island Bridge instead of the Ross Ferry-Big Harbour route. The ferry shuttled 180,000 cars a year.

2001 Canada cut off

A major storm with winds reaching 130 km an hour, washes away large sections of the road crossing the Strait of Canso, causing traffic to back up for several kilometres on both approaches. On the other side of the island the Newfoundland ferries are kept tied up in port. Thousands of Cape Bretoners are left without power and nearly 200 homes in Whitney Pier lose their phone services due to flooding.

November 9

1836 Mammoth bone
An immense thigh bone, believed to be from a mammoth, is found in Cape Breton and is donated to the Mechanics' Institute in Halifax.

1968 NDP
Jeremy Ackerman is elected leader of the provincial New Democratic Party.

1972 Fresh Yankee
Fresh Yankee is honoured at the Sports Centre tonight. This prize-winning mare was bought for $900 in 1965 by Duncan MacDonald of Sydney who, together with R. J. "Dick" Logue and Mrs. Logue comprise the Down East Farms Ltd. The yearling was to be sent to Cape Breton to be trained and raced locally, but she missed connections with the van and was placed under the training of Sanders Russell, renowned for turning out champions.

She began to break world records. In 1969, she won $195,686, the most money ever won by a trotting mare in one year. She ran the fastest mile by an aged mare on a five-eighths mile track and the fastest mile by a mare on a half-mile track. Her lifetime earnings were $1,294,252.

November 10

1885 Holy Angels
This month, Sister Saint Domitilla of the Congregation of Notre Dame arrives in Sydney with two other Sisters from Montreal to establish a convent boarding school for young girls of Cape Breton County. A smallpox epidemic delays the start of classes until January 1886. The original wooden building of Holy Angels is added to in 1907, and the High School is built in 1959. The Order of teaching Sisters has been involved before with education in Cape Breton with the establishment of a school in early Louisbourg. (See also October 11, 1727.)

1951 Princess Elizabeth
Princess Elizabeth and her husband, Prince Philip, arrive in Sydney aboard the HMCS *Ontario*, Canada's second largest warship. This marks the first visit to Cape Breton by members of the Royal Family since the Prince of Wales' (later King Edward VII) impromptu visit to Sydney Mines in 1860. (See July 28, 1860.) Earlier, on November 6th, when they were visiting Halifax, the Royal couple were presented with handwoven Cape Breton tartans from the Gaelic College at St. Ann's. Princess Elizabeth received a scarf in the Stewart tartan, while Prince Philip received a necktie on behalf of all the Scots in Nova Scotia.

Princess Elizabeth visits St. George's Church, Sydney, and sits in "Nelson's Chair". Following a reception, they tour the steel plant at the special request of the Princess. Tomorrow she will take part in Remembrance Day ceremonies.

November 11

1799 A LITTLE KNOWLEDGE IS A "GOOD" THING

George Peters, condemned to death for grand larceny, pleads "Benefit of Clergy." Handed a Bible, he proves that he can read and, by an ancient law, this makes him immune from capital punishment for certain crimes. His reduced sentence is that he be whipped until his back is bloody. Starting from the jail door, he is whipped as he walks along Charlotte Street in Sydney down to the Esplanade and back again. Then he will be in jail for six months.

Whipping is a common punishment in the early days. Although the route is changed, another man, for example, receives much the same punishment for stealing a pair of shoes.

1918 "PEACE! WAR IS OVER! - 1,570TH DAY OF WAR

"Armistice Signed" - Lloyd George

November 12

1918 CELEBRATE

Cape Bretoners celebrate the Victory of the Allies. About 8,000 take part in the largest parade ever held in Sydney.

1959 COURT HOUSE

The Cape Breton County courthouse in Sydney, built in 1901, is destroyed by fire. The new courthouse is built at Wentworth Creek. In 1983, plans are made to construct a larger courthouse on the Sydney-Glace Bay Highway.

2000 GLEN BRETON WHISKEY

Glen-Breton Rare Canadian Single Malt Whiskey is released by Glenora Distillery at Glenville, Inverness county. Having all the attributes of a Scotch, it cannot be labelled as such because it is not made in Scotland. It is North America's only single malt whiskey. Sales of the 750 ml., $75 bottle is brisk, with many buying it as a gift or as an investment.

It is described by an award winning travel/cuisine journalist: "This spirited malt crafted from a small distillery in the highlands of Cape Breton, Nova Scotia—New Scotland—earns instant classic status. The pure waters of the distillery's MacLellan's Brook result in an exceptionally clean, light malt. Yet lightness in no way means lack of character or complexity. Single malt fanciers will prize the all around balance of this rich yet smooth and subtle dram."

Colour: amber gold
Nose: big bouquet, fresh, warm and heather floral
Body: medium
Palette: zest of heather-honey, assertive yet gentle in taste, slightly dry in texture, medium depth, lots of flavour development.
Finish: rounded, lingering, faintly sweet, merest whisper of peat.

November 13

1869 Turning the sod

A. C. Morton, president of the International Coal and Railway Company, sums up the company's goals. "Our mission is to tear down the rocks and trees, and to build the railway, and to prepare a coal shipping pier."

Starting from the Harbour Lime Kiln Point at the northern tip of Sydney, a first-class railway will run twelve miles to connect with the International mines at Bridgeport. And a 1,000-foot pier will project into the Harbour.

Cape Bretoners take part in the railway custom of helping to turn the first sod. Three cheers are given for the railway and, after more speeches, local residents are invited to turn the sod. Shovels and wheelbarrows stand ready nearby. Miss Dodd volunteers to try her hand at shovelling. She is followed by Judge Dodd, Rev. Dr. MacLeod, Miss Weeks, Miss Bourinot, Miss Uniacke, Miss Dickson (Dixon), Miss Rachel Burchell and others.

2000 Volunteers

Cape Breton volunteers are preparing for next year's International Year of the Volunteer. This United Nations initiative recognizes the importance of volunteers—anywhere in the world. There are an estimated 7.5 million Canadian volunteers. Cape Breton has about 2,300 volunteer organizations. That works out to several thousand volunteers and countless volunteer hours.

November 14

1883 Enterprising Millers of Glendyer

The new Glendyer Woolen Mill opens with one-third larger capacity and four power looms. Fire last July destroyed the mill, known throughout the province for its quality tweeds, unions and homespuns. The new three-storey mill is lit by sixty-four windows. Like its predecessor, it attracts business from all over Cape Breton and eastern Nova Scotia, exchanging goods for cash or wool.

The three MacDonald brothers follow in their father's enterprising footsteps. Donald MacDonald came from Pictou in 1848 and named the place Glendyer. He started the first, and for some years the only, fulling-mill on Cape Breton. Six years later, he built a grist mill and had the first shingling machine on the island. He died in 1866, leaving his three sons, sixteen-year-old Walter being the eldest, in charge. In 1871, they imported the first spinning machine to Cape Breton and a year later the first power loom.

1965 Bomb scare

A Capitol Airlines Super Constellation makes a successful emergency landing at Sydney Airport just six minutes after the airport received the news that a bomb is aboard. Fire crews reach an isolated section of an unused runway within 60 seconds of hearing the alert. There is no panic among the passengers who are soon enjoying a lunch provided by Aero Caterers at the terminal. The bomb scare is a hoax.

November 15

1761 *L'Auguste*

After thirty days of a storm-wracked voyage from Quebec, en route to Europe, the sailing ship *L'Auguste* is smashed ashore near Aspy Bay with the loss of 114 officers, cadets, soldiers and passengers, including 17 children. There are 7 survivors, including Saint-Luc de la Corne, who leads them in search of help.

After a week's travel, the survivors reach some deserted houses at Niganiche (Ingonish) where two of the survivors stay, too ill and exhausted to travel further. Days later, the remaining five will be discovered by Indians near St. Ann's Bay. These Indians provide the survivors with food and shelter and with canoes and a couple of guides who lead them to the Acadian community of St. Peter's, where they arrive December 8. In the shipwreck, Saint Luc de la Corne loses his brother, two nephews and his two young children.

November 16

1905 Up to Boston

The Plant Line at North Sydney offers a direct passenger service to Boston. Sailing will be on Wednesdays at 8 a.m. to Boston via Halifax.

1933 Oysters to Montreal

A carload of Bras d'Or oysters leaves Orangedale Station to fill the order of one of the largest fish and oyster firms of Montreal.

2001 Tar pond report

After hearing the testimony of 372 residents of the tar pond/coke oven sites, Nova Scostia's associate medical officer of health, Dr. Maureen Baikie, reports that "residents living near 'Canada's worst toxic waste site' are exposed to lead and arsenic as often as other Canadians, Americans and Europeans."

November 17

1961 Switch to oil

The Sydney and Louisbourg Railway switches from coal to oil. The conversion to oil has been delayed as long as possible, as the S & L's main function has been to serve the coal industry. Originally, each steam locomotive had a name: *Henry M. Whitney* and *The Louisbourg* were two. The heaviest locomotive, No. 102, weighed 311 tons. The total track mileage is some 199 miles. Sir Wilfred Laurier was one of the Line's distinguished passengers, but the most colourful events were the miners' picnic excursions around the turn of the century when the flat cars had railings put on the sides. (See also June 17, 1895.)

1977 Hall of Fame
Jimmy Trott, who played ball for No. 3 Colliery team in Glace Bay in 1905, is inducted into the Nova Scotia Sports Hall of Fame.

November 18

1883 Time change
Cape Bretoners join others in the Atlantic Zone at midnight tonight in setting their clocks and watches to conform with the first operation of Standard Time in North America.

1929 Earthquake
Shortly after 4:30 this afternoon, an earthquake rumbles through Cape Breton. Born on a fault under the Gulf of St. Lawrence some four hundred miles south of St. John's, Newfoundland, it lasts here about two minutes and causes minor damage. About four hours later, an eight-foot-tidal wave sweeps over the shoreline of Sydney Harbour and causes a great deal of damage.

Western Union cables running from North Sydney to New York and to St. Pierre are broken. The Marine slip is washed clean of everything movable and several wharves are destroyed. The highway between North Sydney and Sydney is impassable, with the flood waters reaching three feet in places. The road at the foot of Campbell's Hill, Northwest Arm, is flooded for about two hours and is blocked by trunks of trees and other debris washed in by the tide, causing traffic to pile up. Mike Sullivan's bus detours through fields to get to usable parts of the road.

In Sydney, the streets are flooded, while around the Island, earth slides and earth cracks cause considerable damage to the roads. The 300-foot bridge near Isle Madame crumples in the quake, and several large boulders, weighing as much as two-and-a-half tons are strewn around like marbles.

November 19

1872 "Best and cheapest"
The North Sydney *Herald* is established. In 1892 it is advertised as "the best and cheapest paper in the Maritime Provinces," with three new presses and a circulation of 4,000. The four-page weekly is typeset by hand and costs $1 a year. By the 1930s, the *Herald* has more subscriptions in New England than in North Sydney.

1923 Kiwanis formed
About fifty businessmen in Sydney gather at a luncheon to form the first Kiwanis Club in the Maritimes.

1932 Bootleg coal
Recommendations from the inquiry in Glace Bay into the death of two Sydney boys in a cave-in of a bootleg mine at Low Point, Wednesday, are that bootleg mining should be supervised and that boys under the age of sixteen shouldn't be allowed to work the pits. Legally, anyone mining coal in Cape Breton must have a licence.

Earlier this winter, two miners were killed in a cave-in at Lingan, and last summer a young man died of injuries from a Sydney Mines' pit accident. The recent deaths demonstrate the dangers of bootleg mining, but it's become a "racket" now.

At first, the Coal Company looked the other way when a man mined coal for his own use. But now, scores of men and dozens of trucks are actively engaged in bootleg mining. For many people it's their only income. Hundreds of pits are being mined around the area and on the Northside. Some mines are properly timbered but others, like the one the boys were in, are not. Besides cave-ins, there is also the danger of breaking through to old workings and the possibility of a gas explosion.

Bootleg coal is of inferior quality, but it's also cheaper. The recent price war has brought some of it down as low as $3 a ton. These operations are making heavy inroads into the regular sales of the Coal Company.

1987 Olympic torch

The Olympic torch, lit by the rays of the sun in Olympia, Greece, and carried to Canada in three miner's lamps aboard a Canadair Challenger, arrives in Cape Breton on its winter journey to Calgary and the 1988 Winter Games. On November 17, the torch arrived in Newfoundland. Now, it will travel in the longest relay in Olympic history, some 18,000 kilometres, in 88 days, carried by over 6,500 torchbearers, a kilometre at a time, by foot, wheelchair, dogsled, helicopter and snowmobile to arrive in Calgary. The torchbearers have been chosen by lottery and range from 4 to 86 years of age. Thousands of spectators line the route.

1967 Parade of concern

More than 20,000 persons, including religious leaders, housewives and school children, as well as the steelworkers, join together on an historic two-mile parade of concern to protest the imminent closure of the steel plant. (See also October 13, 1967.)

Fig. 11.5 St. FX Junior College students listen skeptically, 1967. Raytel Photography.

2004 Membertou Convention Centre

Membertou Trade and Convention Centre opens. The modern building, overlooking Sydney, contains a large dining room, reception areas and several meeting rooms, each named for a Mi'kmaq legend. The entire area will benefit by this fine centre.

November 20

1731 Splurge

A merchant in Louisbourg splurges and entertains a number of sergeants at the Hotel de la Marine. Costing 7 livres, it is the most expensive meal on record. To put it in perspective, in 1737, a soldier is paid 9 *livres* a month before food and clothing is deducted. A pair of fishermen's boots cost 15 *livres*, a wool blanket 12 *livres*, a Negro slave 300 *livres*, a horse 300 *livres*, a pig 24 *livres*, a sheep 10 *livres*, a chicken 1 *livre* and a bottle of Bordeaux wine, 1 *livre* 5 sols.

1928 Boiler explosion

Glace Bay's worst explosion since 1907, when one man lost his life, is heard today all over town. A boiler explodes and a three-ton section of it catapults through a twelve-inch wall into the compressor powerhouse, injuring a number of men. Boilers provide power for the collieries of the Glace Bay district and for the operations of No. 2 and 9 Collieries.

1994 Residential Society's first home

Lynda Bonnar, returns to her hometown, New Waterford, and sees her dream come true. The Cape Breton Residential Society she spearheads helps mentally challenged adults find a new lease on life. It "creates homes that provide a safe and secure environment, while at the same time encouraging individuality and freedom of choice for the residents." By the 10th anniversary, the number of homes operated by the Society rises to six.

November 21

1914 "Patriotic records"

Just received! Patriotic Disc Records at Smith and Smith, the Piano Merchants, Sydney. "*God Save the King,*" "*Sons of the Sea* -1914 War Edition," "*Rule Britannia,*" "*Boys in Khaki, Boys in Blue*" and "*Land of the Maple.*"

1928 Diptheria on Northside

North Sydney's Health officer, Dr. A. K. Roy, says that the North Sydney diptheria situation is under control. There are only seven cases and no more than one in each home. A few days ago, sections of the Regent Street school were closed while the rooms were fumigated. A few children had developed diptheria after being at school.

November 22

1748 New ballad

Newspapers and pamphlets in New England and Britain bitterly denounce the government's decision to return Louisbourg to France. The following satiric verse appears in the *London Evening Post*:

New Ballad, on the Glorious Times (to the tune of Derry Down)

"Cape Breton's expensive, as well hath been prov'd
And therefore, the Burthen is wisely remov'd
Which Burthen French Shoulders we settle again on
And add our own Stores, Our Provisions and Cannon."

November 23

1900 First coke

The first battery of coke for the blast furnace is turned out today.

1928 Batteryless and worryless

The Radio Club is two weeks old and Nathanson's wants Cape Bretoners to buy radios. You can buy a Westinghouse—"Batteryless and Worryless. The modern way of radio is designed for reception under Canadian conditions. $200 and $265. Plug in on your electric light current and use your radio any time or all the time. Nathanson's will pay your fare to Sydney from any point in Cape Breton, easy terms."

1928 Real girls

The 10th Annual Review of the popular Dumbells, the Canadian ex-army entertainers is held at the Strand Theatre in Sydney tonight. Real girls are used in the show, instead of female impersonators. Admission is $1, $1.50 and $2.00. The New Waterford train will be held until 11:15 p.m.

2001 Last shift

There is an air of sadness as the final piece of coal is mined from the last Cape Breton colliery, Prince Mine at Point Aconi. Actual production ends around 12:30 p.m. on the 7 a.m. to 3 p.m. shift. Those working the next shift conduct the gas tests and safety checks.

Coal has been mined in Cape Breton for hundreds of years. The honeycomb seams worked under Sydney Harbour extend kilometres under the sea.

November 24

1784 *Blenheim* arrives

The *Blenheim* and 129 settlers arrive at Spanish Bay (Sydney Harbour) in a heavy snowstorm. A frigate from Halifax helps the settlers unload their supplies at Point Edward. Temporary shelters are erected. Gov. Des Barres won't arrive until January 7th. This first winter, food is rationed out and is supplemented by fresh moose meat supplied by the local Micmacs. The settlers are paid in provisions for their work. Joseph Rudderham builds a limekiln at Point Edward.

1916 Colliery stable fire

Fire early this morning destroys the Dominion Coal Company's large stable at No. 21 colliery. A large quantity of hay, feed and harnesses are lost. Two horses are burned to death.

1923 J. B. McLachlan

J. B. McLachlan, deposed secretary-treasurer by virtue of being sentenced to imprisonment for sedition, is unanimously elected president at the convention of the provincial Independent Labour Party in Sydney Mines. His first important resolution deals with an educational policy. He wants the advisory council dismissed and a department of education established. He wants free education and free textbooks for the public schools.

1968 Pinaud dies

Walter Pinaud, well-known Baddeck yacht designer, dies just before his 88th birthday. Born in Charlottetown, Mr. Pinaud moved in 1906 to Cape Breton where he started his own boatyard in Westmount. In 1912, he went to Baddeck to work with Dr. Alexander Graham Bell. One of his projects was the HD-4, the famous hydrofoil. (See September 9, 1919.) He was superintendent of shipyards in Virginia for a few years but he returned to Baddeck to start his own boatyard. He designed many prize-winning yachts and was Commodore of the Bras d'Or Yacht Club from 1929-31.

1986 Oldest movie theatre

Olive MacDonald, owner of the Royal Theatre in Dominion, is honoured by the Canadian Picture Pioneers. The Royal is the oldest family-owned-and-operated movie theatre in the country. In 1994, Hollywood actor Cliff Robertson joins others in a special tribute to Olive and her family.

November 25

1850 Slow heart

A writer in the local paper comments that the town of Sydney, with a population of one thousand, has only 50 children in school. "If the heart beats so slow in the centre, what can be said of the extremities?"

1911 Police get guns

The Sydney police are to be armed.

1918 U-Boats

Naval authorities reveal that last summer three giant German submarines operated just off the coast. There were also three merchant ships which had been converted into raiders. The U-boats and the raiders carried torpedoes and mines, which they sowed off Sydney Harbour. These are being swept up.

1931 Belle Cote ladies

Calling itself the Belle Cote Ladies Club, a group in Inverness tries to fill in the gaps between the home and the education system. This is the oldest Home and School Association in Inverness County.

1950 Glace Bay to Grey Cup

Eddie Norvack used to play English rugby with Glace Bay High. Today he's playing in the Grey Cup final at Toronto with the Winnipeg Blue Bombers.

2003 "To the church!"

Malagawatch United Church starts down the highway to travel on a 38-metre barge on a four-day journey from its home at Malagawatch in the River Denys Basin, across the Bras d'Or to a wharf at Iona, then onto Highway 223 and up a steep hill to its new home in the Highland Village. Constructed as a Presbyterian church in 1874, it has undergone many changes over the years, including a vote in 1925 when the majority of the congregation chose to become part of the newly established United Church of Canada.

Fig. 11.6 Malagawatch Church, 2003. Cape Breton Post.

When the church reaches its final destination, representatives of the museum and the contractors (Superport Marine Service, Port Hawkesbury), led by local author and historian, Jim St Clair, gave a toast with wine from Malagawatch grapes. "To the Malagawatch Church, to those who gave it, to those who moved it, and to those who cared for the project, *slainte*—To The Church."

November 26

1723 To control prostitution

Louisbourg's Governor Saint Ovide tries to control prostitution in the town. He recommends to his superiors in France that the few married soldiers be discharged and allowed to become settlers as they have such a disruptive effect on the other men.

1907 Sydney Mines first

The first dial telephone in Canada starts in Sydney Mines. But the service will revert to the magneto (Manual) system next year as the dial system isn't reliable. Sydney Mines again on October 7, 1939, will become the first Cape Breton community to have a dial system.

1962 Boom times at the Strait

Nova Scotia Pulp Ltd. heralds a new industrial era for the Port Hawkesbury area. At full production, the new mill will use about 250,000 cords of pulpwood a year with 100,000 cords of this coming from private woodlot owners. The logs will be barked, chipped and chemically processed. The new industry has added impetus to the development of Port Hawkesbury, whose population has doubled since the Causeway opened.

November 27

1938 First co-operative house

Mary and Joe Laben of Tompkinsville (Reserve Mines) move into their new house. It is the first cooperative house in North America. They have moved into their unfinished house because Eastern Light and Power will not hook up power for the families to work on their houses unless one of the houses is occupied. By January 1, everyone is in his new home. The cost: $1,408 each!

On December 14, 1982, the Labens are visited by Gov.-Gen. Ed and Mrs. Schreyer, who are in the area for the celebration of the 80th anniversary of Marconi's sending and receiving signals by wireless radio and telegraph.

1963 *Highlander*

The first edition of the weekly *Cape Breton Highlander* is published. This family-operated newspaper runs until the end of 1976. In the early 70s, its circulation reaches about 15,000, to make it the biggest weekly east of Montreal.

November 28

1792 Indians in Westmount

Lt.-Gov. Macarmick grants Chapel Island to the Indians. Micmac chiefs Francis Baske and Michael Tomma obtain leave to build a church there. Chiefs Baske and Tomma are well-known and live in what is now Westmount. They trade in Sydney and there is a story that one day Chief Baske and his wife paddled their canoe over to sell moccasins and baskets. Chief Baske had very long hair. He was very insulted by a young Sydney man who matted his hair with some oily substance. Retracing his steps back to Wentworth Creek where his canoe was, he went back across the Harbour to report the ill treatment. That same evening, some tweo hundred men, headed by their chiefs, crossed the Harbour to revenge themselves on the offender. The people of Sydney managed to calm them down by persuasion and gifts. (See also August 12, 2003.)

November 29

1721 Early liquor law

One of the many ordinances trying to control the sale of liquor is passed in Louisbourg. So that work can progress on the fortifications, liquor is not to be sold to men on workdays.

1979 Gaelic whiskey

Ian Noble, Scottish whiskey blender, is a guest of the Mabou Gaelic and Historical Society. He has founded a Gaelic College on the Isle of Skye. He also created a new whiskey, Te Bheag, the only Gaelic-named whiskey in the world.

2004 Oldest woman dies

Annie Samson, a native of River Bourgeois in Richmond County, aged 113 years, 9 months and 24 days, dies today in the Convent of Les Filles de Jesus in Moncton, NB. Annie, who had taken her vows as a nun in 1917, was believed to be the oldest woman in Canada and the eighth oldest in the world. (Earlier this year The Guniness Book of World Records recognized a 114-year-old Puerto Rican woman as being the world's oldest.)

November 30

1851 Chief Dies

Word is received that earlier this month, Michael Dennie, 90 years of age, died at Crow Harbour, Guysborough County. He was a chief of the Micmacs in Cape Breton.

1933 Flying club

Every Thursday night members of the Cape Breton Flying Club teach rolls, loops and spins in the air and the classroom. Pilots on the roster include two commercial pilots, 6 private pilots, 7 who have gone solo, 4 just about ready to solo, and 10 others in various stages of instruction. The Club is preparing for winter, constructing two pairs of skis to use in landing.

The Club leases 1,500 acres at Reserve and has two runways, 1,800 feet and 1,500 feet long, that will accommodate almost any type of aircraft. A hangar is available for six folding-type planes.

1940 War convoys

Residents around Sydney Harbour are used to seeing the harbour crammed with vessels in the evening but empty the following morning. The convoys depart at night. On one occasion this month, the vessels forming up were joined by a Halifax-U.K. convoy taking shelter, and the Harbour was filled with 127 ocean-going ships. This month, 1,528,000 tons of shipping were in port. Next September another record is set with the harbour sheltering some 416 ships, of 1,728,000 gross tons, the greatest recorded in the war.

Fig. 11.7 War convoys, c. 1940.

December

My Home, It's Here

One day, he said to me:
"Come to the city, you will awaken.
Quickly you will forget this half civilized corner of the world."
"What," I replied, "me, forget my home?
Forget the mountain winds which sing me to sleep…
Forget the splendour of a field of oats waving their heads in the sun…
Forget the perfume of a freshly cut field of hay…
Forget the hope with which the morning sun wakes the valley…
Forget the wisdom of the full moon illuminating the dark of the mountains…
Forget the sea, the rocks, each pebble of the shore…
Forget the dandelions, the daisies, each blade of grass…
Forget that which old Joseph told me:
'Remember, here you are at home'".

One day he said to me:
"Come to the city, you will awaken.
Come, forget this half civilized corner of the world
"My poor friend,"
I said to him,
"Let's talk of other things."
Translation – David Parkes

Fig. 12.1 Mabou Ridge, c. 1910.

Mon Pays, C'est Ici

By Nicole Le Vert

Un jour, il me dit:
"Viens a la ville, ti seras ruse.
Vite to oblieras ce coin de terre motie-civilise!"

"Quoi," responds-je, "Moi, oublier mon pays?"
Oublier le vent des montagnes qui chante le soit pour m'endormie…
Oublier la splendour d'un champ de foi fraichement coupe…
Oublier l'esperance qu'inspire le soleil matinal reveillant la valee…
Oublier la sagesesse d'une pleine lune illumninant la noirceur des montagnes…
Oublier la mer, les rochers. Chaque caillou de cote…
Oublier leas pissenlits, les marguerites, chaque bring d'herbe…
Oublier ce que le vieux Joseph m'a dit:
"Souviens-toi qu'icitte, tu es chez vous."

Un jour, il me dit:
"Viens a la vile, tu seras ruse.
Vit to oublieras ce coin de terre moitie-civilise."
Mon Pauvre ami.
Je lui a dit,
"Parkons d'autres choses!"

Fig. 12.2 Whycocomagh Harbour, c.1914.

Home of our Hearts

Fig. 12.3 River Bourgeois, 1994. Paul Prendergast.

Fig. 12.4 Margaree Valley, c. 1950. Nova Scotia Bureau of Information.

Fig. 12.5 Arichat postcard, 11-Sep-12.

Fig. 12.6 Baddeck, c.1900.

December 1

1914 94th Regiment
The 94th, an old Cape Breton Regiment, is put on active service for home defence. Their headquarters are in North Sydney, and their duties include guarding the cable office.

1936 Regiment formed
The North Nova Scotia Regiment is formed.

1982 Christmas trees galore
A Christmas tree producer in Inverness County has shipped more than 2,500 trees, the biggest shipment ever of cultivated trees from one woodlot on Cape Breton. Carmen Campbell's Western Star Christmas Tree Farm in Glengarry employs as many as twenty men during the harvest.

1997 Unama'ki Tribal Police
The three-year old Unama'ki Tribal Police Force is to get new facilities, with the headquarters to be built in Eskasoni and satellite stations in Membertou, Chapel Island and Waycobah.

December 2

1854 Soggy mail
Cape Bretoners complain about their mail service. Mail often arrives wet and soggy because covered carriages aren't required, as they are on the mainland, and horses often have thirty to forty miles to travel between stops.

Fig. 12.7 Mail from Down North, 1920s.

December 3

1864 L'Eglise St. Pierre
Pierre Fiset is ordained. He comes to the Cheticamp area in 1875. (His brother, Napoleon, is Cheticamp's first resident doctor.) In 1893 Father Fiset starts the building of the new church. Parishioners haul stones by horse and sled across the harbour ice from Cheticamp Island to build L 'Eglise St. Pierre, named in honour of Father Fiset's patron saint. Quebec bricklayers receive $2 a day while other labourers get 50 cents. The church, 212 feet long by 74 feet wide and 180 feet high at the belfry, becomes the dominant landmark in the area.

1913 SS *Electronic*

Fig. 12.8 SS Electronic *1910.*

The SS *Electronic*, launched from Portland, Maine, crosses the Bay of Fundy today on her way to Sydney Harbour in the worst storm in years. In their last decade, the *Peerless* and the *Electronic*, calling at Westmount, make thirteen crossings between Sydney and North Sydney (9 a.m. - 10 p.m.) on weekdays and fourteen from North Sydney to Sydney (8:10 a.m. - 10:45 p.m.). The ferries call in at Point Edward when tides permit. On Sundays they make only five trips a day, the last at 6 p.m. The *Peerless* is discontinued two years after the *Electronic* as the new bus service between Sydney and North Sydney grows in popularity. (See also December 25, 1930.)

1981 Razed barn raised again

The Skye Glen barn raising is completed. Herman Van Den Heuval of East Skye Glen lost his barn last August 31 in a fire. In the barn raising, a revival of an old custom, manpower was provided by the community and over 12,000 bales of hay were contributed from around Cape Breton.

1983 Training centre

A "hands on" training centre for Devco coal miners and mechanics opens today in the Adult Vocational Training Centre in the University College of Cape Breton complex. This centre, with its simulated longwall face, is believed to be one of the most advanced in North America.

1988 Celebrities to Centre 200

A celebrity tennis tournament takes place at Centre 200. Chris Evert, Martina Navratilova, Mike Tyson and Robin Givens are among the celebrities. The Centre's promoter, John Graham, has also been able to book the Ice Capades and the Harlem Globetrotters.

1997 Utopia?

Canadian Pioneer Estates, a Canadian real estate company owned by Port Hawkesbury native Kelly Bouman and her husband Rolf, has been selling developed lots in several subdivisions and larger parcels of land in Cape Breton for twelve years. Their customers include mostly Germans, Swiss and Austrians seeking "uncrowded living, clean air and water, low or no crime, convenient international flight schedules and filling most of their need for half the price."

1999 Utopia?

A marketing campaign to induce people to retire to Cape Breton is working. Launched in 1996, some 300 people have chosen to retire to Cape Breton. They come from Ontario, Newfoundland, Quebec, Halifax and area, Saskatchewan, Alberta, British Columbia and the U.S. to the Sydney area, Bras d'Or, Boularderie, Arichat, East Bay, L'Ardoise, Iona, St Ann's and Christmas Island.

December 4

1828 Same old story
In 1822, Thomas Meyers of the Royal Military Academy at Woolwich, England, published a work, with statistical tables and maps, that has become a standard and it has now reached Sydney. A Sydney man complains about wrong information. According to Meyers, Nova Scotia has 50,000 inhabitants and Cape Breton 1,000. "The soil of the latter is, we are there told, swampy, or covered with moss and unfit for cultivation." The critic contends that Cape Breton at the moment supports about 25,000 people, four fifths of whom are dependent upon agriculture alone "from the swamps and moss I suppose."

1839 Steam link needed
Arichat's population, wealth and commerce are all increasing and a regular steamship service between Sydney, Arichat and Newfoundland would benefit everybody, claims a letter to *The Nova Scotian.*

1914 No tents in December
The new barracks near the Marconi wireless station are nearly completed. For the past two weeks, soldiers have been living in unfinished quarters, but which are more comfortable in December than tents.

1987 Cold ducks
Lorena Warneck of Sydney speaks out for the ducks and other waterfowl that spend the winter in Wentworth Park. The city agrees to take the birds inside for the cold winter months.

1988 ECBC
Devco's Industrial Development Division becomes Enterprise Cape Breton Corporation—not to be confused with Enterprise Cape Breton.

December 5

1780 Prenties cast ashore
The brig the *St. Lawrence* founders in a heavy snowstorm off the west coast of Cape Breton near the mouth of Margaree Harbour. Her rigging is caked with ice and the seams of her hull, opened by the storm, have been desperately caulked with small chunks of beef.

The *St. Lawrence* left Quebec on November 17 with twenty-five aboard, including Ensign Samuel Walter Prenties of the 84th Regiment of Foot. He is carrying important dispatches from the British forces at Quebec to Sir Henry Clinton in New York. The Captain is drunk and hasn't left his bunk and the crew has been bribed by Ensign Prenties with wine to keep the pumps working, when the ship runs aground.

Ensign Prenties reaches shore in a lifeboat with his servant, two sailors, the mate and a boy passenger, who dies in the night. Their clothing is frozen. There is no food or fire. And the shelter of woods is two hundred and fifty yards from the shore through waist-high snow. Ensign Prenties and the mate are forced to beat their companions with branches to keep them from falling asleep and dying.

At daylight tomorrow, the survivors on land help the men still on the boat to shore. The storm continues until December 11. By then the survivors have saved some onions and salt beef and have made a roofless shelter out of planking. On January 4,1781, Ensign Prenties, his servant, the useless Captain, the mate and two sailors set out northward in a patched up lifeboat to find "civilization." (See also February 28, 1781.)

December 6

1918 First Ordained

Rev. Leo O'Connell is the first young Sydney man to be ordained a priest. He celebrates his first Mass at the Church of the Sacred Heart, where he has been a member all his life.

1937 Princess tragedy

A runaway trip in Princess Colliery crashes into and kills three miners, narrowly missing their companions. This is the worst fatality on the Northside in more than twenty years. Following the tradition of the day, on hearing the news, fellow miners drop their tools and return to the surface.

1938 Tragedy strikes again

A runaway rake in Princess Colliery early this morning sends sixteen miners to their death and scores more injured to the hospital and their homes.

This disaster has come just one year to the day of a similar accident in the same Colliery. The death toll is to climb to twenty miners, making it the worst mining accident in Cape Breton since 1917, when 65 miners perished in a New Waterford mine explosion.

For years afterwards, the miners of Princess Colliery will not work on December 6. For years, coal miners acted on other superstitions. For example, five men are allowed in the cage, but miners won't travel with two members of the same family in the cage—in case the rope breaks. If miners see a bird in the shaft while they are going down, some will return to the surface. And, if they see a woman on the street when they're going to work at that early hour of the morning, they will go home.

1999 Sisters of St. Martha

The Sisters of St. Martha celebrate their 100th anniversary.

December 7

1745 Death for mutiny

In Rochefort, France, two Swiss soldiers who had been involved in the mutiny at Louisbourg about a year ago (see December 27, 1744) are hanged. Two days later, another is beheaded just hours after the conclusion of his court-martial. Later, five French soldiers are hanged, one dies in prison and two are sentenced to life terms as galley slaves.

1795 Deserting Sydney

To strengthen defences on the mainland, companies of the 33rd Regiment stationed in Sydney have been withdrawn to Halifax. Only one subaltern and twenty men remain at the barracks at northend of Sydney. Many settlers, fearing that France will again attack to regain

Louisbourg and the gateway to the St. Lawrence, decide to seek greater safety in other colonies. Only 121 people remain in Sydney and of these 26 are preparing to depart. Fear is expressed that soon Sydney will only be inhabited "by those receiving their income from the government."

1999 Deck the halls

It's been a successful season for the Cabot Trail Wreath Exporters in Belle Cote and North Sydney. They export 18,000 wreaths, 5,000 kissing balls and some 2,000 table decorations which are made from local materials and sold in New England.

December 8

1906 Crashing bell

A 2,000-pound bell is blessed and placed in one of the towers of Stella Maris Church in Inverness by the League of the Cross. It will stay there until early March 1977, when it crashes down on the corridor floor while being rung for the 11 o'clock Mass.

1950 Franklin Mine

General Manager David Burchell and assembled guests watch as A. H. MacKinnon, Minister of Mines, presses the button on an electric switch and starts the operation of the first and only Air-Sand-dry coal cleaner in Canada. The Bras d'Or Coal Company recently installed the cleaner in the Franklin Mine, making it the first fully mechanized mine in Nova Scotia. The new 45,000-pound machine cleans coal through a system in which air-blown sand plays a major part in the cleaning operations, while stone is also eliminated from the coal. The dry-cleaned coal will provide the type of coal that finds a ready market in central Canada.

1975 Beaton Institute

The Beaton Institute of Cape Breton Studies is named in honour of Sister Margaret Beaton, who was killed recently in a car accident. In 1957, Sister Beaton, the librarian of Xavier College started collecting Cape Breton treasures: newspaper clippings, manuscripts, old letters, pictures and books, and under her leadership this collection grew and is continuing to expand. A combination of Cape Bretoniana and the University College of Cape Breton Archives, the Beaton Institute broadens its initial scope to include research, ethnic folklore, and the social and cultural history of Cape Breton. In August 1976, Cape Breton historian, Dr. Robert Morgan becomes director of the Beaton Institute. He has worked as a senior historian and researcher at the Fortress Louisbourg. Among many historical works on Cape Breton, Dr. Morgan is continuing to write biographies of early Cape Breton personalities such as David Mathews, Major General Despards and Lt.-Gov. Des Barres for the *Dictionary of Canadian Biographies*.

1989 Port Hawkesbury celebrates

Port Hawkesbury celebrates its 100th anniversary.

1990 High unemployment

Unemployment on Cape Breton is at 13.9 per cent.

December 9

1886 Strong woman of Benacadie
It is said that Catherine Cameron MacInnis of Benacadie, daughter of "Big" John Cameron, is the strongest women the area has ever known. She gains her reputation one market day. Without a team to haul goods two miles away to the boat, her husband Donald starts off carrying two large bags of oats on his shoulders. He is surprised to hear Catherine coming behind him through the woods with a carcass of pork on her shoulders.

1997 Wilderness sites
Thirty-one wilderness sites around the province are being protected. "The Wilderness Areas Protection Act prohibits the construction of hydroelectric facilities, utility lines, pipelines, bridges and roads and the cutting or removal of trees, agriculture or aquaculture within the designated wilderness." Wilderness activities such as hiking, canoeing and kayaking are to be encouraged, while snowmobiling will be allowed only in certain areas. Jim Campbell's Barren near Cheticamp, Middle River in Inverness and Victoria counties, Pollett's Cove, Aspy Fault and Sugarloaf Mountain are among the protected sites.

2000 Native science program
A native science program at UCCB receives $160,000 investment research grant from Sable Offshore Energy Inc. The money is to be used toward the development of the program which integrates the traditional Mi'kmaq world view with modern science principles.

December 10

1765 New County
Cape Breton is made a county and is entitled to send two members to the House of Assembly in Halifax. But in 1766, the two representatives elected are refused admission to the House because Cape Breton land is held by lease and not by freehold and so, according to those in Halifax, no Cape Bretoners are eligible to vote. Cape Bretoners are angry. With no representation, they argue, they shouldn't have to pay taxes—especially the rum tax, a lucrative source of income to the province.

In 1775, Cape Bretoners are expected to raise one-fifth of troops for new infantry companies and to help pay their costs. In 1776, most of the troops are sent to Boston with only a few remaining to guard the coal mines at Sydney Harbour and Cow Bay. As the merchants and rum peddlers leave soon afterwards, the small settlement at Louisbourg virtually disappears.

1989 Fish farming
Salmon and rainbow trout are now being raised in the Aqua Nova Scotia Salmon Ltd. fish farm at Lingan using sea water combined with heated water from the new multi-million dollar Lingan power plant.

1997 High tech for kids
MediaSpark Information Technology Solutions Inc. of Sydney receives funding under a new fund developed by MT&T and Telecom Applications Research Alliance (TARA). One of the

products to benefit from the funding is GoWebster, an Internet browser for the classroom. In February 2005, MediaSpark announces yet another high tech for kids, this time it's "GoVenture MyFirst series for infants who are old enough to play on a keyboard but too young to use a mouse."

1998 Silicon Island
Silicon Island, Cape Breton's showplace of high tech companies, officially opens. The state-of-the-art facility is housed in the former Cape Breton county courthouse which was transformed by local entrepreneurs, Donnie Snow and Ken MacLeod. Now it will be a thriving centre for multimedia and digital technology.

2004 Order of Canada
Irving Schwartz of Sydney is appointed an Officer of the Order of Canada at an investiture ceremony in Ottawa. He is the most recent Cape Bretoner to receive the national recognition of lifetime achievement.

December 11

1788 Convicts dumped
The Captain of the *Providence*, finding the season too advanced to get his ship to Quebec, anchors off Main-a-Dieu. Here he removes the irons from his eighty convict passengers, men, women and children from England, hoists out his small boats and lands them on a deserted shore about two miles from Main-a-Dieu. It is long after dark before they are all ashore, stranded with no food or water. Most of the convicts find their way to homes and shelter in Main-a-Dieu, but seven get lost in the woods and die of exposure.

The others are sent on to Sydney, where they are supplied with food and shelter. Still suffering from frostbite, a number are hospitalized. In the spring, they are free to go. Some leave and some stay. No action is taken against the Captain of the *Providence.*

1833 Tough times
The Nova Scotia Legislature sends relief to the settlers in Cape Breton. Crop failure this past summer has caused a great deal of hardship. (See also March 18, 1848.)

1988 Prisoner escapes
Cape Breton's Correctional Centre leads the province in prisoner escapes.

December 12

1881 Great Fire of North Sydney
At 7 a.m., a fire is discovered on the second floor of W. H. Moore's store in North Sydney. Horses haul the hand-pumped fire engine to the warehouse. Bucket lines form and the Sydney firemen arrive by the ferry *Lady of the Lake,* but the whole block, on both sides of Commercial from Archibald Avenue to Caledonia Street, is burning.

All winter supplies come into town by water during the summer and fall and are stored for the winter. In the past two weeks, large shipments have been delivered to W. H.

Moore and Co., the latest being just two days ago. The fire means the loss of dry goods, crockery, 950 barrels of flour, 300 of oatmeal and cornmeal, 5 tons of butter and several hogsheads of sugar. The Atlantic Street Hotel and many businesses burn. (See also May 4, 1913 and May 17, 1916.)

1932 Credit Union

Farmers, miners and others brave cold, sleet and snow to attend meetings last night at the Broad Cove schoolhouse and the Inverness Miners' Hall and tonight at Reserve Mines. They organize the first three Credit Unions. An Act recently passed by the Provincial Legislature, the first of its kind in the Maritimes, authorizes Credit Union organization in Nova Scotia.

1976 Mission Church burms

Fire destroys the St. Anne's Mission Church, an historic Indian church on Chapel Island.

1997 "Yes, Eileen, you can play hockey"

Fifteen-year old Eileen Boutilier of Westmount is to be able to play boys' hockey with the Cape Breton County Bantam "A" Islanders. Previously, the Nova Scotia Hockey Association had ruled her ineligible because of ACHA rule that girls cannot play boys hockey above a certain level if girls hockey is available in their area. Under threat of a lawsuit and a formal complaint to the Nova Scotia Human Rights Commission, the original ruling is overturned and Eileen wins a battle against the Canadian Hockey Association.

2000 *New Waterford Girl*

New Waterford Girl, the successful film shot in Cape Breton in the fall of 1998, which has already won the top award at the Atlantic Film Festival in 1999, is nominated for seven Genie Awards. These include best motion picture, editing, art direction and costume design. The film is "a coming of age tale set in mid-1970s New Waterford where screenwriter Trish Fish spent her formative years. The story centres around 15-year old Moonie Pottie, a misfit who can't wait to leave the small, Catholic coal-mining town for the bright lights of New York City." (The awards are to be handed out Jan 29 on CBC-TV.)

December 13

1851 Exports to Scotland

Victoria County is enjoying prosperity. E. J. Campbell of Baddeck is exporting staples, including butter, to Glasgow, Scotland.

1882 Tanneries flourish

It is reported that North Sydney butcher J. W. Peppett has in the past week, butchered 153 animals. The nine tanneries in town are able to produce leather from the hides. Some of the leather is used by the local shoe factory, the rest in other parts of the Maritimes and as far away as St. Pierre and Montreal.

1950 Happy ending

Twenty-one passengers and ten crewmen walk away safely from the wreck of their Swiss Airline DC-6, which crashed early today at Sydney Airport. The plane was on a flight from Shannon Airport to New York and crashed in heavy fog. The flight's youngest passenger is seventeen-month-old Ronald Rehorek, going to join his parents. Rescuers were attracted to the crash site by Ronald's laughing and shouting.

1971 New radio station

CHER radio begins broadcasting in Sydney.

1974 No separation

Cape Breton feels alienated from decision-making in Halifax, and municipal leaders hear talk about becoming Canada's eleventh province. But economist Rev. John Capstick believes that "becoming a separate province is not the answer.... There will always be that separatist feeling in Cape Breton because it's an island."

These separatists are not the first or the last to feel this way about Cape Breton. Cape Breton's latest exponent of separation is General John Cabot Trail. (See also October 16, 1820 and September 4, 2002.)

December 14

1908 "Gem of Canada"

In a recent booklet, issued by the Department of the Interior, naturalist Prof. Macoun has written about Cape Breton in glowing terms: "I consider Cape Breton the gem of Canada. The climate is grand ... never too hot, never too cold."

1913 Tram cars

The Cape Breton Electric Company's new electric cars are in use. They are much longer and roomier, with interior lighting so that passengers can read. The lower steps are more convenient in these modern "pay-as-you-enter types."

1928 Peddlers

"Let the buyer beware." Businessmen are warning Cape Bretoners about peddlers, with their "smooth talk and shoddy merchandise." But many people prefer to buy from their homes and for people in the rural areas it's almost a necessity. They think that talk of shoddy merchandise "smacks of jealousy."

1979 First quads

Believed to be the province's first quadruptlets, Kelly, Bradley, Shannon and Rinus Van de Ven are born in Halifax to Rinus and Lynn Van de Ven of Judique. Two of the heavier babies will leave for their Cape Breton home on January 6, 1980. Born within a span of four minutes, the babies weigh between 2 lbs. 14 oz. and 4 lbs. 6 oz.

2000 Little Buck

A half-hour animated children's film, *Little Buck's Christmas,* is shown to an enthusiastic audience at the Boardmore Playhouse, UCCB. Created by Virtual Media Productions (VMP), a Sydney animation company, the film is based on Christmas Island author Mary MacNeil's book of the same name. Little Buck "bravely treks to the North Pole to deliver a friend's letter to Santa; in the process he saves Christmas from a massive snowstorm." It will be aired this holiday season on CTV, CBC and nationally on Bravo.

December 15

1722 King forbids gambling

The King of France, in an attempt to control gambling in his colonies, forbids it. Although officially prohibited, gambling at Louisbourg is accepted as a social grace and tolerated as a fact of life.

1902 "The patient waiter"

The message, "The patient waiter never loses" is sent from Table Head in Glace Bay, to England, by Gugliemo Marconi. This first transatlantic wireless contact is promptly followed by a message from the *London Times* correspondent conveying greetings to England and Italy. This is followed by an exchange of greetings between King Edward VII, Lord Minto, the Governor General, and King Alfonso of Italy.

By 1907, transatlantic wireless traffic becomes commercial and on one day, October 17th, 10,000 messages pass between the Marconi Towers near Glace Bay and the sister station at Clifden, Ireland.

Fig. 12.9 Marconi and train to Table Head, c.1905.

Eighty years after the first message, on December 15, 1982, Gov.-Gen. Schreyer commemorates the event with Mrs. Gioia Braza, Marconi's daughter, with a message from Glace Bay to the President of Italy. A portable earth satellite station at the Miners' Museum carries the television signal to the Anik Satellite, then beams it to the World Satellite via Montreal and down to Rome, Italy.

In July 1989, the Marconi National Historic Park opens in Glace Bay. (See also July 28, 1999.)

1939 Huge gypsum trade

Shipping operations for the season have stopped. This has been one of the National Gypsum Company's busiest and most successful seasons. The company, with headquarters in New York, reports that more than 100,000 tons of crushed gypsum from their plants at Dingwall and Cheticamp have been shipped. The gypsum at Dingwall is said to be of the finest quality. With the increase in market potential, the harbour facilities have been improved and the channel deepened.

1977 Inverness station to close

CNR plans to phase out the station building at Inverness. The agent has already been moved to a warehouse. The Inverness station is the only place in Cape Breton besides Sydney where it is possible to wire money.

1992 Heritage businesses

Four Cape Breton heritage businesses are recognized by the Atlantic Canada Opportunities Agency (ACOA) for their many years in business and their long commitment and contributions to their communities.

1. The Telegraph House in Baddeck was built in 1860 and has been operated ever since by the Dunlop family. James Dunlop came to Baddeck while working for the cable company that was laying a cable across the Atlantic. The company moved its headquarters to the Telegraph House and some of the first telegraph messages were sent and received from here.
2. Robin Jones & Whitman Inc., Cheticamp, was founded about 1766 to supply fishermen with basic necessities and take the catch to markets around the world. Possibly the second oldest company in Canada, it is no longer involved in the fishing industry. One unusual business problem in the early days was being "bothered by privateers" during the American Revolution.
3. North Sydney Marine Railway recently expanded, started in 1865 by Archibald and Company.
4. MacKeigan's Pharmacy, Whycocomagh. Over the past 125 years the building has housed MacPhail's General Store. Later Wattling's Whycocomagh Supply Company, Gillis Brothers, and today, MacKeigan's Pharmacy.

All four companies have been proclaimed "Heritage Businesses."

December 16

1767 Island census

Statistics show that on Cape Breton there are 271 men and 141 boys, 128 women and 161 girls. There are two Negro men and two Negro women and two girls. There are 420 Roman Catholics and 287 Protestants. There are 170 from the American colonies, 169 Irish, 70 English, 21 German and related nationalities, 6 Scots and 271 from other countries.

1841 New newspaper

The newspaper, *Spirit of the Times*, replaces the *Cape Breton Advocate*.

1861 Wet wheat for sale

A public auction is held at Plaister Cove (Port Hastings) starting at 10 a.m. and continuing until everything has been sold. Goods are from the ship the *Czar*, John Langwell, Master. The terms are cash. There are about 35,000 bushels of wet wheat and Indian corn and 600 barrels of flour, among other goods.

1951 Really united

The enlarged United Protestant Church at Sydney River is formally opened. Many people with varied church backgrounds cooperated to build the church. This is the only church in Canada that has merged five denominations: United, Presbyterian, Baptist, Anglican and Lutheran.

1994 Give it back

Harvard University Archives would like to give the Louisbourg Cross back to the Fortress. Harley Holden, curator of the Massachusetts university archives, believes the cross found its way to Harvard when some of the members of the invading troops in the siege of 1745 were Harvard graduates and they brought the cross home with them. The item survived a fire in the 1840s, but the inscription citing its origins were destroyed. The curator says, "Every time someone comes back (from visiting the Fortress) they say, 'My, we should give them their cross back."

December 17

1958 New invention at DOSCO

George Reid, master mechanic in DOSCO's open hearth department, develops a stainless steel tipped steam-atomizing open hearth furnace oil burner that will eliminate the need of water cooling.

1994 Junior Achievers

JASP, the Junior Achievers of St. Peter's High School, win, for a second time, the national Junior Achievers Award for best company of the year. Company president Trudy Hiltz said the 21-member company created Tuiteanus (Gaelic for "chance"), a Cape Breton board game. It's a combination of cribbage, Monopoly and Trouble and sells for $35. As you travel around Cape Breton, you learn about different places and historical facts.

December 18

1754 Louisbourg obsession

Playing cards are extremely popular in Louisbourg. The town's permanent population of about 5,000 increases to about 8 or 9,000 in the summer with the arrival of more fishermen and sailors. Some 7,200 decks of cards have been imported. That's almost enough for everyone to have his own.

1800 Preserving morals of Cape Breton

Gov. Despard decides to raise money for the Colony through taxation, even though without a House of Assembly, this can't really be legally done. It is thought that the 2,500 residents of Cape Breton consume some 10,000 gallons of black rum every year. Despard receives permission to tax the incoming rum at between two and three shillings a gallon, a measure taken to "preserve the Health and morals of the Inhabitants of Cape Breton."

1895 First Home and School

Mabel Hubbard Bell, wife of Alexander Graham Bell, organizes the first Home and School Association in Canada at Baddeck. At a meeting of the Baddeck Young Ladies' Club, Mrs. Bell proposes the development of a parent-teacher program similar to those being formed in the United States. The goals are to promote the welfare of children and youth and to raise the standards of home life.

1899 Night telephone

Night telephone service begins in North Sydney. Commercial telephone service began in Cape Breton in 1890. In 1901 a main trunk line is built to the Strait of Canso to connect with the lines of the Nova Scotia Telephone Company, which helps share the cost of getting a cable across the Strait. By 1905, there are 406 miles of telephone poles and 916 phones in operation on Cape Breton.

1976 Last operator

With the coming of dial telephones to Eskasoni, an era ends on Cape Breton. It is not until June 30, 1981, that the last manual service is discontinued in the rest of Nova Scotia on the Northport Exchange, owned by the Cumberland Rural Telephone Company. This is the last of the 254 connecting rural co-ops which operated between 1952 and 1981 and over which Maritime Tel and Tel has now assumed responsibility. The telephone operator, an integral part of the community, and always a goldmine of information, will be missed. A way of life has disappeared.

1994 Too big

Critics of the recent amalgamation say the regional government is too big.

December 19

1908 Rampart cement

Sydney's "Rampart Cement" is the only business of its kind in Canada. The cement is much like the old Roman cements, and the iron embedded in it helps assure permanency. Over the past three years, Rampart Cement was used at the county jail, the Cape Breton Asylum, schools, the high piers of the S & L Railway and the crossing of the Intercolonial Railway as well as in several big jobs around the Maritimes.

1908 Teeth Pulled For 25 Cents

Maritime Dental Parlours in Sydney and Glace Bay advertise that their $9 teeth are equal to many $15 sets. Teeth will be extracted without pain for 25 cents. When the work is five dollars or more, patients from Sydney Mines and points in between will have their return train fares paid.

1964 Pulp for Norway

Williams and Simpsons, pulp exporters, are loading over 1,000 cords for Norway on board the 2nd Russian ship to visit Baddeck in the past two weeks, the *Chernjakhousk*, owned by the Baltic Steamship Line of Leningrad. Before coming to Baddeck, she had delivered a cargo of trucks, cars, combines and vegetables to Cuba from Russia.

December 20

1838 Gaelic Bible

Margaree schools receive Gaelic Bibles and schoolbooks in Gaelic and English from the Glasgow Colonial Society of North America.

1901 Dolls
Dolls for Christmas are available in bisque, kid, rag, wool, rubber and china.

1994 Early settlements
Historical artifacts in the Englishtown area are still being found and may cause a diversion in the approach to the new proposed bridge between Englishtown and Jersey Cove. Blue-green glass pieces may be 18th-century French, bits of 19th-century plates and stoneware, foundations of farm buildings. Over the years people have found cannonballs and a French broad axe along the road. Local resident, Nelson Edge, says "A lot of people don't realize this area was settled thirty years before Louisbourg." The site is near the mid 1600 settlement of Port Dauphin.

December 21

1885 Firefighters
North Sydney's first firefighting unit is organized.

1964 A lot of snow
Today's snowfall of 58.7 centimetres is more than the monthly average of 57.7 centimetres.

December 22

1909 Coal and gypsum
Farmers at McKinnon's Harbour have applied to headquarters for a search lease so they may exploit the coal they believe might be under the "cradle humps" in the area. Meanwhile, gypsum mining at nearby Ottawa Brook will be suspended when winter sets in, unless the company repairs the pier pilings damaged by sea worms. Construction of the railroad from the quarries to the pier took longer than expected this fall and shipping has been delayed.

December 23

1930 Eight-hour day
Beginning the first of the New Year, the eight-hour day will be put into effect at Sydney's steel plant. (See also January 28, 1929)

1933 Early winter
Allan's Ice Company of Upper North Sydney has already completed cutting all its ice, about 20,000 tons. Stored in saw-

Fig. 12.10 Ice cutters, c. 1938.

dust and hay, about half of it will be left until summertime. Delivered by horse and wagon, and later by truck, a five-cent chunk will fill your icebox.

This winter has started exceptionally early and will cause great hardship to communities around Cape Breton, especially those which have been unable to receive their winter supplies.

1994 Cellular safe talk

Driver education programs are advancing with the times, as "cellular safety" is established. MT&T is sponsoring a $60,000 program to teach Nova Scotia high school driver education students the importance of using cellular phones both safely and for safety.

Called "Cellular Safe Talk" the program is the first of its kind in Canada, and by the new year it is expected to be underway in 22 high schools across the province.

2004 Hope for Donkin Mine

There is hope that the Donkin Mine may be developed and opened again.

December 24

1927 First outside lights

Mr. and Mrs. Moffatt, of 42 Archibald Avenue in North Sydney, become the first in town to decorate a tree outside with Christmas lighting. The tree's lights are turned on at dusk.

2003 Special decorations

The Radtke family of Sydney River continues to put up its annual Christmas decoration display, which gives the passers-by so much pleasure. This year there are more than 5,000 coloured lights and 125 lawn ornaments.

Decorating their home and yard for the past 27 years, the display took on special meaning in 1992. In June of that year their 16-year-old son died of brain cancer. He had expressed his wish that the family continue their traditional decorating, saying, "No, dad, I'll be in heaven. You make sure you put them up so I'll be able to see them."

December 25

Christmas past

Cape Bretoners start preparing for Christmas—in November. Mincemeat pies (with real meat) and white and dark fruit cakes are made.The smells of Christmas baking continue to fill the houses through December. In the kitchen, molasses taffy is "pulled" while it's still hot by kids with buttered hands.

Years ago, Cape Breton families didn't have much money, but they always had enough to eat, lots of love and a "good feed of music," from family singalongs to fiddle music. Christmas was a time for the closeness of family and neighbours and for much visiting. There were no "store-bought" decorations then. Spruce boughs for wreaths and foxtails (foxpaws), long trailing evergreen vines, were brought in from the woods to decorate over the doors and handles.

There might be a tree at the school, but in the days before central heating, there was usually no room for one in the house. The front living rooms, used for winter storage, were too cold. When the trees did come into the house, they were real ones from the local woods. Tree decorations were all homemade: empty spools of thread covered with the tinfoil from the packages of tea, sometimes homemade candles, acorns or buttons covered with tissue paper, little cookies and gingerbread men.

Homemade stockings were hung by the chimney, over chairs, back of the stove, or on the clothes line in the kitchen. A child might get one small toy, which would be treated like gold throughout the year. But there was always something in the stockings—hard candies and apples, and occasionally an orange; perhaps a scribbler and a pencil, a pair of mitts, a sweater, maybe a pair of skates.

In later years, children in the industrial area listened anxiously to the radio for reports of Santa Claus's progress from North Sydney to Sydney on the top of Mike Sullivan's bus. Those were still the days primarily of horse and sleigh. Cars, if you had one, were put up for the winter, and the neighbours kept the sleigh track open on the road. Sleigh bells, the sounds from each set distinctive, were laid across the horses' backs, while others stretched along the sides of the shafts. People huddled under robes and some had hardwood blocks, heated earlier in the oven, wrapped in an old blanket to keep their feet warm.

To many, Midnight Mass on Christmas Eve was the highlight of the holiday season. Fasting after supper, people went by horse and sleigh up to eight or ten miles to their churches. Everyone turned out for church services and, depending on the area, there could be as many as forty to sixty horses and sleighs tied up outside the church.

Some people wouldn't get home until three or four in the morning. The Acadians always had their traditional rabbit pie and other mouth-watering meat pies. Others returned home to a pork roast and mashed potatoes.

On Christmas Day in Sydney, people dressed up and paraded along Charlotte Street in their horse-driven sleighs. Though Cape Bretoners may have lacked material wealth, spiritually they made Christmas the richest of seasons. Merry Christmas, everyone!

1894 Glace Bay to Sydney

Engineer Ed Muggah takes the first passenger train from the S & L station in Glace Bay to Sydney. Before this, passengers could go to Sydney by way of the International Railway from Bridgeport or from Reserve on the road now used by the tram line.

1897 First Mass

The first Mass is said at the dedication of St. Mary's Church in Mabou.

1901 The first day of Christmas

This Christmas Sunday an unusual assortment of names sits in one pew at St. Matthew's Presbyterian Church in North Sydney. There is a Bird, a Crowe, a Pidgeon and a Partridge.

1930 Mike Sullivan's bus

Mike Sullivan's new bus line starts its run from North Sydney to Sydney, leaving North Sydney at 8 a.m. The bus service takes the place of the Cape Breton Electric Company's ferry service, which was discontinued last night.

December 26

1837 U.S. Consul appointed

American president, Martin Van Buren, appoints John J. D'Wolf as United States consul for the port of Sydney, Cape Breton and for all other ports which may be nearer to Sydney than to the residence, of any other Consul.

1912 Many thanks

The *Bohemia*, loaded with salt cod, out of Newfoundland bound for Halifax, founders in a storm off L'Ardoise. Men from L'Ardoise rescue the crew and in the morning salvage the codfish. The fish is stored in a nearby barn before being shipped by sledge to St. Peter's, and on by rail to Halifax. Next year, the *Bohemia* is repaired and relaunched. The man who got the lifeboat into the water is rewarded $500. Those who hauled the fish to the barn are paid 10 cents an hour for their labour, and those who had rescued the crew are all awarded watches by the Federal government in recognition of heroic service.

1918 Demonstrate their superiority

Marshal Haig commends the men of mine tunnelling companies. "At their own special work, mine warfare, they have demonstrated their complete superiority over the Germans and, whether in the patient defensive mining ... or in the preparation for the offensives of the Sommes, Arras and Ypres, they have shown the highest qualities both as military engineers and as fighting troops."

The Canadian No. 1 tunnelling Company, Cape Breton section, was recruited and taken to France by Lt. George Morley, of the Dominion Coal Company Glace Bay. In a sapping contest open to the world, six men of the No. 1 Company, all miners from the Caledonia pit, win first prize and set a world's record. The Canadian No. 2 tunnelling company, commanded by Major Roy Spencer of Glace Bay, also took part in the competition.

2004 Tsunami

The world's most powerful earthquake in 40 years triggers massive tidal waves that slam into villages and seaside resorts across Asia, killing more than 150,000 people in five countries.

People all over the world begin sending money for relief. Here on Cape Breton, schoolchildren, individuals, community groups, churches and businesses help. Two Cape Breton women, Cpl. Angela Townsend of North Sydney, and Master Cpl. Noelle Fraser, of Sydney, go to Sri Lanka as members of Canada's Disaster Response Team (DART). Landmine expert Terry Long, with the Decommissioning Consulting Services in Sydney has also gone to help in Sri Lanka.

December 27

1744 Mutiny

In the early hours at Louisbourg Fortress, Swiss soldiers mutiny and give their officers a list of grievances concerning unpaid labour, their failure to collect legitimate booty following an earlier raid against the English at Canso, and also the problem of rotten vegetables. The Swiss, joined by French soldiers, march armed through the streets with drums beating, and they threaten to blow their officers' heads off. Some officers are roughly handled, and order is restored when the officers concede to the soldiers' demands.

The confrontation lasts only a few hours but may have helped prompt the attack by the New Englanders in May, 1745, for they had heard of smouldering rebellion at Louisbourg. After the New Englanders had captured the Fortress, the garrison was sent to Rochefort, France, where eight mutineers were executed. (See also December 7, 1745.)

1977 Archivist retires

C. Bruce Fergusson, of Port Morien, has just retired as Provincial Archivist in Halifax. He joined the Archives staff as an assistant in 1946.He was a lecturer in contemporary history at the Nova Scotia Technical College and in 1957 became an associate professor of history at Dalhousie. He has worked on a number of publications, including the Diary of Samuel Perkins, celebrated Nova Scotia privateer, books on Joseph Howe, W. S. Fielding and the establishment of blacks in Nova Scotia.

1989 Murder

Sydney teenager Walter Gorman is charged with second-degree murder of retired Salvation Army major, Ralph Sexton.

December 28

1965 Dingwall survives

In 1960, Dingwall was in danger of becoming a ghost town. More than half the population of 500 had left. The harbour had been closed since 1957 because shifting sand had silted up the entrance to the port. The National Research Council was called in, and their plans for the town saved the day. A dam diverted the Aspy River from the harbour, and a new channel was dredged. The village is prospering again. Dingwall Fish Company is to install new equipment to handle increased catches.

1969 Production record

Sydney Steel establishes a 70-year production record as its one-millionth ton is poured. Premier Smith says it is "a wonderful accomplishment, not only for Cape Breton, but for the entire province." Sydney Steel was threatened by closure only a year ago.

December 29

1901 School days

The yearly school report shows the following statistics:

COUNTY	SCHOOLS IN SESSION	TEACHERS	PUPILS
Cape Breton	162	163	8,215
Inverness	131	131	4,790
Richmond	75	75	3,014
Victoria	60	60	2,054

1947 Cape Breton Israeli

Lionel Druker of Sydney is elected president of Canadian Young Judea. He resigns in February 1948 to go to Israel where he joins the tank regiment of the Israeli Defence Force, fighting with it in the War of Independence. After the war, he becomes co-founder of the United Tourists, which becomes the largest privately operated touring company in Israel.

1967 A whale of a problem

Port Caledonia has a problem. The carcasses of ninteen whales have been stranded on the shore. Each whale is more than fifteen feet long and the carcasses are practically frozen, making disposal extremely difficult. Wildlife biologist, Modena Gunch, believes the carcasses are not yet a health problem.

December 30

1901 Great shipping record

The insurance losses on "hulls and cargoes" of steamers to and from the St. Lawrence have been compiled by the Montreal Marine Underwriters Association. The number of steamers entering and leaving "the two Sydneys" is equal to the number entering and leaving the port of Montreal. Yet of total losses over the previous ten years of ten million dollars, the losses incurred in Cape Breton were only $142,000.

1901 First steel

At 9 p.m., the first cast of steel is made from No. 10 Open Hearth Furnace. Shortly afterwards, three ingots, each weighing 6,000 pounds, are reduced to billets of various lengths. Arthur J. Moxham, general manager, reports to the directors that "Everything worked well."

1969 The man with a highland heart

Neil MacNeil, successively assistant national editor, foreign editor, city editor and assistant night managing editor of the New York Times, dies at the age of 78.

Born in Boston but raised in Cape Breton, Neil MacNeil joined the *Times* after service with the U.S. Army in the First World War. He is best known on Cape Breton for his book *A Highland Heart in Nova Scotia,* a story of growing up on grandfather's farm in Washabuck. Mr. MacNeil, after his retirement in 1951, became editorial director of the second Hoover Commission on the reorganization of the U.S. government. Later he was named one of the literary executors of former President Herbert Hoover.

1991 New Fortess older than old Fortress

The Fortress of Louisbourg needs lots of money, some $10 million, to make repairs. Worn by time and weather, the reconstruction is now older than the original Fortress. Damp local conditions favour the rotting of wood, rising water levels threaten sills, natural forest regeneration is destroying the remains of siege camps and underwater archaeological treasures are threatened by natural forces and divers.

December 31

1784 New Colony of Cape Breton

Cape Breton is now a separate colony. The Micmacs have been on the island for generations and they help the settlers through the difficult early months. There are isolated settlers and fishermen around the Island. Jersey fisherman, Ramon, lives at South Bar and Jersey-based Charles Robin has established a fishery in Cheticamp. Ann and Donald MacIntyre and their child Jane have arrived in Princeville from Scotland.

There are Loyalists at St. Peter's and at Louisbourg. There are Loyalists and settlers at Sydney Mines and a few at Point Edward, where the supplies are stored, and these settlers are "encamped ...in the woods with temporary huts for the winter." John Meloney, credited with being Sydney's first settler, is over on the Sydney side of the harbour. Lt.-Gov. Des Barres is due to arrive in early January.

1898 - Report Of Licence And Police Committee

Your committee on Licences and Police beg to report that from figures supplied by the Stipendiary the cases tried in his court were as follows:

Assaults	17
Drunk and incapable	16
Cattle at large	11
Causing disturbance on streets	8
Jail breaking	1
Riding on sidewalk	5
Carrying firearms	1
Malicious injury to property	1
Polluting water of reservoir	1
Threatening language	1
Bastardy	1
Offences against public health	2
Profane language	1
Abusive language	2
Challenging to fight	1

The poundkeeper's report shows that 73 cows, 5 horses and 10 sheep were impounded. Very great complaints are made as to the many animals wandering at large.

Charles McKinnon

E. C. Hanrahan

D. MacDonald

1902 Report Of The Stipendiary Magistrate

The following cases have come before the Public Court, for the year ending December 31st, 1902.

Assault	98
Trespassing at railroad	60
Drunk	594
Causing disturbance on street	79
Malicious injury to property	14
Profane language	28
Disorderly conduct	18
Cattle going at large	47
Riding bicycle on sidewalk	6
Stealing	38
Furious driving	6
Carrying firearms	13
Shooting with intent to wound	3
Lunacy	5
Vagrancy	38
Trading without license	11
Assaulting policeman in discharge of his duty	7
Keeping house of ill fame	3
Sanitary laws	3
Driving on sidewalk	2
Sureties	19
Destruction of sidewalks	16
Exposing person in full	2
Obscene language	3
Peddling without license	2
Trucking without license	12
Bastardy	5
Driving passengers without license	1
Resisting arrest	11
Fighting	3
Assault grievous harm	5
Refusing duty on ship	5
Stowaways	2
Nuisance	1
Riding bicycles without lights	14
Refusing to pay railway tickets	2
Keeping vicious dogs	2
Riding on sidewalk	3
Interfering with police officer	1
Neglecting to support family	2
Desertion from ship	11
Neglecting to clean sidewalk	13
Cruelty to animals	1
Causing disturbance on electric car	12
Murder	1

Frederick Moseley
Stipendiary Magistrate

1902 Health report

D. K. McIntyre, Health Officer for Sydney reports: "so far as the general health of the citizens is concerned, Sydney ranks second to no other town of its size to-day in Canada. We are at present entirely free from all acute diseases; and this fact must be a source of great satisfaction to the public when it is remembered that within the past two years we have had several outbreaks of Diptheria, Scarlet Fever, Small Pox, Measles and Typhoid…" Tuberculosis (32 cases) still heads the list of deaths, with Children's Cholera (22), Pneumonia (21) and Stillborn (15) following.

1947 *The Little Mary*

After thirty years of service, the ferry *The Mary*, nicknamed *The Little Mary*, makes her last run from Dobson's wharf in Westmount to the Cape Breton Electric Company wharf in Sydney. The forty-ton *Little Mary*, fifty-nine feet long and fourteen abeam, had seating accommodations for thirty-five passengers. It was built in Mahone Bay as a sailing pleasure yacht. J. M. Dobson converted her to a gasoline-operated ferry. He was enraged that the *Peerless* stopped only briefly at his wharf at Westmount on her trips between North Sydney and Sydney. Many passengers had to wait three or four hours for the next time she called at Westmount.

Fig. 12.11 Little Mary, *c. 1900.*

When the *Peerless*'s American owners wouldn't make improvements to the service, Mr. Dobson, along with other local men, formed their own ferry service. *The Little Mary* left every hour from Westmount to Sydney. There she stayed for ten to fifteen minutes before returning to Westmount. School kids going to the Academy rode the ferry to school for five cents and grown ups for a dime.

1962 High Hopes For Service

A new passenger service starts between Halifax and Sydney. The fast rail-liners will cut an hour and twenty-five minutes off the journey.

1967 SYSCO

At midnight, the Sydney Steel Corporation becomes SYSCO, now operated by the Nova Scotia government. The steel plant's name has changed a number of times. Incorporated in 1899, DISCO, the Dominion Iron and Steel Corporation, was the first. In 1908, DISCO amalgamated with the Dominion Coal Company and became DOSCO, the Dominion Steel and Coal Company. In 1920, it became BESCO, the British Empire Steel and Coal Company, in 1928 the Dominion Steel and Coal Corporation and, in 1957, the Hawker-Siddley Corporation.

1984 Celebrations

Cape Bretoners start celebrating the Centennial of North Sydney and the Bicentennial of Sydney with New Year's Eve dances, fireworks, and a torchlight parade in Sydney on New Year's Day.

1991 Barra Strait

Tenders are called for the overpass over the CN rail tracks on the Grand Narrows side of the crossing, another stage in the Barra Strait fixed crossing.

1994 Casinos are good for us

According to Premier John Savage, "Casinos will have a positive impact on developing the downtown area and we have confidence, a positive impact on the economy. Whether or not people approve of casinos in Cape Breton, they have to realize there is a major opportunity there, including for employment."

Some Sydney club owners are not rejoicing.

1999 Hope fading

Hope is fading that the province will be able to find a buyer for SYSCO. The Premier insists that it must be sold or closed by midnight. The steel plant is to close in January, almost one hundred years after the first steel cast was made (on December 30, 1901).

1999 Millennium celebrations

Millennium celebrations are held! Police and technology companies are prepared for any Y2K technological problems as commuter systems switch over to 2000. The Nova Scotia Liquor Commission assures customers that there will be enough champagne for the celebrations.

Fig. 12.12 Millennium Fireworks. Raymond Fahey.

List of Figures

12.3 Paul Prendergast. River Bourgeois, 1994. Courtesy Beaton Institute. 94-1094-25609.
12.4 Nova Scotia Bureau of Information. Margaree Valley, c. 1950. Courtesy Beaton Institute. 77-82-216(a).
12.5 Arichat postcard, 11-Sep-12. Courtesy Beaton Institute. 84-609-14709-P.522.
12.6 Baddeck, c.1900. Courtesy Beaton Institute. 96-1095-27783.
12.7 Mail from Down North, 1920s. Courtesy Beaton Institute. 86-149-16246.
12.8 SS *Electronic*, 1910. Courtesy Beaton Institute. 80-752-4932.
12.9 Marconi and train to Table Head, c. 1905. Courtesy Beaton Institute. 78-926-2676.
12.10 Ice cutters, c. 1938. Courtesy Cabot Archives. 79-692-3672.
12.11 *Little Mary*, c. 1900. Courtesy Beaton Institute. 77-586-720.
12.12 Raymond Fahey. Milennium Fireworks.